Viktoria Ritter
Job Love

Steinbeis-Edition

Viktoria Ritter

Job Love

An empirical Analysis of the Concept of Love for
a Job, its Measurement and its Antecedents

Imprint

© 2021 Steinbeis-Edition

Viktoria Ritter
Job Love. An empirical Analysis of the Concept of Love for a Job, its Measurement and its Antecedents

1st edition, 2021 | Steinbeis-Edition, Stuttgart
ISBN 978-3-95663-258-7

Likewise Steinbeis University, dissertation 2021
This book is also available as an e-book: ISBN 978-3-95663-259-4

Layout: Viktoria Ritter | Technical Editing: Steinbeis-Edition
Production: e.kurz+co druck und medientechnik gmbh, Stuttgart

The platform provided by Steinbeis makes us a reliable partner for company startups and projects. We provide support to people and organizations, not only in science and academia, but also in business. Our aim is to leverage the know-how derived from research, development, consulting, and training projects and to transfer this knowledge into application – with a clear focus on entrepreneurial practice. Over 2,000 business enterprises have already been founded on the back of the Steinbeis platform. The outcome? A network spanning over 6,000 experts in approximately 1,100 business enterprises – working on projects with more than 10,000 clients every year. Our network provides professional support to enterprises and employees in acquiring competence, thus securing success in the face of competition. Steinbeis-Edition publishes selected works mirroring the scope of the Steinbeis Network expertise.

215561-2021-12 | www.steinbeis-edition.de

Foreword

Since I started my psychology studies, I have questioned myself what drives people, especially what drives people at work. What makes people get up in the morning, give their best at work, fully engage with what they do, and remain loyal to the company which they work for? Research as well as business practice have been interested in this question, mainly focusing on topics such as employee attachment, commitment, and employee happiness. Yet, one driving force of human behavior has been widely passed over in employer-employee relationship research: *love*. Love can be described as the most intense form of a relationship. When love is present, usually people experience a number of desirable outcomes: people who love and feel loved in return feel more energized, are more willing to invest in their partners, and feel more fulfilled by and satisfied with their relationships. In the context of employer-employee relationships, job love is suggested to have similar outcomes that are beneficial for both – for those who love their jobs and for employers with employees who love their jobs. Although 'Job Love' may sound like a win-win situation for both, employers and employees; when starting to research the topic of love in the context of work, many critical voices arose, stating love not to be suitable for a job relationship. It is an interesting question to ponder: Is a job to be loved? What does it mean when a person loves a job, and what leads to love or hinders people from loving their jobs?

Over the course of the years while writing this dissertation, one of the first questions I asked most people I met – whether at dinner parties, in late Berlin bar evenings, on work conferences, or family gatherings – was: "Do you love your job?". Interestingly, regardless of whether the answer to my question was 'yes' or 'no', or whether people thought that a job *should* be loved or should not be loved, most people stated: 'I think, one *can* love a job'. This dissertation therefore does not discuss whether a job should be loved or not, but why people love their jobs and what companies can do to foster job love to create this win-win situation. When I think about my own job of writing this dissertation, I come to the conclusion that I *loved* my job. The dissertation was written during my time as a research assistant at the Deutsche Post Endowed Chair of Marketing and Dialogue Marketing at Steinbeis University. Having the possibility to read interesting books on (love) relationships and researching what drives people at work was a great joy and passion for me. Writing this dissertation was also one of the best things I did in life, while also being one of my biggest challenges so far.

This work would not have been possible without the great support of my supervisor Prof. Dr. Dr. Schneider, one of the most inspiring people I had the pleasure to meet and work for. Not only was he the one pointing to the topic of love, but his constant ideas and out-of-the-box thinking helped to change perspectives and to see the big picture as well as the details to focus on. Therefore, I first want to thank him for his great supervision, for the interesting discussions and fruitful exchange that brought this dissertation to a successful finish. Second, I want to thank my team at Steinbeis University: Thank you, Markus, Ann-Kathrin, Frederick, Anja, and Claudia for being there for me and giving your great ideas to this dissertation. Third, I like to thank my second reviewer Prof. Dr. Kirchgeorg for his opinion and valuable view on this dissertation. Fourth, I want to thank all those that contributed to the dissertation taking part in my qualitative as well as quantitative studies, whether as interview partners, focus group participants, or study respondents: without you, this research would not have substance.

Finally, I want to thank all my family and friends. I thank my parents, who always encouraged me to go for my dreams and to not give up, and my sisters and my grandparents who always had an open ear for me and believed in me. I also want to thank my friends and partner who I see as my second family and who were there for me to build me up when I was down and who were there for me celebrating the successes in life. Thank you for your interest in my work, our uncountable discussions, your inspiration and advice, and your support. I am grateful for each person I am blessed to share life with. Not only have I received so much love, but I was also constantly reminded that life is nothing without love and that you always gain by giving *love*.

Berlin, 2021
Viktoria Ritter

Table of Contents

List of Figures

List of Tables

List of Abbreviations

ANOVA	analysis of variance
AD	Anno Domini (in the year of the Lord)
Art.	Article
BL	brand love
BLS	Brand Love Scale
C	Commitment
CEO	Chief Executive Officer
CFA	confirmatory factor analysis
CFI	Comparative Fit Index
DV	dependent variable
e.g.	exempli gratia (for example)
Ed.	edition
Eds.	editors
EFA	exploratory factor analysis
engl.	English
et al.	et alii, et alia, et alteri (and colleagues)
etc.	et cetera (and so on)
Exp(B)	exponentiation of the B coefficient (odds ratio)
H	hypothesis
i.e.	id est (which means)
IV	independent variable
JL	job love
JLS	job love scale
KMO	Kaiser-Meyer-Olkin
NIV	New International Version
NPS	net promoter score
nr.	number
OCA	Organizational Commitment – Affective Commitment (subscale)
P	passion
p.	page
PLS	Passionate Love Scale
Sig.	Significance
SD	standard deviation
Std.	standardized
SPSS	Statistical Product and Service Solution
SRMR	standardized root mean square residual
TLI	Tucker-Lewis-Index

V	Verbundenheit (Connection)
VIF	variance inflation factor
Vol.	volume
Wald	Wald test
WOM	word of mouth

List of Symbols

α	Cronbach's Alpha (probability of error)
β	regression coefficient
&	and
d	Cohen's d (effect size)
df	degrees of freedom
F	test variable in the F-test
lv	latent variable
M	mean
n	sample size
p	probability of error
r	correlation coefficient
R^2	coefficient of determination
SD	standard deviation
SE	standard error
t	test variable in the t-test
$\chi 2$	chi square
$-$	negative relationship
$+$	positive relationship
$\neq$	unequal

A   INTRODUCTION

The first chapter of this dissertation discusses the significance and relevance of the chosen research topic. It identifies people as a central factor in organizations and emphasizes the importance of considering the factors that motivate people in organizations to commit to their jobs and to stay loyal to their employer. It analyzes concepts that have already been researched and defines a new concept for research: job love. Based on these arguments, insights are presented into how this dissertation can contribute to the scientific world, as well as business practices, through empirical research.

1   People as a Central Factor for Organizations

Problem Description

In today's economy, it is difficult for companies to both attract employees and to develop and retain them – in order to maximize and maintain a competitive advantage. The ongoing competition for talented and highly skilled workers, described as a "war for talent" by Bartlett and Ghoshal (2002), has forced companies to think more intensely about employer attractiveness and how to gain and keep high-potential employees (Kirchgeorg & Günther, 2006; Kirchgeorg & Müller, 2013). Moreover, industrial development has produced an enormous change in the workplace, with a growing portion of the workforce now occupying the role of "knowledge workers" (Drucker, 1959) – employees who must be capable of handling multiple, complex tasks and remain intellectually motivated and engaged in the workplace. Stotz (2007) argued, "The ability of a company to use its *human capital*, its *intangible assets*, efficiently and effectively, distinguishes more and more successful from less successful companies" (p. 1). It is, therefore, only a matter of time before the human capital of a company is counted as a component of its assets, with motivation and performance of the workforce as key criteria (Stotz, 2007). A meta-analysis published by Gallup in 2019 showed that employees who are highly engaged in their work and who feel connected to their employer are more likely to come to work every morning, generally take fewer sick days, and are more productive. Moreover, engaged employees display a greater commitment to the quality of their work,

1

which results in improved performance in comparison with those of a lower level of engagement. Nevertheless, the proportion of the workforce that is truly engaged, either in the USA or in Europe, is relatively low: a study conducted in 2019 by Gallup showed that in Germany, only 15% of all employees felt emotionally connected to their work, while the majority (69%) had a weak emotional connection to their employer. The remaining 16% of the employees, which Gallup estimates at around 5.9 million in Germany, did not feel any emotional connection to their work at all. Of these, approximately 47% did not expect to remain with their current employer in the following year, and 11% were even actively looking for a new job. These alarming statistics indicate that the cost of failing to engage employees is high for companies: Gallup estimates German companies accrue 105 to 122 billion dollars per year in losses from fluctuating costs and low performance by unengaged employees (Gallup, 2019, p. 7).

Solution: Investing in Employer-Employee Love Relationships

These considerations have encouraged companies to invest in the well-being of their employees and strategies to maximize engagement and loyalty among their workforce. Researchers, as well as practitioners, are highly interested in finding a magic formula that will incentivize people to give their best at work, fully engage with their work, and remain loyal to the company for which they work (Bakker, Albrecht, & Leiter, 2011). In this context, the focus of personnel marketing has shifted over the past years: while it was limited exclusively to the acquisition of potential employees, today, personnel marketing is increasingly understood as an expanded, more holistic concept which also includes current employees (Scholz, 1995). The topics studied in research environments are multitudinous, as are the contexts in which they are encountered in modern business practice. Numerous constructs – such as employee commitment, employee attachment, employee happiness, and employee engagement – have been assessed with regard to their potentials for improving employer-employee relationships. In some cases, these efforts have already led to a greater understanding of the significance of the employee-employer relationship in maintaining the competitive advantage of organizations (Stotz, 2007).

Whilst research in employer-employee relationships is mainly focused on the aforementioned qualities like attachment, commitment and happiness, among others, one driving force that is discussed in virtually all other interpersonal relationships has been widely passed over in employer-employee research: *love*. Regarding interpersonal relationships, people yearn for love, they restlessly seek the perfect partner they can love, and – at least in Western culture – most people marry for love (Fisher, 1992). Love has been identified as the highest and most intensive emotional basis possible in a relationship, and when present, it generally leads to a myriad of desirable outcomes for the individuals involved: people who love and feel loved in return are more energized, more willing to invest in their partners and feel more fulfilled by and satisfied with their relationships (Sternberg & Sternberg, 2018).

When it comes to the field of marketing, both practitioners and researchers have identified love as a key component of successful consumer relationships. The old picture of homo oeconomicus, the species of consumer that makes decisions based solely on rational reasoning, has aged badly (Scheier & Held, 2006, p. 53). Brain research has shown that people think and behave based on emotions, not on cognitive processes and profit motives alone (Langner & Kühn, 2010). Therefore, it is clear to marketers that although a consumer may be subjectively satisfied and consciously aware of the advantages and qualities of a particular product, he or she will not necessarily remain loyal to any one brand (Jones & Sasser, 1995). Even satisfied consumers may (and do) switch to other brands and products (Reichheld, 1996). For true brand loyalty to take hold, the consumer needs to have an emotional connection to a brand. Kevin Roberts, a former CEO of the marketing agency Saatchi & Saatchi, introduced the concept of Lovemarks in his famous book *Lovemarks – The Future Beyond Brands* (2004). He describes why he believes that companies need to build emotional consumer-brand relationships in order to build successful brands and why it is important to build brand love among consumers. The intensive research on the concept of love for a brand, which will be described in Chapter B, has shown in numerous studies that people who love brands buy *loved products* more often, are willing to invest significantly more into their *love brands,* and are keen to recommend these products to others – even if the loved brand or product does not perform as well as it did before they had formed their unconditional loyalty to it.

What, then, if people could come to love their jobs with a similar fervor? – to feel the same emotional connection with their job as they feel with a favorite brand and, therefore, be prepared to commit to the job, to be loyal to their company, and to be vocal about their loyalty? People who love their jobs could be good for the performance and success of a company, but they would also be healthier and happier at work: people who love products are more satisfied with the products, they idealize these products and experience strong positive emotions from owning them. Hence, it stands to reason that people who love their jobs feel significantly more positive emotions towards their work than those who do not. Regarding those positive effects of love, it is not surprising that love has found its way to the job marketing world: a marketing campaign conducted by Stepstone, one of Germany's leading job platforms, was already advertising its service in 2011, almost a decade before this dissertation, with the slogan *"You too can find a job that you love."*

Research Gap

Surprisingly, at least in the fields of human resources management and personnel marketing research, the concept of love in an employer-employee relationship has not yet been the subject of formal study – likely because the word *love* is loaded terminology and by any definition, carries strong emotional charges considered unsuitable for a professional context. While similar concepts have found broad appeal among researchers, the "job you love" has not been identified as a research topic (see Figure 1).

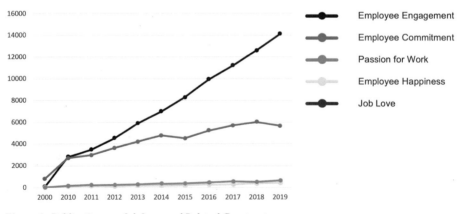

Figure 1. *Publications on Job Love and Related Constructs*

As Figure 1 shows, one of the similar concepts that is beginning to be explored, is employee engagement – where we find 14,000 relevant publications in the year 2019 alone.[1] Employee commitment has also been widely researched over the past ten years, but, judging by the rate of recent publications, the topic seems to be stagnating. One of the potential explanations could be that a committed workforce alone is not sufficient to guarantee the success of a company; companies need employees who not only stay with the company but who are willing to go the extra mile and who are engaged and passionate about what they do. Hence, alongside the skyrocketing interest in employee engagement, other highly emotional concepts such as passion for work and employee happiness are finding more and more interest among researchers.

---

[1] Results were collected from a Google Scholar search on 2020, July 4.

2   Why Job Love?

"The only way to do great work is to love what you do," said Steve Jobs, co-founder and former CEO of Apple, in 2005, addressing the graduating class of Stanford university – young adults with their entire working careers ahead of them (Stanford, 2008). "Work," he continued, "is gonna fill a large part of [...] life and the only way to be truly satisfied is to do what [you] believe is great work" (Stanford, 2008). And his is a valid argument: A typical career spans approximately 80,000 hours (Todd, 2016), and, as the hours spent working comprise a large part of almost everyone's life, it is natural that people should seek enjoyment and even fulfillment in their working lives. A growing number of publications such as *How to Get a Job You Love* (Lees, 2018) and *Put Your Mindset to Work: The One Asset You Really Need to Win and Keep the Job You Love* (Reed & Stoltz, 2013) reflect public interest in the topic of how to find and keep the job you love.

Definition of Research Relevant Terms

But what do we mean by love? The Oxford Learner's Dictionary defines love as "a very strong feeling of liking and caring for somebody/something, especially a member of your family or a friend."[2] The classification of love as a feeling or emotional state is widespread and many researchers view love in this light as well (Buck, 2002; Burkett & Young, 2012; Izard, 1992; Lazarus, 1991; Panksepp, 1998; Shaver & Hazan, 1988). Although the terms are often used interchangeably, emotions and feelings are distinct concepts. *Emotions* are reactions of the brain to external stimuli and they manifest in the unconscious mind (Ekman & Cordaro, 2011). They help human beings survive by enabling the body to react quickly to threats, rewards, and environmental signals without requiring slow and costly rational analysis. In short, emotions are physical reactions of the body to a stimulus. They can be measured by facial expressions, body language, blood flow and brain activity (Ekman & Cordaro, 2011). *Feelings*, on the other hand, are the cognitive reactions to an emotion, or the interpretation of the emotion (Manstead, Frijda, & Fischer, 2004). They,

---

[2] The Oxford English Dictionary (2020) defines love as: "A feeling or disposition of deep affection or fondness for someone, typically arising from a recognition of attractive qualities, from natural affinity, or from sympathy and manifesting itself in concern for the other's welfare and pleasure in his or her presence (distinguished from sexual love at sense); great liking, strong emotional attachment; (similarly) a feeling or disposition of benevolent attachment experienced towards a group or category of people, and (by extension) towards one's country or another impersonal object of affection. With of, for, to, towards."

contrary to emotions, are the conscious experience of an emotion. As an example, if someone reacts to a threat with the emotion termed anxiety (often accompanied by the physical presentations of sweating and widening of the eyes), a feeling will provide the brain with a more nuanced assessment of the severity of the danger and suggest a wider range of potential physical reactions than the simple "fight or flight" impulse. When a mother sees her baby smile, her reactive emotion and feeling can indeed be love, but viewing this as an emotion or feeling is a very reductive view, drastically reducing an immensely complex process to a simple reaction to a stimulus.

Love cannot be viewed purely as an emotional state but must also be seen as a form of social relationship (Heinrich et al., 2012). A relationship is formed and develops over time and can be accompanied by various emotions and feelings. A love relationship can have intense positive emotions (joy, vigor) while also producing negative emotions from time to time (separation anxiety, jealousy). In contrast with the conception of love as an emotion, it can be thought of as a description of a particular form of a relationship encompassing many differing emotions. As these emotions are all intensive, love itself is considered by some to be the most intensive form of a relationship. In social psychology, there are different theories about love (Aron & Aron, 1991; Lee, 1977; Maslow, 1943; Reik, 1944). One of the most talked about theories is the Triangular Theory of Love introduced by Robert Sternberg in 1986. According to his theory, love can be described as a triangle involving three dimensions: intimacy, passion and commitment (see Figure 2).

While *intimacy* is the emotional component of love and involves feelings of closeness and connectedness to the partner, the *passion* component is described as the motivational component of love, because it motivates the loving one to invest into the loved partner. Passion is accompanied by highly positive emotions and feeling towards the partner, a tendency to idealize them and a motivation to be close to them and to care for them. The third dimension of love is the cognitive decision to love: *commitment* includes the rational thought that the relationship is the right relationship and the wish to maintain this relationship in the future.

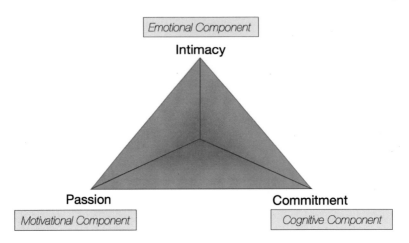

Figure 2. *Sternberg's Triangular Theory of Love*
Note. Own illustration adapted from Sternberg, 1986

These three dimensions, taken together, produce eight distinct types of love relationships, or what Sternberg called love types, depending on which of the dimensions are at play in an individual. Non-love occurs when none of the three dimensions are present. The three love types "liking," "infatuation" and "empty love" are types where only one dimension is present (intimacy, passion and commitment, respectively). Three further types, such "companionate love", or "romantic love" include two out of three dimensions present in the individual. According to Sternberg, only when all dimensions of love are present in the individual, is it "real love" or, to use his own terminology, *consummate love*. Sternberg's love theory has been applied to the marketing context: e.g., Shimp and Madden (1988) build their brand love theory on Sternberg's triangular love model showing the possibility of a transfer to other contexts than the interpersonal relationship. Therefore, for this research, it seems interesting to look at Sternberg's model as a possible basis for the research on love in the context of a job.

Delimitation from related Concepts

When transferring Sternberg's love model to the work context, it seems obvious that certain dimensions of Sternberg's model should seem analogous to already researched concepts in the context of employer-employee relationships: Passion can be naturally equated with what is termed passion for a job, commitment with employee commitment and intimacy with employee connection. In an employment context as well, love may be a multidimensional, rather than a unidimensional concept – involving all three dimensions, passion, commitment, and connection present.

In the course of discussing a new concept in personnel marketing research, the inevitable question arises as to whether job love is actually a necessary concept to be introduced, or whether already existing constructs might not already be able to adequately depict the job love concept. As stated above, there already exist a multitude of established concepts which can be used as indicators for an emotional relationship between an individual and one's job. However, these concepts are suggested to be different from this novel concept of job love.

Employee Commitment. While employee commitment is defined as "a psychological state that (a) characterizes the employee's relationship with the organization, and (b) has implications for the decision to continue or discontinue membership in the organization" (Meyer & Allen, 1991, p. 67), the focus of the concept is rather on commitment (a cognitive process) than behavior at work. It can explain why someone might stay in the organization, but *not* how much effort an employee puts into her/his job, or how strongly the person is excited about a job. For example, continuance or normative organizational commitment reflect the desire to stay in an organization because of a lack of alternatives and feelings of obligation. Affective organizational commitment (Allen & Meyer, 1990) is, in a sense, also cognitive in nature, as it finds emotional reasons to stay connected to work. Love, or job love, on the other hand, is suggested to include more than just a commitment to stay with the job, but more: passion and connection.

Passion for Work. The concept of passion for work, or employee work passion, is rather focused on the job itself and not on the commitment to the job and the organization. Vallerand and Houlfort (2019) describe passion for work as a strong inclination or desire toward a job, that someone finds important, and that someone wants to spend time and put energy in and that someone sees as part of their identity. Passion therewith reflects a strong motivational perspective, highlighting the motivational component of passion. The two concepts, passion for work and job love, have considerable overlap: Love also has a motivational component that leads to the wish to invest into the loved one. Also, the loved one is considered as very important. Still, compared to love, passion is not connected to the commitment necessary to engage in a long-term relationship (Vallerand & Houlfort, 2019). The "state of intense longing for union with another" (Hatfield & Rapson, 1990, p. 9) can vanish quickly, as arousal and energy that keep motivation high in a passionate individual vanish as time goes by. Hence passion cannot describe relationships in the long run. Therefore, it is suggested that passion for work cannot reflect all aspects of a love relationship, and consequently cannot fully explain the phenomenon of love for a job.

Employee happiness. Happiness in general can be defined as "the property of feeling happy at a time" (Raibley, 2012, p. 1108). It typically reflects a state, although there is an ongoing discussion about how much of an individual's level of happiness is already predisposed as a trait (Sheldon & Lyubomirsky, 2004)[3]. Employee happiness can be defined as "an experience of subjective well-being at work reflected through a high amount of positive individual (e.g., highly valuing one's work, feeling engaged to work) and organizational (e.g., providing supportive work environment) experiences and low amount of negative individual and organizational experiences." (Singh & Aggarwal, 2017, p. 1440). Employee happiness is suggested to differentiate from job love in two points: First, happiness is a rather unidimensional concept, ranging from being unhappy to being happy, while job love is considered a multidimensional concept. Second, happiness describes a state that changes over time: when an individual experiences an unhappy event at work, employee happiness is low, while on another day, when something exciting happens, the employee might be happy. The concept can therefore only reflect a small window of an employee's state at a time, but not their attitudes in general, their motivation to invest into the job, or their commitment to stay in the organization. Job love, on the contrary, is considered to reflect a broader view on an employer-employee-relationship that reflects a constant motivation to do the best at work and staying committed even on an unhappy day.

---

[3] Sheldon and Lyubomirsky (2004, p. 131-133) describe three factors that influence an individual's personal happiness level: they describe that 50% of the happiness level are predetermined, 10% are determined by life circumstances (e.g. material status, employment status, income), and 40% are the result of intentional activities that a person engages in. Those may be cognitive (e.g. practicing positive thinking), behavioral (e.g. physical exercise), or volitional (e.g. engaging in meaningful activities).

Employee Engagement. The last concept to be discussed, employee engagement, might be the closest concept to job love. The Gallup organization has defined an engaged employee as someone who is "involved in, enthusiastic about and committed to their work and contribute(s) to their organization in a positive manner" (Gallup, 2017, p. 12). Bakker and Demerouti (2008, p. 209–210) add that engagement is a state of mind that is positive and fulfilling and that an individual who is engaged can be characterized by vigor, dedication, and absorption. According to Gallup, engagement can be described in three states: engaged, disengaged, and actively disengaged. While actively disengaged employees are unhappy with their work and are not committed to their employer, engaged employees are motivated to do their best at work, and highly committed to work. Yes, what employee engagement is not measuring, is how connected employees are to their job and to the organization. Even the highly engaged employees can feel disconnected to their organization may start looking for options outside. On the contrary, for people who love a job, the job is suggested to be "the one and only job", the job they love, and they have the desire to stay with and invest their best.

The preceding explanations indicate that love for the job, analogous to love for a person, describes an independent concept and thus the need to research the construct of job love. As job love has not been researched as a concept itself, generally accepted definitions and operationalizations do not yet exist. This study will, therefore, seek to understand the concept of love in the context of work. Through this, it will contribute to the search for the "magic formula" of what makes people give their best at work, stay engaged and stay loyal to the company they work for – which should pay dividends not only to employers but also to the workforce itself.

3   Research Questions and Research Design

Research Questions

There are many questions to be asked when researching the concept of love for a job. Some may even be skeptical about researching the love for a job, because love may be a strong term when thinking about a job. If there is nobody who actually loves their job, research on the topic would necessarily be focused on inducing job love in the individual who is currently apathetic toward his employment, or such research would not make any sense at all as there is no one to research. Therefore, a first question to ask when researching the concept job love, is *(1) "Does job love exist?"* Once we have some conception of whether there are people who love their jobs and what job love might look like in an individual, we can then turn to the question *(2) "Is it possible to measure job love?"*. Only by first evaluating *whether* people love their jobs, a study can safely proceed to measuring the factors that might play a role in determining the presence or absence of job love in an individual. A further and third question is then *(3) "Why do people love their job?"* as a means of investigating possible antecedents of job love.

Research Design

In order to answer the research questions posed above, this dissertation developed across various steps, as shown in Figure 3. Chapter A provides an introduction to the topic and describes how the research exploring job love could be both relevant and rewarding: *relevant* because companies are desperately seeking more effective means of attracting, developing and maintaining talented people in their organization; *rewarding* because love of a job could be instrumentally beneficial to both the organization in its quest to attract and maintain staff, and to the employees themselves – who thrive in positions they love and who experience a greater sense of well-being and happiness in such roles. A further inquiry into what love is brought into focus the paucity of available research on the topic. This research void cries out to be filled.

In Chapter B, the theoretical framework for the understanding of the concept of job love is constructed. First the history of the concept of work and what lay people think of as a job today are evaluated. A definition of what a "job" is culturally defined as is provided.

Next, the concept of love is analyzed, first in its original context of the interpersonal relationship, then in the brand-consumer relationship. Theories on how conventional love is developed are examined and transferred to the domain of job love – by comparing and contrasting findings from interpersonal love and brand love research.

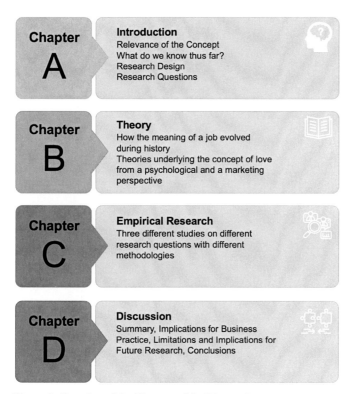

Figure 3. *Overview of the Chapters of the Dissertation*

In Chapter C, the research questions proposed in this first chapter will be answered. Therefore, three different studies are planned and conducted – each answering a different research question with a different methodology, as shown in Figure 4. In Study 1, a first question was investigated: *Do people who love their jobs even exist?* Therefore, social media research was conducted that analyzed posts from people using tags such as *#ilovemyjob* on Instagram. Additionally, a pre-study was programmed in Typeform asking people to rate whether and how much they love their favorite hobbies, brands, their most important persons and their jobs. By comparing those objects with each other, within and between variance could be analyzed. To shed even more light on the question of whether people love their jobs, the researcher conducted several in-depth interviews and a focus group gathering more qualitative data on the topic. Different opinions on what job love is and why people might love what they do are presented in this study. In Study 2, the question of *Can job love be measured?* was answered. Therefore, a theory-based model of job love is developed and, based on the theory, items measuring job love are developed and tested on a scale. In a systematic process, the scale is validated and tested for reliability. In Study 3, the third question *Why do people love their jobs?* is answered. Therefore, hypotheses are derived from both qualitative research and pre-existing studies then included in a hypothesis model containing eleven potential antecedents of job love. All those are tested in their impact on job love.

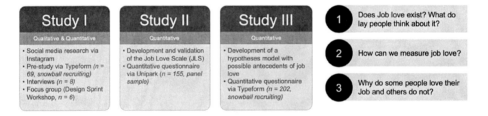

Figure 4. *Overview of Empirical Studies in Chapter C*

In Chapter D, all insights from the empirical research are summarized and their potential impact and relevance for both the scientific world and the practical world are discussed. The results of all three studies presented in Chapter C are summarized and implications for business practice are discussed. To manage this, a systematic implementation process is presented in the final chapter that companies can follow to foster job love in their workforce. As every dissertation has its limitations, the possible weaknesses of the research are discussed frankly. Implications for further empirical research are explored and, in conclusion, a final consideration is presented.

B   LITERATURE EXPLORATION

In this chapter, the reader will be given a general view on the theoretical concepts that already exist in the context of the research object job love. The first part, theories underlying the concept of job will be analyzed and the meaning of work in history from the Old Testament through today are presented to give the reader the possibility to understand what is meant by the term "job," why job love is a new concept to be researched and why the love for a job may play a role today while it did not in previous times. The second part of this chapter focuses on the concept of love and the underlying theories that explain love from psychological and marketing perspectives.

1   On the Development of the Job Concept

What we know as a "job" today did not exist until quite recently, in a linguistic-historical sense. People spoke about work in a more general sense: one "did work" but didn't necessarily work at a job. The definition of a job, and what we think of it today, will be discussed further in the chapter. When looking into literature about the meaning of work across time, two main topics stand out. The first "is the degree of *acceptability* of work as meaningful activity across cultures and times" (Andersson, 1992, p. 95), which developed from a predominantly negative acceptance to a positive acceptance of work. The second topic is the *rewards* people got from a job. Across time, there has been some kind of reward for labor of someone who performed work, but the kind of reward and the significance people placed on the reward(s) have changed over time (cf. Caplow, 1954; Eells & Walton, 1974; Hall, 1975; Levenstein, 1964; Marx, 1887; MOW International Research Team, 1987; Neff, 2017; Tilgher, 1962). Two trends emerge when tracing the evolution of work across history: acceptability and rewards. These two ideologies have changed in diverse ways, which is discussed in the following sections.

1.1 The Historical Development of the Job Concept

The Concept of Work in the Old Testament

Already in the Old Testament we find evidence of work as a punishment that God put on human beings. In the beginning of Genesis, the first book of the Bible, the story of Adam and Eve tells us that humans lived in the Garden of Eden, the single perfect place on Earth where there was no sorrow or burden. After Adam and Eve sinned, God "sent [them] out from the garden of Eden to work the ground from which [they were] taken." (*Holy Bible, New International Version*, Genesis 3: 23). Thus, work can be interpreted as a punishment that distinguishes life in paradise from the world in which humans now live. To emphasize their situation, God said to Adam and Eve: "By the sweat of your face you shall eat bread, till you return to the ground, for out of it you were taken; for you are dust, and to dust you shall return." (Genesis 3:19). Through contemporary times, some Jewish people and sects believe work to be a curse that God brought to mankind because of its disobedience and ingratitude. Interestingly, though, early Christians thought work could be used to eliminate the original sin of mankind and to regain dignity. Augustine, said in 396, "From this cup of sorrow, no one may be excused. The cup that Adam has pledged, must be drunk." (cited after Hollingworth, 2013, p. 4). The hope: To look forward to the next life in God's kingdom.

Work in Greek Literature

In Greek literature, work was described as the doing of the people who were slaves. People saw work as a punishment that was placed on Earth from the Gods. The Greek word for work "*ponos*" (ancient Greek: Πόνος *Pónos*) means **sorrow** or **hardship**. The personification of work in Greek mythology was Ponos, the god of hard work and soil (Caldwell, 1987). All of Ponos's siblings were personifications of wrongdoings of mankind, including Forgetfulness (Lethe), Lies (Pseudea), Dispute (Amphillogiai), Manslaughter (Androktasiai), Pain (Algea), and War (Makhai) (Caldwell, 1987), emphasizing the negative connotation of work to the ancient Greeks. Manual labor was not for the rich, who spent their time pursuing warfare and the "liberal arts"; thus, work was exclusively reserved for slaves who had neither rewards nor power in return for their hard work.

Work during Protestant Reformation

The Protestant Reformation initiated many changes that diverged from Catholic faith traditions, including perspectives about work. For hundreds of years, the Catholic Church had dominated Medieval Europe, until, in 1517, Martin Luther, a German priest, denounced corruption in the Church. He *re*conceptualized work as something that is not negative but beneficial to both the individual and society. In Luther's view, one can serve God through his/her work. Before, people believed the work that was the most pleasing to God was becoming a monk. But Luther proposed that the common work of a servant or a handmaiden can be even more pleasing to God than the fasting and works of monks and priests. Hard work, discipline and frugality became new values in the mindset of the Protestant belief. Luther pointed out that God has equipped every human being with special talents that every individual can use to serve others and to do good for each other, which demonstrates God's love in the individual. Through service to others, people can fulfill the highest commandment of the New Testament: "Love your neighbor as yourself" (Mark 12:31, NIV). Martin Luther's ideas changed society deeply. With the Protestant movement, work became a desired medium to gain life satisfaction and to serve God on Earth (Eells & Walton, 1974; Marx, 1887; Tilgher, 1962).

The Job Concept during Industrial Revolution

During the 18th century, Western societies began using machines for manufacturing processing and developed streamlined and efficient factory systems. In 1786, Adam Smith published his widely recognized book *An Inquiry to the Nature and Causes of the Wealth of Nations*. In his book, he defined necessary conditions for economic growth and proposed the division of labor as the key to an efficient economy and prosperity (1786, p. 18-20). Before the Industrial Revolution, people mainly worked and lived in the same location and community. They worked as farmers, as shoemakers, as crafters; they bought products from people they knew, they produced and traded goods inside their community, and they saw how their products were used and consumed by people they knew. Hence, the process of work was closely connected with the outcome and purpose of the goods and services individuals produced and provided. When industrial manufacturing began, people were encouraged to seek work in factories that promised good pay for their work. Adam Smith famously described work in those manufacturers like this:

One man draws out the wire, another straits it, a third cuts it, a fourth
points it, a fifth grinds it at the top for receiving the head. . . I have seen a
small manufacturer of this kind where ten men only were employed. . . .
They could make among them upwards of forty-eight thousand pins a
day. . . . But if they had all wrought separately and independently . . . they
certainly could not, each of them, make twenty. (cited after Schwartz,

Barry, Why We Work, Chapter 1, p.1-kindle edition)

Organizing labor by dividing work into simple, repeatable, easy to run units was an economically successful idea that resulted in productive efficiency mankind had not known before. But by leaving each individual with the same small tasks to fulfill every workday, people got separated from the outcome of their work. With diminishing responsibility, the desire of people to participate declined. So why would people work this way? The reason was, according to Smith, money. He was convinced that human beings are lazy by nature and would not work unless they are given rewards – without (monetary) rewards, people would have nothing. Adam Smith's ideas made him known as the "father of economics." His philosophy of free markets fundamentally changed the way that business was conducted and set the milestone for a change in the work environment.

Still, there were great thinkers criticizing the ideas of capitalism. One of those was Karl Marx, who wanted to end the division of hand workers and brain workers as proposed before. He finished his *Economic and Philosophic Manuscripts* – a series of notes on capitalism containing some of his most interesting thinking about work – in 1844. Marx criticized capitalism not only because employers failed to compensate workers fairly but also because their work was boring and did not develop their characters through work, which is the core of Marx's criticism of capitalism. He noted that, although he enjoyed work, most workers work in conditions that allow no enjoyment. His idea of communism, in contrast to capitalism, was to bring back enjoyment to work, not totally eliminate work.

At the end of the 19th century, another great thinker, Max Weber, published his ideas. Weber lived during the turbulent formation of the first German national state, so he focused on ideas like rationalization, bureaucracy and social stratification. Weber analyzed the way society was changing from traditionalism to modernity. Traditionalism is understood as a cultural view in which one accepts the condition(s) of the world as it is inherited, while not seeking to change one's own position or roles in society. Modernism, in contrast, included thinking about one's own actions, reflection, and rational thinking. Weber saw religion as the reason for the shift to modernization in society. In his book *The Protestant Ethic and the Spirit of Capitalism,* which he wrote in 1904 (published in English in 1930), Weber argued that the transition from traditionalism to modernity began with the Protestant Reformation that rebelled against the ideas of Catholicism. In the Catholic belief, everything in this world is set to operate how God intended it and that the choices and actions of single individuals do not matter, and therefore, people worked because they had to work but with no bearing on their destiny. The Reformation, though, brought up the idea that one's work and how well one performed his/her work is important. Combined with Calvin's idea that human beings are determined to be saved by God or not, and that wealth and success are proof of being "elected" by God, Weber concluded that if an individual has financial success, that was seen by society as a sign that they were blessed by God. The social consequence of the Protestant Reformation was, in Weber's view, that work became an end in itself: work was important because it proved one's worth. Society transformed from a communal, traditional society to an individualistic, capitalist society – a society focused on economic success.

Weber identified bureaucracy as a key part of the transition from the traditional to the modern state. Bureaucracy was what made public administration, government, and businesses extremely efficient. He identified that the ideal-typical bureaucracy is characterized by: a hierarchical organization (a clearly defined structure of positions) with a rigid division of labor and a clear chain of command; fixed areas of expertise of workers; regular and continuous execution of assigned tasks with regulations that guide all decisions; worker development through training based on qualifications, with qualifications evaluated by organizational rules not individual rules/preferences; and workers treated universally the same, disregarding personal, individual characteristics of workers. Weber did not see bureaucracy as solely or inherently positive. In his view, bureaucracy also threatens individual freedom. He worried that people would become locked in what he called an "iron cage" of bureaucratic capitalism, living a soulless life of continuous interactions based on rationalized rules with no meaning.

The Job Concept in the Past Century

In the beginning of the 20th century, Frederick Winslow Taylor published *The Principles of Scientific Management* (1911), a book that ended up as one of the most influential management books of the twentieth century (Bedeian & Wren, 2001). On the basis of the knowledge provided by Adam Smith, Taylor refined the factory to be more standardized, encouraging workers to be part of a well-oiled machine by working harder, faster, and more accurately. He thereby redefined the role of the worker and their supervisor by suggesting that competent teachers should train their subordinates into new working habits (Taylor, 1911). In his view, there was one best way to do a task, a "standard," and every worker should do each task exactly the same way, or "to standard," in order to boost productivity. Through selection and training, workers could become "first-class employees" excelling at their one designated task. Taylor also believed in hierarchy; thus, control of the performance of tasks should be given to managers who are mentally alert, intelligent, and would plan the work process, while the monotonous labor work should be done by a type of employee who just follows the directions of the leader. Workers became doers, while managers became thinkers.

Taylor also emphasized the role of rewards for the performance of employees: While the most productive worker should be paid more, less productive workers should be fired. Hence, in his mind, people work better when they get more money, building the basis of the idea of seeing work as a pure exchange of performance for pay.

After the Wall Street Crash of 1929, a great depression, a period of economic crisis followed. In some parts of the world, it left almost a third of the working population without a job. The resulting economic chaos caused Bertrand Russel (1872-1970) to think about the meaning of work and to re-evaluate the ethics of work. He pointed out the struggle between classes, which he titled as following a hierarchy of virtue and heavily criticized the class system that resulted from the division of labor. "The morality of work is the morality of slaves, and the modern world has no need of slavery", he stated in 1932. He criticized the existence of social classes in which manual laborers were considered as less virtuous than the intellectual workers of the middle class. The system, he argued, regarded intellectual work as "higher" than manual labor and left unemployed people with no assigned virtue at all.

Other great thinkers engaged in researching the question of the meaning of work. Psychologist Abraham Maslow states that people have the need for a life that is meaningful, which he argued included the need for work that brings meaning to life (1943). Hence, people who cannot see their work as meaningful will be less likely to develop their full potential and are less motivated to perform their best (Chalofsky & Krishna, 2009). According to Guion and Landy, work motivation comes from the appraisal of the job as gratifying and as positive (1972, p. 311). Baumeister and Wilson (1996) see four needs as the basis of the search for meaning: (1) the human need for a *purpose*, meaning that individuals can see their actions lead toward their goals (e.g. graduation, wealth) or to *fulfillment* (e.g. happiness, salvation), (2) the need for *value* and justification, being able to distinguish between what is right and wrong, (3) the need for *efficacy*, being able to make a difference, and (4) the need for *self-worth*, to have a positive view of oneself.

1.2 The Job Concept in Current Times

In the 1970s, a new concept of work was introduced into scientific discourse: New Work. Frithof Bergmann, called the inventor of the concept New Work, began to think about the freedom of the individual and how a job can be combined with the idea of a free individual. Automatization and the way people worked in this system was, in Bergmann's view, contrary to the idea of freedom (1990). Since the Industrial Revolution, the purpose of work activities has primarily been to complete a specific task – for example, a work step on the assembly line. The means to achieve this end was the working man, who thus functioned as a mere tool. For Bergmann, New Work, or the ideal work, is instead to do a job that provides meaning and that is chosen freely by the individual. In short, Bergmann said, "New Work is the work that a person "really, really wants.""

But what is it that a person really, really wants? In his writings, Bergmann assumed that what people really, really want is a high degree of independence, freedom, and participation (Bergmann, & Schumacher, 2005).

Even today, the concept of New Work is hotly debated. New Work is no longer used to solely signify Bergmann's ideas; it is now understood as a collective term for future-oriented and meaningful work. Moreover, New Work is understood as a synonym for the change of the work concept in general, in which the question arises of how we define and organize work innovatively in order to continue to make an increasing contribution to corporate strategy. The socio-demographic changes, including demographic change, digitization, globalization, and change in values results in a changed view on what we think of work and jobs (Hackl et al., 2017). The technological change, including Industry 4.0, digitization, machine learning/KI and decentralization, moreover, leads to a change in the possibilities of how people work together and how work can be organized: classic concepts of a job – in terms of time, space, and organization are being disrupted. The classic "nine-to-five job" is hypothesized to be a relic of the past in many organizations and positions in the future. Also, fixed places to work from, fixed times to work in, and fixed structures in organizations will diminish. More and more people will not work in fixed roles but project-based and self-employed. The fast-moving world will result in more agile work processes, providing the possibility to react quickly to change (Bergmann & Schumacher, 2005).

In the New Work movement, employees are seen as the greatest asset of a company. In times of scarcity, talented employees are hard to find and to attach to the organization. The attachment of employees to the job hence becomes more important, as fast-changing environments lead to diminishing employee loyalty. Therefore, Bergmann (1990) points out that a job should be, as stated before, what employees really want. Work should no longer be a dull activity to earn a living but should be fun and fulfilling: work to live instead of live to work.

1.3 Defining the Job Concept

Before, the concepts of "work" and "job" were used relatively interchangeably with no marked distinguishing definitions or features. This is, because, traditionally, "there has been no distinction made between the concepts of work and job" (Andersson, 1992, p. 89). In general, "work" or "job" both described the action of using one's time and energy on a task in return for a social, financial or psychological reward (Andersson, 1992). The problem with this definition is the insufficient ability to distinguish work and non-work activities, as the definition would describe an employee at a company as well as a person working as a teacher in school, the student learning to prepare for university or the mother using her time and energy at home to take care of her kids. Andersson asks about artists who sell their paintings: "Do they have a job, do they work, how do they perceive themselves in regard to work and job?" (Andersson, 1992, p. 90). Andersson's inquiries indicate that a job is not easy to define as a distinct construct.

When we look closer, there are even more concepts one can bring to the table: profession, vocation, career, and even calling. People frequently say, "Some people have a calling, but most of us just have a job" in an attempt to differentiate between the different levels or forms of employment, with a calling considered the highest form among the rest. To have a calling, something you are called to do, is the highest form of work. To better distinguish the concepts and to differentiate the job concept from other concepts, the following section provides definitions.

Profession. A profession typically describes a group of people who all perform a common type of work, e.g. teacher, doctor, or lawyer. In this type of work, workers are professionals, which means they share certain standards by which they can be judged as professionals. No one can easily proclaim "I am a professional lawyer" and go to court for a client without even having passed the bar exam – this would not be considered "professional." What "professional" is is always determined by the community of professionals that set the standards.

Calling. The wording "calling" stems from Christian belief that God called human beings to love, serve, and follow him. The word comes from the Greek word *kaleō*, which means call, invite, demand. Vocation means the same as calling; stemming from the Latin word *vocare*, which means voice, to call. Vocation indicates the call to follow God's voice, or to do what people are called to do. In the New Testament of the Bible, written both in Greek and in Latin, several verses describe the calling, e.g. "All things work together for good for those who love God, who are called according to his purpose." (Romans 8:28, NIV). Hence, calling is connected to a purpose. Books such as "Make your Job a Calling" (Dik & Duffy, 2013) explore the idea that every person can find meaning and purpose in their work and hence a sense of calling. In a study by Davidson and Caddell (1994), 15 percent of their sample stated that they view their work as a calling, indicating that having a calling matters to people.

Career. While the job is what you do for others, i.e. a company, the career is what individuals build for themselves. The Oxford Dictionary defines career as "the series of jobs that a person has in a particular area of work, usually involving more responsibility as time passes." People with a career orientation tend to think long-term when selecting a job and set goals they pursue.

Job. A job is defined by Ilgen and Hollenbeck as a "set of task elements grouped together under one job title and designed to be performed by a single individual" (1992, p. 173). Hence, the job is not a thing everyone can do; a job means the specific setting of one single individual that is made up by the tasks the individual must do in a specific organizational setting. Organizational setting refers to all components included in a job, which comprises: the specific tasks that are involved in the job, the organization an individual works[4] for, the workplace surrounding the individual and the other people the individual works with (e.g. colleagues, supervisors) or for (e.g. clients, patients, students). Hence, a job has elements that are all reconciled into one unified image the individual has of their job (see Figure 5):

---

[4] If the individual works for a big enterprise or if the individual is self-employed, the person is their own organization.

Figure 5. *Job Elements*
Note. Own Illustration.

Hence, the job is never just about the tasks of the job but has to be viewed in context of characteristics of the job, workplace conditions, and relationships that come with the job.

2   Theories underlying the Concept of Love

Love is a topic that has been of high interest from prehistoric times to the present day, creating a fascination not only among scientists but also among philosophers, poets, historians, songwriters, and artists. Cave paintings of loving couples, old scriptures talking about love, and today's use of modern technology to investigate people's brains when they think about the people they love indicates that nearly every human being on Earth might have experienced or thought about love in life.

Although a topic in literature for decades, in the scientific world, for a long time, the topic "love" was a taboo topic. Any researchers who even touched the topic "were denounced by irate politicians, religious leaders, people-on-the-street, and even their own colleagues" (Berscheid & Walster, 1978, cited after Hatfield, 1982, p. 267).

And understanding love is not easy. It is a complex phenomenon and it took some time to remove the magic that paralyzed people from touching it and finally approach the subject for a deeper analysis.

In this chapter, the reader will learn about two perspectives on love: First, the psychological viewpoint is discussed. The most famous theories on love are presented. Then, the marketing viewpoint is expressed as a first try of the use of interpersonal love theory in other contexts than the person-person context. Love in the consumer-brand relationship, called brand love, is introduced and the most relevant studies are discussed.

2.1   Love for a Person – Love from a Psychological Perspective

In psychology, researchers have long hesitated to touch the topic of love. In the 1950s, psychologists almost gave up on the research of love. Harry Harlow (1905-1981), famous for his controversial experiments with rhesus monkeys, stated in 1958: "The little we [as psychologists] know about love does not transcend simple observation, and the little we write about it has been written better by poets and novelists" (p. 673). Yet, the interest in the topic of love was constantly growing, so that today we see a variety of research up to the point that it is possible to identify a unique psychological perspective of love.

2.1.1   Love as a Social Need (Abraham Maslow, 1943)

One of the first researchers who talked about love was Abraham Maslow. He started his research in the 1930s and became famous for his research on human needs, later known as the Hierarchy of Needs (1943). In contrast to earlier psychologists who were interested in abnormal behavior and mental illness, like Sigmund Freud, Maslow wanted to research how humans can achieve their full potential and meet their needs. Based on Henry Murray's conceptualization of human needs (1938)[5], Maslow found five basic sets of needs:

1. **Physiological needs:** Food, water, shelter, warmth, sex, sleep, etc.

2. **Safety needs:** Security, order, law, limits, stability, etc.

3. **Social needs:** The need to belong, to be loved, family, affection, relationships, etc.

4. **Esteem needs:** achievement, self-esteem, mastery, independence, status, dominance, prestige, responsibility, etc.

5. **Self-actualization needs**: self-fulfillment, personal growth, living one's potential

Maslow's idea was that human beings are motivated by unsatisfied needs. He described certain needs of the individual that must be satisfied in order to strive for the satisfaction of "higher" needs. He states that, before someone needs love, someone wants to have "basic needs" fulfilled. Those unsatisfied needs need to be satisfied in a hierarchical order: basic needs have to be fulfilled before other higher needs can be addressed. The need for love, in Maslow's hierarchy, belongs to social needs, step three of five in the

---

[5] Murray (1938) identified the following needs: abasement, achievement, affiliation, aggression, autonomy, counteraction, deference, dependence, dominance, exhibition, harm avoidance, inavoidance/inviolacy, nurturance, order, play, rejection, seclusion, sentience, sex, succorance, superiority, and understanding.

hierarchy. He even put the need for love before esteem needs and self-actualization needs. In Maslow's view, people want to belong, they want to be loved and be in loving relationships. This need, if not fulfilled, hinders people from continuing up the hierarchy, yearning for achievement and growth.

Despite the simplicity of Maslow's theory and the appeal of an easy transfer to the other contexts (such as the work context, e.g. by Cherrington, 1994), not all researchers have uncritically accepted his ideas. Berl et al. (2013) argued that several studies and replications of the model have found no evidence for Maslow's theory. They criticize the universality of teaching Maslow's theory in universities across several subjects, like psychology, management, and social science, without further reflection upon the result that the student is leaving "college with the false impression that he/she has been provided with insights into what motivates people." (2013, p. 38). Other researchers argue that Maslow does not differentiate needs from motives (Köthemann, 2013), which leads to confusion. Still, as the spreading of the theory in research has shown, Maslow's ideas contribute to the understanding of human theory, and the concept of love as a human need.

2.1.2 Loving vs. Liking (Rubin, 1970)

One of the first scientific researchers of the concept of (romantic) love was the psychologist Isaac Max "Zick" Rubin. Romantic love, compared to love for a need, indicates the view of love as a form of relationship between two people. Rubin started researching the phenomenon of (interpersonal) love for his doctoral thesis at the University of Michigan after recognizing that social psychologists had paid "virtually no attention" to the topic (1970). His research began with asking people about their attitudes toward other people, including questions about physical attraction, idealization, needs and the desire to share feelings. He then formed an item pool containing the answers of the participants and further included items derived from already existing theoretical and empirical literature on interpersonal liking. He let all the items be sorted by two distinct panels of students and faculty judges according to whether they reflected "liking" or "loving." The extracted 70 items were given to 198 students to be rated when thinking of their partner and when thinking of a good friend. The consequent factor analysis could show the two hypothesized distinct factors describing "liking someone" and "loving someone" (Rubin, 1970). The final scale contained 26 items – 13 items measuring "liking" and 13 items measuring "loving." The "liking" items included a feeling of respect and favor for and the perception of similarity to the liked person, while "love" was shaped by the three different components (1) attachment, (2) caring, and (3) intimacy. Rubin's conceptualization of romantic love defined the three components in the following way:

1. **Attachment** is the need to be with another person and to be cared for by this person. It can be enhanced by physical contact and by appreciation of the loved person.

2. **Caring** includes that a person values the loved person's needs and happiness over his/her own feelings.

3. **Intimacy** is built up by sharing feelings, desires and thoughts with the loved person.

Building on his research, Rubin defined love as "an attitude held by a person toward a particular other person, involving predispositions to think, feel, and behave in certain ways toward that other person." (1970, p. 265). He concluded that love is much more than just a more intense form of "liking" or an "emotion" or a "need," contrary to what he thought other researchers had reduced love to (e.g. Heider, 1958). While he characterized "liking" as a form of a platonic relationship, he assumed that a romantic relationship includes both "liking" and "loving." The amount a person loves or likes their partner can be measured with his Loving and Liking Scale, differentiating items that measure when someone (only) likes another person versus items that measure the love for a person.

Rubin's work in the research field of love can be considered highly valuable as his research marked a significant step forward in today's understanding of the phenomenon of love. He was not discouraged by previous researchers such as Harry Harlow, who said researching love would be senseless. Instead, Rubin became a pioneer, introducing love as a multifaceted construct. He was widely credited as the author of the first empirical measurement of the complex feeling of love. Enriching prior research, he introduced the concept of love as not only containing emotional, hence affective, elements, but also cognitive elements (e.g. recognizing the other people's needs) and motivational elements (e.g. the desire to care for the other). Moreover, he provided evidence for love being more than intensified liking. Although the scales of Rubin have become outdated (Masuda, 2003), his research provided a basis for further taxonomies of love.

2.1.3 Passionate and Companionate Love (Hatfield & Walster, 1978)

Another researcher who became interested in the field of love was Elaine Hatfield, a young researcher at Stanford University in the 1960s and 1970s. Together with G. William Walter, she published the book *A New Look at Love* (1978) in which they asked the question: "What is this thing called love?" Hatfield and Walster found that people distinguish two kinds of love, passionate love and companionate (also called compassionate) love. The two are distinguished by the depth of the feelings toward the loved person and how deep someone is involved with the other.

Hatfield and Walster define passionate love as following:

> A state of intense longing for union with another. Reciprocated love (union with the other) is associated with fulfillment and ecstasy. Unrequited love (separation) with emptiness; with anxiety or despair. A state of profound physiological arousal (Hatfield & Walster, 1978, p.9).

Passionate love, "sometimes called 'romantic love,' 'obsessive love,' 'infatuation,' 'lovesickness,' or 'being in love,' is a powerful emotional state" (Hatfield, Pillemer, O'Brien, et al., 2008) and comes with distinct cognitive, emotional and behavioral characteristics that are described in detail below:

1. **Constant thinking about the loved person:** People who experience passionate love have intrusive thoughts about the partner, from which they cannot unwind. These thoughts are persistent and can come at any time during the day or night.

2. **Strong emotions:** Passionate lovers have strong positive emotions towards the loved person when everything in the relationship is going well. They feel extremely well and happy when they are with the loved one or when they think

about them. Contrary, when things are not going well, or the loved one even rejects them, passionate lovers are devastated and develop emotions, such as anxiety and despair.

3. **Desire for emotional closeness:** People who are in passionate love want to be with and know everything about their partner. They also want to self-disclose and become emotionally intimate with the loved one to create the feeling of being close to one another.

4. **Desire for physical closeness:** In addition to the emotional attachment to the loved one, passionate lovers want to be physically close and feel high sexual arousal.

5. **Idealization:** The passionate lover views the loved person as their "perfect match." The other person is idealized as perfect and seen with no flaws. Even if the loved person does something wrong, the other person tends to reinterpret or talk down the misdoing and forgive mistakes.

While passionate love is characterized by its intense emotions and feelings, companionate love is more about the level of intimacy. Hatfield and Walster define it as the "affection we feel for those with whom our lives are deeply entwined" (Hatfield & Walster, 1978, p. 9).

Passionate love is predominant in the beginning phase(s) of a relationship, but in a long-term relationship, companionate love subsumes passionate love, taking over with feelings that are more centered on caring about another person and being and staying committed to the loved one for a long time. Hence, feelings of mutual respect, trust, and affection become more prominent (Fehr, 1988; Hendrick & Hendrick, 1989; Mikulincer & Goodman, 2006; Sternberg & Weis, 2007).

Companionate love has distinct cognitive, emotional and behavioral characteristics that include the following:

1. **Intimacy:** As people disclose themselves to the other and share more thoughts with the other, they become closer, and the level of intimacy between them rises.

2. **Trust:** With a high level of intimacy, trust in the loved person also becomes stronger.

3. **Long-term Commitment:** Finally, companionate love is characterized by a commitment to the other person – in good as well as in bad times.

Passionate Versus Companionate Love

According to various researchers, people in almost all cultures differentiate between passionate and companionate love (Fehr, 1988; Fischer, Shaver, & Carnochan, 1990; Hatfield, Rapson, & Martel, 2007). Lay people usually feel there are two kinds of love: "being in love" and "loving someone" (Myers & Berscheid, 1997). People who are high on companionate love are still passionate about their partners but not as intensely as people with high passionate love. In a long-term relationship, the passion between two loved ones usually declines, while companionate love becomes stronger. While passionate love may quickly fade, the level of companionate love remains stable or even rises over time (Hatfield, Pillemer, O'Brien, & Le, 2008). This process happens mostly within the first one or two years of a relationship. Hatfield and Walster described this process, saying "Passionate love is a fragile flower – it wilts in time. Companionate love is a sturdy evergreen; it thrives with contact" (1978, p. 125).

Interestingly, one of the attributes differentiating passionate and companionate love, according to Hatfield and Walster, is the existence of negative emotions, which exist when love is unrequited by the loved one. Hence, negative emotions are an element of passionate love, while companionate love only includes positive emotions (Hatfield, 1978, p. 207). Still, in a romantic relationship, Hatfield and Walster argue, both kinds of love exist or people even "drift in and out between the two" (1978, p. 10). Together with Susan Sprecher, Hatfield developed the Passionate Love Scale (PLS) (1986), a scale that has been of worldwide interest among the researchers of love. The scale was designed to assess the cognitive, emotional and behavioral components of love and was originally used in family therapy. The PLS consists of 30 items (15 items in the short version), measuring the cognitive (intrusive thinking, preoccupation with the partner, and idealization), emotional (attraction, positive feelings when things go well, ambivalence/negative feelings when things turn bad or when people are reflected by the loved one, the desire to be loved and for complete union), and physical (sexual) arousal and behavioral components (maintaining physical and emotional closeness, serving the other) of love.

2.1.4 Color Theory of Love (Lee, 1973)

Another researcher who dared to tackle the topic of love was John Alan Lee, a professor at the University of Toronto from 1971-1999. He started to look at love by examining and analyzing literature on the topic of love, from romantic poems to philosophical writings (1973). After reviewing literature, he interviewed hundreds of people with a method he developed called the "Love Story Card Sort." In this method, he showed people different phrases like "The night after I met X…," which the subjects then had to complete by choosing from different sentences like "I could hardly sleep after meeting X." Lee found that love can have different expressions or styles in a relationship, which he divided into primary, or "pure" styles, and secondary styles, which he found to be a combination of the three primary ones. He argued that every person has his/her own love style and that it would be helpful to know what kind of love style oneself has and to find out and respect the love style of the partner.

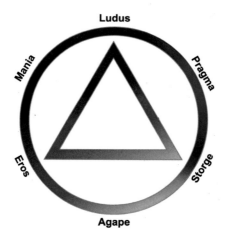

Figure 6. *Colors of Love Theory by Lee (1988)*
Note. Own illustration based on Lee (1988, p. 54).

Lee assigned those love styles to a color wheel (see Figure 6) with the three primary love styles (eros, ludus and storge) aligned with the colors red, blue and yellow, respectively, and the three secondary styles (mania, pragma and agape) assigned to the three secondary colors green, orange and purple.

Primary Types of Love

Eros (passionate love), from the ancient Greek ἔρως *érōs* that means "love" or "desire," is based on romance. It usually begins with strong physical arousal and an immediate powerful attraction, a fascination by the image of the beloved as a vision of ideal beauty, and a hint of recognition of one's true love.

Ludus (game-playing love) is based on conquest. People with this love style are best described as those who see love as a game. They want to "win" as many partners as possible. The focus is on having fun at the moment and therefore the relationships of people with a ludus love style tend to be rather short-term than long-term.

Storge (friendship love) is based on friendship. This style of love grows slowly out of friendship and is based more on similar interests and a commitment to one another rather than on passion.

Secondary Types of Love

Pragma (logical love) is a combination of ludus and storge styles and is based on practicality. People with this love style are practical and realistic and are searching for the perfect compatible partner with whom they can share common goals.

Mania (possessive, dependent love) is a combination of eros and ludus styles and is based on obsession. People with a mania love style tend to have a low self-esteem and a high need to be loved by their partner and to be completed by them. Lovers of this sort usually become very possessive and jealous and experience great anxiety about being left or rejected by them.

Agape (all-giving, selfless love) is a combination of eros and storge styles and is based on selflessness. Agape lovers are ready to do anything for the loved partner; their love tends to be unconditional and altruistic.

In Lee's view (1977), the love type of a couple can change over time and can transform into another love type. Lee's approach provided another view of love as a multidimensional construct and has been widely recognized in scientific literature (Langner & Kühn, 2010).

2.1.1 Love Attitudes Scale (Hendrick and Hendrick, 1986)

On the basis of Lee's typology of love styles (1973, 1977), Clyde and Susan Hendrick developed a scale measuring the love style of a person in a relationship. Their theoretical background utilized Lee's typology because of its multidimensionality and because Lees' love types already included several other theories, building a good basis for their research. For example, they identified the pragma love style to be based on exchange theory (Lee, 1973; 1976), the Agape love style on Clark and Mills' (1979) description of communal love, the Eros love style on Berscheid and Walster's (1978) passionate love and the Storge love style on companionate love as proposed by Kelley et al. (1983).

The Love Attitudes Scale (LAS) Hendrick and Hendrick developed in 1986 has six subscales that each measured one of the six styles of love proposed by Lee. The seven statements for each love style are scored on a five-point Likert scale ranging from "1 = strongly agree" to "5 = strongly disagree." Examples of some of the items are shown in Table 1. The scale has been tested several times and found to have excellent psychometrics (Hendrick, Hendrick, & Dicke, 1998). The higher a person scores on one of the subscales, the more of that kind of love someone has for their partner. The love style can differ from partner to partner, as the love style of the loved partner also influences the relationship and hence the love style shown by an individual. Other factors, such as stage of life and sociodemographic features, can influence the love style (Sternberg, 1986).

Table 1. Example Items of the Love Attitudes Scale

Love Style	Measurement Item
Eros	My lover and I were attracted to each other immediately after we first met.
	I feel that my lover and I were meant for each other.
Ludus	I try to keep my lover a little uncertain about my commitment to him/her.
	I can get over love affairs pretty easily and quickly.
Storge	The best kind of love grows out of a long friendship.
	My most satisfying love relationships have developed from good friendships.
Pragma	I try to plan my life carefully before choosing a lover.
	It is best to love someone with a similar background.
Mania	Sometimes I get so excited about being in love that I can't sleep.
	When I am in love, I have trouble concentrating on anything else.
Agape	I would rather suffer myself than let my lover suffer.
	I am usually willing to sacrifice my own wishes to let my lover achieve his/hers.

Note. Items stem from the Love Attitudes Scale (Hendrick & Hendrick, 1986)

2.1.5 Love as a psychological state (Aron & Aron, 1986, 1996)

In contrast to Lee's multidimensional concept of love, the researcher couple Elaine and Arthur Aron describe love as a psychological state where an individual extends one's own self onto the loved one's self (1986, 1996). Their self-expansion model states that every human being has a desire to expand themselves and that self-expansion can be achieved in close relationships that allow the inclusion of the other person into one's own self.

In their view, love is "the constellation of behaviors, cognitions and emotions associated with the desire to enter or maintain a close relationship with a specific other person" (Aron & Aron, 1991, p. 26). According to Aron and Aron, this love feeling can be attributed to any close relationship, including friends and family. They developed the Inclusion of the

Other in the Self Scale (Aron, Aron, & Smollan, 1992), which became one of the most frequently used tools to assess interpersonal closeness. A visual picture of Aron and Aron's idea of different levels of closeness between a couple is shown in Figure 7.

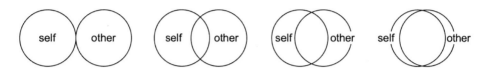

Figure 7. *Love as a Psychological State of Interpersonal Closeness*
Note. Own illustration based on Aron & Aron (1986)

2.1.6 Triangular Theory of Love (Sternberg, 1986)

One of the todays' most recognized theories of love stems from Robert Sternberg, an American psychologist who is ranked the 60th most cited psychologist of the 20th century (Haggbloom et al., 2002). His initial questions regarding his research on love, were "What does it mean to love someone? Does it always mean the same thing, and if not, in what ways do lovers differ from each other? Why do certain loves seem to last, whereas others disappear almost as quickly as they are formed?" (Sternberg, 1986, p.119). In line with previous researchers (e.g. Lee, 1977; Hendrick and Hendrick, 1986), Sternberg sees love as a multidimensional construct. In Sternberg's Triangular Theory of Love (1986), love consists of the three dimensions passion, intimacy, and decision/commitment, with each dimension forming one vertex of a triangle. This triangle is rather a graphic metaphor than a geometric model, as the three dimensions are not independent, but influence each other. On top of the triangle is intimacy, left of it is passion and right is commitment/decision. The theory suggests that people can have different levels of each of the dimensions that result in distinct forms of love. Only when all three dimensions are at a high level, Sternberg argues, do they have "consummate love." Hence, the three dimensions are not substitutional for each other: A higher level of passion cannot compensate for the lack of commitment and vice versa.

The three dimensions each have distinct characteristics:

1. **Intimacy**: In loving relationships, intimacy describes feelings, such as closeness, connectedness and warmth. Therefore, Sternberg refers to intimacy as the "warm" and *emotional* dimension of love (1986). Sternberg and Grajek (1984) argued intimacy can be potted into ten different clusters: (1) The desire to want the best for the loved one, (2) happiness when being with the other, (3) high regard for the other one, (4) ability to count on the other in times of need, (5) mutual understanding, (6) willingness to share possessions, (7) emotional support received from the loved one, (8) emotional support provided to the loved one, (9) intimate communication and (10) high value for the loved one. Intimacy develops over time as couples get to know each other better, and it is a process in which self-disclosure plays a major role (Sternberg & Grajek, 1984; Sternberg, 1986).

2. **Passion**: is the *motivational* dimension of love. Passion is closely related to physical attraction, arousal and feelings of romance, which explains why the dimension is also called the *hot* component of love. Passion can be described as "a state of intense longing for union with the other" and involves the fulfillment of needs for self-esteem, dominance, and the need to avoid negative experiences such as loneliness.

3. **Commitment**: Commitment is the *cognitive* dimension of love and includes two aspects: The short time aspect, which is the decision to be with and to love someone at the current time, and the long-term aspect, which is the willingness to maintain the love relationship in the future. The two aspects of commitment do not necessarily have to exist both together as someone can also decide to love a person only within a short-time commitment without committing to forever. Adding to this, the commitment dimension also comprises cognitive thoughts, such as the assumption that the loved one is a good partner to love. As this dimension is based upon rational thoughts the dimension is also called the *cold* component of love.

The three dimensions result from different processes. While intimacy derives from emotional investment into the loved one, passion stems mostly from motivational involvement, and commitment comes from the cognitive decision for the relationship.

Still, as stated above, the three dimensions of love are not independent, as they can interact with each other. To measure the dimensions, Sternberg developed the Sternberg Triangular Love Scale (STLS, 1997). It consists of 72 items with 24 items measuring each of the three dimensions of love, including feelings about and behavior towards the partner. Research shows that the three dimensions interrelate, as intimacy and passion are closely related (e.g., Sangrador & Yela, 2000; Weigel, 2010; Graham, 2011). How they are related is not yet clear. While more studies identify intimacy as the driver of passion (Aron & Aron, 1986; Baumeister & Bratslavsky, 1999; Birnbaum et al., 2016; O'Leary et al., 2012; Reissman et al., 1993), other studies find that passion causes intimacy (Ratelle et al., 2013). And although previous research could not show a clear casualty of one dimension to the other, Hendrick and Hendrick (1989) found a high correlation between Sternberg's dimensions. This can explain why, when passion towards the loved person is high, intimacy also increases. The reasons might be that with high passion, motivation to invest in and to spend time with the loved one is high and by spending time together, intimacy might rise, potentially causing the level of commitment also. In the negative example, when passion is still high but commitment is very low, the level of intimacy might decline due to the lack of commitment to spending time with each other.

Sternberg admits that there are multiple ways to divide the complex construct of love (1986, p. 119), but his choice of dividing love into intimacy, passion and commitment would be the most promising for understanding the phenomenon of love in close relationships.

Properties of Sternberg's three dimensions of love
As an outcome of the combination of different levels of the three dimensions, Sternberg recognizes eight different kinds of love that can be extracted, with each having distinct characteristics (for an overview see Figure 8).

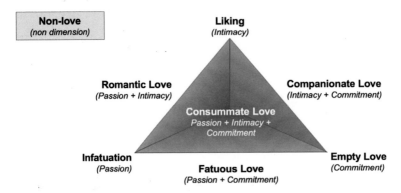

Figure 8. *Sternberg's Love Types*
Note. Own illustration based on Sternberg, 1986

Sternberg defines the types in the following way:

1. **Non-love** is a state where all three dimensions are absent. This type characterizes the majority of relationships with people that one does not know deeply or with whom one simply does not have a love relationship.

2. **Liking** can be described as simple sympathy without being passionate about someone or committed to them. This is true for relationships people have with acquaintances or close friends.

3. **Infatuation** is the kind of love someone experiences when only passion is high. It is also described as "love at first sight" and characterized by high physical arousal without even liking the person or being committed. Typical psychophysiological reactions are an increased heart rate and increased hormonal secretions. This kind of love occurs primarily at the beginning of a relationship when enough time has not yet passed to develop intimacy or commitment. It can also occur if someone loves a person who does not know about or rejects the affection shown by the passionate lover. Tennov (1979) called the phenomenon of obsessed love "limerence," a strong desire for the reciprocation of one's feelings, which can last quite some time.

4. **Empty love** exists only when commitment is high, but passion and intimacy are low. It can be found sometimes in long-term relationships when two partners have lost their passion and mutual emotional connection with each other. In Western society, empty love is often the end stadium of a marriage or relationship, while

in other cultures, for example in areas with arranged marriages, the mutual commitment to love each other can be the setting stone of a relationship with intimacy and passion developing in the future.

5. **Romantic love** is the love Hollywood waits for: it is the kind of love relationship one can see in movies and read about in literature, and that is sometimes referred to as "true" love. Probably the most famous example of such true love is Romeo and Juliet, who were even willing to die for each other. In a romantic love relationship, passion is high and so is intimacy. Commitment is not necessarily high in a romantic relationship and feelings can easily fade without it.

6. **Companionate love** is the kind of love that derives from a combination of intimacy and commitment without the passion dimension. A long-term, committed friendship can be characterized by companionate love as well as marriages where sex and physical attraction play a minor (if any) role.

7. **Fatuous love** is the love that exists when passion and commitment are high, but intimacy is low. Sternberg gives the example of a couple who meets, gets engaged the day after and marries the next month to describe this kind of love. It is love based on emotion and passion but not a stable involvement with the other person. It can also characterize a beginning relationship, as passion can be high from the beginning, while intimacy needs time to develop and flourish. As a result of this fact, Sternberg strongly advises *against* hasty weddings, as they often end in divorce (1986, p. 124).

8. **Consummate love** is the combination of all Sternberg's three elements of love – intimacy, passion, and commitment. It is also called complete love, as most people long for this kind of love in a relationship. Nevertheless, Sternberg states that maintaining consummate love is like maintaining a healthy weight after a weight-reduction program: getting there is easier than staying there.

Changes of Love Over Time

When we look at how love develops over time, Sternberg's three dimensions help us understand which parts of love change. Stating that love changes as relationships change, the components of love also change (see Figure 9).

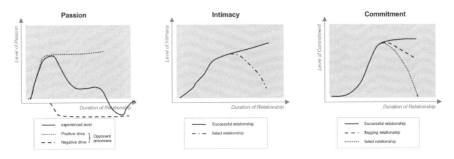

Figure 9. *How Love Changes over Time*
Note. Own illustration based on Sternberg, 1986, p. 126-127.

Sternberg distinguishes successful relationships from failed relationships when he describes the course of single dimensions over time. In a successful relationship, intimacy grows when the partners get to know each other, spend time together, and grow connected to each other. Still, intimacy declines after some time. In a failed relationship, the couple starts with equal levels of intimacy, but the decline is steeper: The level of intimacy declines to an almost lower level than the starting level (Sternberg, 1986, p. 126). Commitment also falls drastically after some time in a failed relationship, while in a successful one, commitment rises to a high level, where it stays (Sternberg, 1986, p. 127). The third component, passion, is, according to Sternberg, the least stable component of love, as Sternberg built his view of passion on Solomon's opponent-process theory of acquired motivation (Solomon, 1980). When it comes to passion, two motivational processes seem to work: a positive process that is "quick to develop but also quick to fade," and a second opponent process that "is slow to develop and also slow to fade" (Sternberg, 1986, p. 126-127). The passion component usually increases quickly but can as quickly peak down. As both processes act, the individual feels a change of passion depending on which process, the positive or the negative, is present. During these processes, passion comes with intensive emotions and feelings. Emotions are a reaction to stimuli that change instantly, also the feelings that come with passion do. What can be summarized from Sternberg's theory is that love changes over time, because the components of love, passion, intimacy, and commitment are subject to change.

Conclusions

Although no theory can completely cover the complexity of the phenomenon of love (Hendrick & Hendrick, 1992, p. 62), research on love measurements shows it is possible to measure love, as many researchers have done previously. Most researchers perceive love to be not unidimensional, but multidimensional, hence the view that interpersonal love is a multidimensional construct is increasingly gaining ground in research. Through today, the most widely known theory of love is Sternberg's Triangular Theory of Love (Langner & Kühn, 2010). Sternberg (1986) therewithin proposed a theoretical approach to the research of love that explains the multidimensionality and the multifaceted diversity of the construct. He suggested that any type of interpersonal relationship can be described as a combination of three dimensions: intimacy (connection, closeness, emotional component), passion (arousal, excitement, motivational component), and commitment (decision, cognitive component). Several researchers have empirically validated Sternberg's concept of love in an interpersonal context (e.g. Chojnacki & Walsh, 1990; Hendrick & Hendrick, 1989; Lemieux & Hale, 2000). The simplicity of the theory helped it become the most talked about and used theory on love in scientific research (Hendrick & Hendrick, 1992, p. 59). Therefore, Sternberg's Triangular Theory of Love is seen as the most suitable for the research of love in the work context and is suggested as a theoretical basis for the empirical research of this dissertation.

2.2 Love for a Brand – Love from a Marketing Perspective

After the discussion of love from a psychological standpoint, it is now necessary to look at the topic of love in marketing. In marketing practice, maintaining good relationships with customers has long been in the focus of marketers (Heinrich et al., 2012). Fetscherin and Heinrich (2014) provide a matrix classifying consumer brand relationships into two dimensions: emotional-based (low versus high) and functional-based (low versus high) connection (see Figure 10).

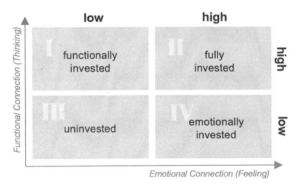

Figure 10. *Classifying Consumer-brand Relationships*

Note. Own illustration adapted from Fetscherin & Heinrich (2014, p. 368)

While a functional connection to a brand is formed when "functional needs" are met, the emotional connection is formed as the result of met emotional needs. *Functionally invested* consumers may be satisfied with their brands' performance, but they are not emotionally connected to the brand. In contrast to the price-sensitive *uninvested*, functionally invested would be willing to pay higher prices for the best functioning product, but if they find a product that has better functionality for a better price, they do not remain loyal to a brand. *Emotionally invested* consumers like their brands as they value the feelings they have for the brand, although the product may not have all the functions or features they would look for in a brand. In this case, fulfilling emotional needs compensates for the lack of function. When consumers are fully invested, high functionality comes with high emotional function. In this type of relationship, consumers show the highest brand loyalty, willingness to pay and extremely positive word of mouth, even "turning a blind eye after service failures" (Fetscherin & Heinrich, 2014, p. 368).

In marketing research, the focus is shifting towards the research of emotional relationships (e.g., Fournier, 1998; Fournier & Yao, 1997; Robinson & Kates, 2005; Shimp & Madden, 1988). Emotional consumer-brand relationships are not always positive in nature. Fetscherin and Heinrich (2014) group emotional relationship concepts by the strength of the relationship (strong versus weak) and the valence of the feelings towards the brand (positive versus negative). As shown in Figure 11, brand love is a concept that comes with strong positive feelings towards the brand and high strength of the relationship. While positive feelings also characterize concepts such as brand satisfaction, high strength of a relationship is also given when consumers start to hate their brands, indicating the strong motivational component of love and hate.

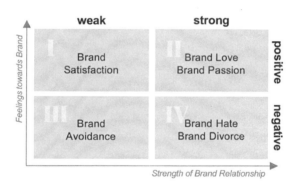

Figure 11. *Brand Feeling Matrix*

Note. Own illustration adapted from Fetscherin & Heinrich (2014, p. 370)

2.2.1 Consumer-Object Relationships (Shimp & Madden, 1988)

In 1988, Terence A. Shimp and Thomas J. Madden, two researchers from the University of South Carolina, introduced a conceptual model of consumer-object relationships based on Sternberg's Triangular Theory of Love. For their transfer of Sternberg's love components (passion, intimacy and commitment) to the brand context, they renamed the dimensions into yearning, liking, and decision/commitment, respectively. Shimp and Madden see yearning as the deep desire consumers have for a brand, and liking as the closeness and connection people feel with a brand. Commitment to the brand describes the decision people make to be loyal to their brand. Analogous to Sternberg's eight types of interpersonal love, they also constructed eight kinds of consumer-brand relationships by combining the single dimensions as presented in Table 2.

Interestingly, the type of love when all three dimensions are present, which Sternberg identified as the only real "consummate love," Shimp and Madden named "loyalty," indicating that they hesitated to use the strong word "love" for their concept. The reason why they have translated love into loyalty, which further emphasizes the commitment facet of love, is left open by the authors.

Table 2. Shimp & Madden's Brand Relationship Types

Sternberg's Triangular Theory of Love (1986)	Shimp & Madden's Consumer-Brand Relationships (1988)	Liking (Intimacy)	Yearning (Passion)	Decision (Commitment)
Non-Love	Non-Liking	-	-	-
Liking	Liking	+	-	-
Infatuated Love	Infatuation	-	+	-
Empty Love	Functionalism	-	-	+
Romantic Love	Inhibited Desire	+	+	-
Companionate Love	Utilitarianism	+	-	+
Fatuous Love	Succumbed Desire	-	+	+
Consummate Love	Loyalty	+	+	+

Note. + means the level is high, - means the level is low/absent.

2.2.2 Relationships between Consumers and Brands (Fournier, 1998)

Susan Fournier was the first researcher to name relationships between consumers and brands "relationships." While others criticized the transfer of interpersonal relationships to the consumer context, she argued that brands are like real "relationship partners" a person can build strong bonds with (Fournier, 1998). With an idiographic analysis, wherein she analyzed qualitative interviews, Fournier identified 112 different consumer-brand relationships out of which she devised 15 relationship types that range from "secret affairs" to "committed partnerships." To do this, she identified seven facets that relationships can be described by: (1) voluntarily or imposed, (2) positive or negative, (3) intense or superficial, (4) short-term or long-term, (5) private or public, (6) formal or informal, and (7) symmetric or asymmetric (Fournier, 1998, p. 361). All 15 relationship types have different combinations of these facets as shown in Table 3.

Fournier showed, with her publication, a first approach of seeing consumer-brand relationships as similar to interpersonal relationships. By naming the types "marriage" and "affair," her research made a big step into researching love in the marketing sphere. It did not take long for practitioners to take on similar language and relationship methodologies.

Table 3. *Consumer-Brand-Relationship Types*

Relationship type	Definition	Examples
Committed partnerships	Long-term relationship that is voluntary and based on love, intimacy, trust and a commitment to be loyal even in adverse circumstances.	Brands that are not given up although other, potentially better brands or products exist because of the strong commitment
Arranged marriages	Long-term relationship that has been arranged by a third party and has therefore not been consciously entered.	Household brands that have been already used by parent; brands that are used by the partner
Marriages of convenience	Long-term relationship that is voluntary, but induced by external social factors	Brands that have been used for a long time, like a car brand that is convenient not to change
Dependencies	Highly emotional, even obsessive relationships with the brand, characterized by feelings of separation anxiety.	Brands that are irreplaceable to the consumer, e.g. football teams that have loyal fans although they leave a league.
Secret affairs	Highly emotional relationships that the consumer wants to keep a secret.	Brands from socially not suitable products, e.g. (unhealthy) products; websites that are frequently visited without the consumer telling others
Flings	Short-term relationships with a high level of emotional affirmation, but without promises and mutual demands	Brands that cover different, situational needs and moods, or are used just to experiment
Courtships	Transitional relationship on the way to a committed partnership	New brands and product launches offering, e.g. special offers or free trial
Best Friends	Voluntary association based on reciprocity and characterized by self-disclosure and high intimacy and honesty and intimacy	Brands with frequent, long-term use and strong integration into everyday life
Compartmentalized Friendships	Friendships with a low level of intimacy and connection but high commitment in special situations	Brands that are consumed/used on specific occasions, e.g. perfume brands

Casual friends/buddies	Friendships where the partners show effort only sporadically, characterized by low levels of intimacy and low expectations for reciprocity	Brands that are very similar to other brands in the same product category that people go to when there are special offers
Childhood Friendships	Relationships that stem from a memory of earlier times, offering comfort and security to former ego	Childhood brands, e.g. sweets such as Nutella; Nostalgia brands; Retro brands
Kinships	Non-voluntary relationships that stem from lineage ties	Brands that the (grand-)parents used
Rebounds/avoidance-driven relationships	A connection that stems from the desire to break out of a current or past relationship	Brands that currently meet the needs of the consumer but would usually not be chosen
Enslavements	Involuntary community completely determined by the partner's wishes; includes dislikes but exists because of the circumstances	Use of brands with a monopoly position so that there is no alternative
Enmities	Intense negative relationships, characterized by aversion and the desire to avoid one's own pain or to inflict pain on the other	Brands with negative memories in which the consumer was highly involved, but was disappointed

Note. **Table retrieved from Fournier (1998, p. 362).**

2.2.3 The Lovemarks Concept (Roberts, 2005)

In 2005, only seven years after Fournier's pioneering "consumer-brand relationships," Kevin John Roberts, former CEO of famous marketing agency Saatchi & Saatchi, introduced a new way of thinking in marketing: that brands can be loved. He identified emotions as the core reason why consumers build strong and lasting relationships with their brands. He stated, "Emotion has become a legitimate subject for serious research. Once the scientists got into emotion it didn't take them long to prove what was obvious to everyone how cared to look" (Roberts, 2005, p. 38-39). Why are emotions so relevant? As Roberts argues, they lead to actions, while reasoning only leads to conclusions. And when emotion and reason battle each other, emotions win (p. 42). He concluded that finding out what satisfies people is not enough to build a strong brand. Consumers, in his view, need to *love* the brand. The special brands that have distinct emotional connotations to their customers he called "Lovemarks," a concept that greatly impacted management-oriented literature.

Roberts later defined Lovemarks as "brands, events and experiences that are loved by people" in his book *The Lovemarks Effect: Mystery, Sensuality and Intimacy at Work* (2006). He states that brands can be distinguished by the two dimensions "love" and "respect" (see Figure 12).

There are brands with *low love* and *low respect:* these products are those that consumers do not really feel attracted to. *High love, low respect* brands are those short-term, trendy products that are hip one day and out the next. Consumers tend to not be loyal to those though they love them for a short time. Then there are brands that enjoy *high respect*, but *no love.* Those are the ones that are comfortable to use but do not cultivate a spark.

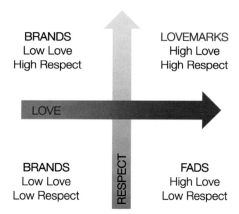

Figure 12. *Lovemarks in the Love-Respect Diagram*
Note. Own illustration adapted from Roberts (2006)

Only brands that enjoy *high respect* and *high love*, can be called lovemarks. Lovemarks contain three dimensions:

1. **Mystery** built with stories, metaphors, dreams and symbols that connect past, present, and future. Mystery gives a relationship texture and helps it stay strong with complexity, layers, revelations and excitement.

2. **Sensuality** appeals to our five senses, which are stimulated by the brand. It is about textures, smells, lovely sounds that bring a smile to consumers' faces when

they think about the brand. By involving all senses, Lovemark brands create unforgettable memories.

3. **Intimacy** is the component that helps grow empathy, trust, engagement and passion with consumers. The close connections to those brands build intense loyalty among consumers as those brands are often remembered long after functions and benefits have faded away.

Roberts's Lovemarks concept found broad interest in the marketing field, but the groundwork was not empirically based, so scientific researchers stepped in to fill that gap.

2.2.4 The Brand Love Concept in Research

The term brand love was first published in 2006 when Aaron Ahuvia and Barbara Carroll published their article *"Some Antecedents and Outcomes of Brand Love"* in *Marketing Letters*. Their research began in 1993 when Aaron Ahuvia published his dissertation on the love for objects. He criticized the approach of other researchers to transfer the love concept of interpersonal relationships to consumer relationships without evidence of the fit, so he proposed a grounded theory approach for researching the matter. Yet, also with his more qualitative approach, he found that similarities exist between love and brand love; in a study published in 2005, Ahuvia compared how people describe love between persons with the ways they describe the love for objects, which were very similar. Ahuvia then partnered with Barbara Carroll, and together, they started researching not only objects but also brands. They defined brand love in their article from 2006 as an emotional relationship between a consumer and a brand that is characterized by passion. Contrary to researchers like Shimp and Madden, who took Sternberg's typology of love as a basis, Carroll and Ahuvia describe brand love as a more unified concept. Their one-factor construct of brand love contains five different characteristics: (1) passion, (2) attachment, (3) positive evaluation of the brand, (4) positive emotions, and (5) declarations of love. Although all five elements of love are separated by their definition, the authors conclude love as one factor, as their factor analysis showed loadings of all elements on only one factor. Six years later, Ahuvia published another higher-order prototype of brand love together with other researchers, Batra and Bagozzi. Using a grounded theory approach, they identified seven core elements: (1) self-brand integration, (2) passion-driven behaviors, (3) positive emotional connection, (4) long-term relationship, (5) positive overall attitude valence, (6) attitude certainty and confidence, and (7) anticipated separation distress (Batra et al., 2012).

Conclusions

Various studies have shown that there is a difference between people who like brands and people who love them (Langner & Kühn, 2010): people are not only more satisfied with loved brands and glorify them, even when a brand is losing performance or cannot be delivered on time, but their loyalty goes beyond that of those who just like a brand. There is the saying "Love makes people blind" and that is part of why people who love a brand differ from people who like a brand: those who love the brand make it part of their identity and build such strong relationships with the brand that they are loyal even if they know that not everything is perfect with the brand (Carroll & Ahuvia, 2006).

Although the concept of brand love has found a tremendous amount of interest among researchers in the marketing field during the past two decades, there is still little agreement on what brand love is. Numerous models of brand love currently exist, with each providing helpful and distinct insight into the relationships between consumers and brands. What we have learned is that although the transfer of the concept of love in interpersonal relationships to the marketing context has been criticized (Langner & Kühn, 2010), various researchers (e.g. Shimp & Madden, 1988; Fournier, 1998; Carroll & Ahuvia, 2006) have shown that consumer-brand relationships indeed have similarities to interpersonal love relationships. A transfer of models that already exist in psychology has shown promising results when being applied within marketing contexts. In contrast, other researchers have tried to introduce completely new theories on brand love using grounded theory approaches. Within a grounded theory approach, researchers start from the "ground" and build theories from data collected exclusively from their experiments and studies. Yet, the outcomes of their grounded theories of brand seem similar to theories published in interpersonal research on love (e.g., Ahuvia et al., 2008), indicating that either way – building new theory and using interpersonal love theory will produce similar outcomes.

3   Conclusions on the Literature Review

Love is a widely researched phenomenon, both in psychology and marketing. Still, there exists neither a unifying theory on its underlying dimensions nor the processes of how love is developed. Therefore, the advantages and disadvantages for approaching the love of a job have to be weighed and the most suitable theory for researching the job love phenomenon must be evaluated.

By far, the most used theory on love is Robert Sternberg's Triangular Theory of Love (1986). There are several reasons for the success of his theory. First, Sternberg describes love as a complex and multi-dimensional construct and not as a simple emotion. Perceiving love as a form of relationship can explain why people who are in love experience different emotions, both positive and negative emotions, such as experiencing joy when being with the other, and having anxiety about losing the loved person. Also, the change of emotions in people who love over time can be better explained by the perspective of love as a form of relationship rather than an emotional state. Moreover, Sternberg's theory provides a clear definition and operationalization of the love between persons. The theory has been applied already successfully in branding theory where consumers who love brands are described as distinct from consumers who just like brands (e.g. Shimp & Madden, 1988). Consumers in a love relationship with their brand are ready to invest time, effort and money into their loved product; are highly loyal and positive when speaking about the brand; and they would even stay loyal when negative events associated with the brand occur. Sternberg's three dimensions of love – passion, commitment and intimacy – are three dimensions of love leading to different outcomes, as they describe motivational, cognitive, and emotional processes. Those three dimensions are not substitutional for each other: A higher level of commitment cannot compensate for a low level of passion. Only when all three dimensions are existent, people experience what Sternberg names *consummate love* for a person. After carefully weighing evidence advocating for and recommending against using Sternberg's model as a basis for the research of love in the work context, it is concluded that Sternberg's Triangular Theory of Love is the most suitable and, especially important, most applicable theory for a study of job love.

Proposed Job Love Model and Operational Definitions

Sternberg's Triangular Theory of Love is used as a theoretical base for this dissertation's job love concept. Job love is defined as:

> **Definition:** Job love is a person's dedication to their work, characterized by a strong passion for work, the feeling of connection with the organization and the people in the workplace, and the decision to maintain the relationship in the future.

Hence job love consists of three dimensions: passion, connection[6], and commitment (see Figure 13).

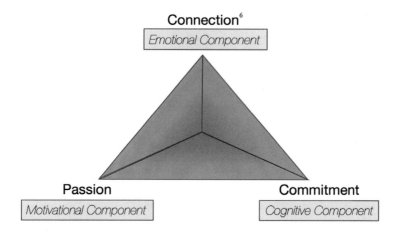

Figure 13. *Job Love Model*

Note. Own illustration adapted from Sternberg's Triangular Theory of Love (1986).

---

[6]Sternberg's dimension "intimacy" had to be renamed and adapted to the work context, because the word "intimacy" could be misunderstood as sexual intimacy. In the job context, the term being connected was seen as more appropriate. Hence the adapted name for the dimension "intimacy" is "connection".

The following definitions of the dimensions passion, commitment, and connection are proposed:

Table 4. Operational Definitions of Job Love Dimensions

Dimension	Operational Definition
Passion	Job Passion is a strong inclination toward work involving intense positive feelings for the work, idealization of the workplace and motivation to invest time and energy into the work. The job is seen as part of one's identity.
Connection	Job Connection describes the emotional connection of a person to the workplace including the feeling of belonging, well-being and feeling emotionally valued and supported by the work environment.
Commitment	Job Commitment involves a conscious decision for the work and workplace, including the knowledge to have a perfect fit job and the wish to maintain the job in the current and in the future.

With the study's definition of job love and its dimensions, this study requires that more questions be answered before suggesting a theory of job love. This study will engage in the ongoing discussion of whether theories of love may be applied to contexts other than the interpersonal context. After exploring whether job love exists among people, job love is being examined in whether it is possible to measure it. After having a model and measurement of job love, other questions can be examined. One can either examine how the concept develops, or how it affects outcomes. According to Schneider and Gerold (2007), there are two different possibilities when conducting research: When we research a concept "from the left," or "from the right" (see Figure 14). When we look at the concept as an independent variable and see how it is related to an outcome, this can be described as "research from the left" (Schneider & Gerold, 2017): from the left, the *in*dependent variable's side, we look to the right side, the dependent variables' side, and see how job love affects variable(s) X.

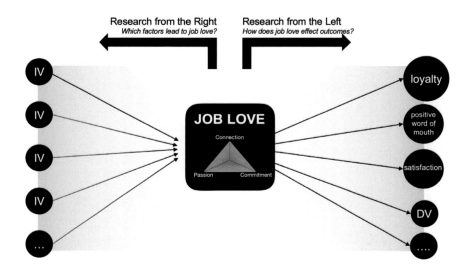

Figure 14. *Overview of the Research Objects*

Note. Own illustration. ID = independent variable, DV = dependent variable

As explained in this chapter, there are several outcomes that stem from the love of a person or a brand. For example, research has shown that people who love brands are highly loyal to their brands and provide extremely positive word-of-mouth recommendations to others (Langner & Kühn, 2010). It has also been shown that people who state they love their partner, show very high relationship satisfaction (Hatfield et al., 2008). There are numerous other (positive) outcomes of love, but as the goal of this dissertation is to give implications for companies of how they can enhance the employees' love of a job, it is more fruitful to look "from the right" side: what leads to job love? In this case, job love is seen as a dependent variable that can vary when different independent variables are put into the equation. Research from the right is especially challenging, as we want to explain a variable by finding possibly all the independent variables that determine a dependent variable. In this research, there is a focus on *research from the right*: The question is: "Why do people love their job?" and hence what leads to job love. The process will be described in the empirical part of this dissertation in the following chapter C.

C EMPIRICAL EXPLORATION

In the previous chapter, the theoretical basis of job love was explained. The concept of the job was explored in its historical development through contemporary work, which provided a foundation of what we understand as a job today. Following, theories on the concept of love in psychology and their transfer into the marketing field were discussed and theories that give insight into what love is and how it shows in the individual were presented.

This chapter provides an empirical exploration of the concept of job love. Three studies are presented, each with a different focus and different guiding research questions. The final focus of this research was the question: "Why do some people love their job while others do not?". Before being able to ask and answer this question, however, it is necessary to provide evidence that job love actually exists. This will be answered in Study 1. Moreover, the study will interrogate if job love exists in people and what laypeople think about job love. If Study 1 determines that job love is existent and that it is possible to love a job, it is necessary to be able to measure it. How to measure job love is investigated in Study 2. Finally, Study 3 explores why people develop love or not their job and identifies and tests possible antecedents of job love.

1 Study 1: Does Job Love Exist and What Do Laypeople Think about It?

There is an ongoing discussion on whether love is a concept that can be transferred to contexts other than the interpersonal context, i.e. person-to-person love.

1.1 Study 1a: Does Job Love exist?

To see whether job love exists, social media research was conducted. On the social media platform Instagram people who state that they love their jobs were researched with the use of hashtags. On social media, people tag statements with hashtags to identify messages on a specific topic. A hashtag is always started with a "#" and followed by a word or phrase that describes what is presented in a posting, whether it is a short message, a picture, or a video. As of June 4, 2020, there were 24.463.968 postings with the Hashtag *#lovemyjob*. More than 14 Million people used *#ilovemyjob*, and *#ichliebemeinenjob* (German for #ilovemyjob) was used more than 93 thousand times, indicating that there are people who *say* that they love their job.

For example, German eCommerce Company Zalando posted on their community account "insidezalando" a picture with a huge balloon in the shape of an eight, stating "8 years. We are impressed. Congratulations!", celebrating the eight-year anniversary of an employee with the hashtag *#ilovemyjob*. Another example found was Susi, a nurse, describing "What I love about my job: first of all, my colleges, we have a lot of fun. #urosisters. 2nd: to help people in their worst moments and make them a little better! 3rd Kathether legen […] ". A third example was Max, a subway driver, who wrote "Long turnaround time and wonderful weather. […] *#ichliebemeinenjob #ilovemyjob.*" Moreover, numerous testimonies were found on Instagram of people who do not only *say* they love their job but also *show* their positive word of mouth by posting testimonies publicly on their Instagram profile. All together those examples give evidence of people who at least express in words they love their jobs.

The question that follows from this is: *Do people mean the same when they say they love their job as when they say they love a person?*

1.2 Study 1b: Can the Love of a Job be compared to the Love for a Person?

The underlying question is whether the love of a job can be compared with the love for a person. The answer to this question is: Yes, it can. Comparing does *not* imply that the result of the comparison will be: Love of the job is the same as love for a person, but the result of the comparison can be. There are some similarities and some differences. Critical voices on the transfer of the love concept to other objects than persons are not new: critics in the marketing field conclude that the transfer of interpersonal love theories, like those of Lee (1977) and Sternberg (1986), to the consumer-brand relationship is inappropriate. Critiques frequently cite the unilateral nature of relationships between a person and a brand as a critical factor because a brand cannot love a person back. This argument can also be used as a critical point in the investigation of job love: Can a job love a person back? Maybe, in the work context, the environment of the job plays a role in this matter, as an employer(s), supervisor(s), colleague(s), and client(s) can love a worker back creating the feeling of being loved by a job.

Some critics also argue brand love is just an intensification of the liking of the brand, with love being the highest possible value on the liking scale. But in fact, people who love brands differ significantly from those who just like a brand: they talk more and more positively about the brand (Langner & Kühn, 2010), they are willing to invest a significantly higher amount of money into the brand (Batra et al., 2012) and they are more loyal to the brand, even in the eye of possible misdoings the brand makes (e.g. the product changing their portfolio, changing prices for the worse, delivering with mistakes, or providing bad products/services) (Batra et al., 2012; Langner & Kühn, 2010).

Procedure

To see to what level people think they love their jobs and to compare it with a subjective measure of love for a brand, and for a person, a survey was conducted asking people how much they love their job, their favorite brand, their favorite hobby and the most important person in their lives. The items were assessed on a scale ranging from *1 = I do not love X at all* to *10 = I love X above all.* The study was conducted between April to May in 2019 with the web-based survey software Unipark. In the study, 69 people joined with 46.3% men and 53.7% women, with a median age of 33.

Results

On top of the ranking of the four variables is clearly the love between people: love for the favorite person had the highest ranking, scoring a mean of 9.52 out of 10, followed by love for a favorite hobby with an average mean of 8.32 out of 10 (see Figure 15). Compared to this, love for a job and a favorite brand were relatively low: the level of love for the job scored a mean of 6.94, closely followed by the lowest average scoring of 6.63 out of 10 for the favorite brand.

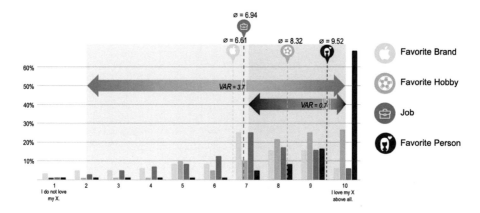

Figure 15. *Job Love Compared to Love for a favorite Brand, Hobby, and Person*
Note. The participants were asked: *"On a scale from 1-10, how much do you love…your favorite brand/your favorite hobby/your job/your most important person?"*

Discussion

The results show that most people have someone in their lives who they love at a very high level. The average level of love for the job was close to the average scoring of the love for the brand. What is interesting to look at, is variance within the variables. While most people (67%) rated the love for the most important person with a 10 out of 10, the lowest stated value among very few people (6%) was 7. Compared to love for work, where only 15% stated they love their job on a 10, the rating went down to 5% who gave their love a rate of 2 out of 10. Hence, the variance between people in the work context was very high ($var = 3.7$), while the variance in the person love variable was very low ($var = 0.7$, see Figure 15). This means, there are people who say they love their job very much, while there are people who say they do not love their job at all. The question is why? What differentiates people with an average of 2 from those with a 7 and those with a 10? How do their jobs differ? Those are interesting questions to ask and worth researching.

1.3 Study 1c: What do Laypeople think about Job Love?

In order to gain a deeper understanding of the concept of love of a job, a further approach was to ask how people actually experience the phenomenon in a qualitative study. The objective of the qualitative study was to gather honest information from laypeople's concept of job love and what people think about the love of a job. Laypeople's perspectives on the matter are important for initial exploration and understanding of the work situations people are in and to find first indicators for the reasons why people develop or have a love of a job or why they do not. The goal of Study 1c was, rather than already explaining the whole concept of job love in total, a first exploration of the concept and possible antecedents and outcomes of job love. Those insights are transferred into assumptions and hypotheses to be tested in further studies.

1.3.1 Method

Interviews. To gain these insights, people were asked in a personal, one-on-one interview setting about their attitudes towards work and about their opinions on people who love their job. Interviews were conducted to get a first impression of job love as it has been constructed in laypeople's minds. As the job typically is an element of one's life that is one spends months to years inside; the whole story of an individual's job journeys could be explored.

Focus Group. In addition to the individual face-to-face interviews, a *focus group* was planned and executed. The method is used to get initial opinions about a topic by conducting interviews in a group setting. Compared to other methods, the focus group is particularly suitable for researching attitudes on a specific topic. As the job is experienced mostly in a group setting in which the worker is present with colleagues and supervisors, researching the love of a job in a group setting is perceived as a good method fit. The interaction in the group can help people to explore and clarify their views in a way that is less accessible in a one-on-one interview.

Sample

Interviews. The interviewees were recruited from the author's personal environment. This made it easier to participate and to identify suitable test subjects. The test subjects for the interviews were selected in terms of their heterogeneity regarding their job, age, and gender (see Table 5). In total, eight people were interviewed ranging from 26 to 68 years *(mean = 37 years),* with four female and four male participants.

Table 5. Overview of Study 1c Interview Sample

				Interview Sample
#	Name[7]	Gender	Age	Profession
1	Mathias	male	32	Logistics Manager
2	Max	male	57	CEO, Sewage Works
3	Ava	female	30	Employee, Customer Operations
4	Peter	male	28	Project Manager
5	Adam	male	29	Sales Manager
6	Sarah	female	26	Nurse
7	Julia	female	34	Singing Coach
8	Janine	female	32	Teacher

Note. All names have been changed in order to protect the respondents' anonymity.

Focus Group. To recruit participants for the focus group, the researcher posted a call to participate on different social media platforms (Facebook and Instagram). The focus group was advertised as a Design Sprint workshop on the topic of "love of job" and interested parties were given further information on the purpose of the research. In total, six people were selected for the focus group, four women and two men, aging from 23 to 43, all with different professional backgrounds, building a heterogeneous sample. See Table 6 for more information about participants.

1.3.2 Procedure

Interviews. The interviews were conducted in a quiet place that the interviewee selected (i.e. a café, at home, or online via video call). The interviews were semi-structured and

---

[7] The names have been changed to allow the anonymity of the participants.

included (1) an introduction of the topic of love in general and job attitudes, (2) questions about the person and their current job situation, (3) questions about the interviewees' attitudes toward their jobs, and (4) significant events that happened over time. In the first part, the interviewee gained an introduction to the goal of the research they were a part of and to the topic in general. They were informed that their data would be anonymized. Then, a few questions about the interviewee and their current job situation were asked. In the following part, questions about love in general and possible factors that can lead to or hinder love were asked from the respondents. The interviews were recorded and transcribed. A uniform written language was used, i.e. colloquial expressions were converted into standard German.

Table 6. Overview of Study 1c Focus Group Sample

				Focus Group Sample
#	Name[15]	Gender	Age	Profession
9	Milo	male	33	Sales Manager
10	Amalia	female	26	Software Consultant
11	Sebastian	male	43	Kindergarten Teacher
12	Jessica	female	25	Office Employee
13	Anna	female	30	Marketing Manager
14	Valerie	female	23	Horticulture Engineer

Note. All names have been changed in order to protect the respondents' anonymity.

Focus Group. For the procedure of the focus group, the researcher did not use the "typical" focus group setting, i.e. giving a certain question or topic to discuss in a group; instead, the researcher conducted the focus group using methods from Design Thinking and Design Sprint. Design Thinking is a defined five-step process that seeks to solve complex problems by approaching them from the user's perspective (cf., Brown & Wyatt, 2010; Liedtka, 2014; Thoring & Müller, 2011). Concluding, Design Thinking is understood as a holistic, people-oriented innovation approach "in which many creative and analytical methods are combined in order to enable the development of new ideas and their testing in a series of prototypes" (Eppler & Hoffmann, 2012). In the context of job love, the user is a worker or an employee, and the "problem" to be solved by the focus group was to find out why some people love their jobs and why others do not.

Subsequently, the research question of this dissertation was transferred into what Design Thinking calls a "challenge." A challenge in Design Thinking is the definition of the solution to the problem that needs to be solved during the process, e.g. "Our challenge is to find out why some people love their jobs and why others do not." A Design Sprint is a concept that follows the Design Thinking method in a five-day time frame, which can be customized into different time frames depending on the goals of the workshop.

Figure 16. *Impressions from the Focus Group*

Note. Photographs were taken during the focus group. The picture on the right shows three positive factors for job love: Spaßfaktor im Büro = fun in the office, Wertschätzung = appreciation, and Annahme = acceptance. The red orange note is indicating a negative factor: Kündigung = termination.

At the start of the focus group, the researcher explained the procedure of the Design Sprint and that the outcomes of the study would be used for research purposes and that the data would be anonymized using pseudonyms for the publication of the research (see impressions of the focus group in Figure 16). Further, the participants were asked for their consent to take pictures and record their answers for the purpose of analyzing the content and presenting the outcomes in presentations and publications of the study, such as the present dissertation. The purpose of the workshop, to find out why people love their jobs and others don't love or even hate their job, was presented as well as to determine how attitudes and feelings towards work change over time. After each of the participants introduced themselves to each other, different steps of the Design Thinking method were followed as shown in Figure 17:

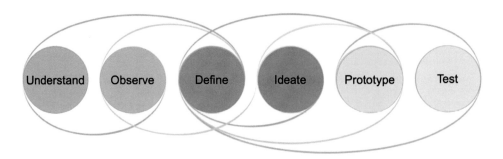

Figure 17. *The Design Thinking Process*

Note. Own illustration adapted from Plattner, Meinel, & Weinberg (2009, p. 114)

1. **Understand Phase**: This step is all about understanding the problem "job love" and the user. Therefore, the participants were asked to think about why people love their job and why they might not love their job and to write these down using brainstorming methods. Then, all the statements were presented in the group.

2. **Observe Phase**: After step one, each of the participants had to do their own qualitative research by doing interviews with the other participants of the group asking about the individual stories of the group members.

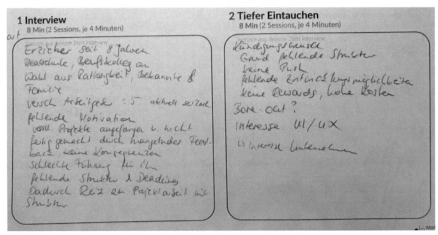

Figure 18. *Design Sprint – Participant Notes from the Observe Phase*

Note. Tiefer Eintauchen = dig deeper.

The result was interviews conducted with each participant by different interviewers. The insights about each of the persons then were shared with the group (see example notes in Figure 18).

3. **Define Phase**: In a third step, user stories were developed. Therefore, different methods, such as persona-building and empathy mapping (see Figure 19), were included. Personas are fictional characters that are created based on the research completed in step one and two that represent different points of views or typical employees, e.g. an employee who is very unhappy in their job and does not love it at all and another employee/persona who loves their job very much. Those personas help to create and develop ideas why people experience different feelings and behaviors, such as job love. The empathy map contains four different fields describing what the persona says, thinks, does, and feels.

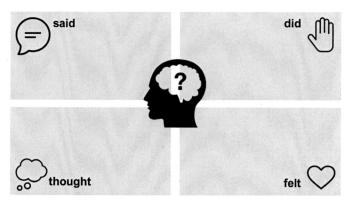

Figure 19. *Design Thinking Process – Empathy Mapping*
Note. Own illustration adapted from Schallmo & Lang (2017, p. 93).

4. In the fourth step, the **Ideation Phase**, the participants of the Design Sprint were challenged to create ideas for those personas to solve their problems. In this case, they thought about how to help people to love their jobs and what companies can do to create surroundings where people love their jobs.

5. The fifth step, the **Prototype Phase**, is usually the sketch of a solution product for the challenge of the Design Sprint. As the goal of the Sprint was to find out why

people love their jobs, the final prototype was more of a structured map of reasons for people to love their job or not. Therefore, a mind mapping technique was used, where the whole group together clustered the ideas into groups or categories – similar to the content analysis process of a qualitative research process. The result is presented in Figure 20.

6. Usually, the sixth step is the validation or **Testing Phase** where the prototype is tested in "real life." This part was excluded from the focus group setting, as the testing of the assumptions derived in step five will be part of Study 3.

1.3.3 Qualitative Findings of Study 3

Studying what laypeople think about a concept, such as job love, is based on the assumption that people have fundamental beliefs about themselves and how the world around them works (Furnham, 1988). When people are asked: "What do you think love is?", the answers are as different as the people themselves.

What is Love?

Peter, project manager in a big corporate, said his definition of love would be that love is:

"an extreme emotion in a maximally positive expression. The most positive emotion one can probably feel, next to the most negative one, hatred."

For other people, love is not just about feelings, it is more about cognitions and a decision(s). Sarah said in the interview:

"I think love is a decision. A decision to really accept something or someone as it/he/she is with all the good things and the bad things and to appreciate that, without wanting to change it."

Another interviewee, Julia, a singer and singing coach, thought love to be more of a holistic concept consisting of divine love, romantic love, and altruistic love. She answered the question of what she thought love is:

"I think you can sub-categorize love. First, there is divine love, which somehow stands above life. The love from which the world was made, from which we are made. and that is what carries me in life, where I feel carried. And [second], of course, I have to think of my partner, and there I find love as a great gift. And [third], there is love for other people. Love is something that unites us all that we have this ability to love."

Compared to Julia, who had a spiritual view on the love concept, Adam, sales manager, pointed out the biological side of love. In the interview, he stated:

"I would always call love a biochemical process, because for me that is just what it does to us, so our brain is one of the greatest mysteries we have, which we have not yet fully deciphered. Which hormones are released there and in what doses; that gives us the feeling of love."

Continuing to think about love, he added:

"This warm, this light, this being happy, one likes to be out and about with this object or this person, or in this atmosphere. Looking back, one also says: 'I loved that time', because you associate something beautiful with it. And I think if you manifest positive feelings in an object, in a memory, then you can say that you love that because somehow you don't want to miss it. A lot also has to do with the fact that one has expenditures. So many things that I love, maybe I don't have them anymore, or I'm afraid that they could be lost."

As demonstrated with those citations from the interviews, the definitions of love can be very different. According to the picture of a concept people have in their heads, they also evaluate things differently. An individual might think, for example, that love is something that is meant to be or not, and that love only exists when a person has found the perfect fit. This view then shapes how the individual perceives different situations or settings. To this individual, a fight between a couple might be a sign the couple is an imperfect fit. Or, a difficult situation at the job is a sign that the job is just not the right fit to cultivate job love. An individual with the contrary view, such as Sarah mentioned in the previous paragraph, who thinks that love is a decision during good and bad times, might see a difficult situation at work not as a lack of love but as something that one has to overcome in the journey of job life. Also, Michael, CEO of a sewage works company, said that love is not something that is meant to be, but that has to develop.

> "Love is also something that changes. I know this from my experience with my wife. Not everything is like it was at the beginning. It evolves. At first, you are totally in love, but real love is something else. It develops."

Consequently, it is important to state that the answers of single individuals to a specific question are always shaped by the individual's views and experiences. What people think love is as a concept might subsequently shape their view on what job love is as a concept.

What is Job Love?

In the following, the insights to questions related to the love of a job are presented in an overview. Additionally, some examples of statements from people of the qualitative sample are collected. All the results provided an initial perspective on what laypeople think about job love in order to build a testable research model for the latter two studies, Study 2 and Study 3.

After discussing general views on what love is as a concept, the interviewees and focus group participants were asked whether or not they personally loved their job. They were then asked to rate their level of job love on a scale ranging from *1 = no love* to *10 = complete love* to give them a starting point to talk about their own attitudes toward their work. Some of the respondents said they loved their job, while others said they did not, and the reasons they named were different.

When asked about the possibility, in general, for one to love a job, the majority of the qualitative sample said, no matter whether they personally loved their jobs or not, they believe it is definitely possible for an individual to love a job. Peter, for example, said:

> "[What is job love?] is a difficult question – you can definitely have an extremely positive emotionality and that could also be love, but I'm not sure myself if *I* would call this love [of a job]. But that you can feel this extreme positive feeling of love, I think is possible. It's about the wording."

Also, Adam said he thinks it is possible to love a job. He stated:

> "Yes. I think you can love your job. Complex answer: I think there are different facets to it that you have to add up: I think you can love parts of the job. But you can also love the work in itself. I would differentiate there."

When the study participants were asked to imagine someone who loves their job, most people thought of someone who found their dream job – a person having extremely positive emotions about the job. Being passionate about what they do were stated as signs for someone who loves their job. Michael, one interviewee said that he loved his job. He specified this saying:

> "I have found my dream job. I think the love for a job is comparable to the love for my wife. It grows and grows more every year. It wasn't like that from the beginning. But I learned to love my job. It's perfect for me."

Another example of a job-lover was Sarah. She said in the interview:

> "I realized that I love my job when I felt like I had arrived and felt home at work. I became part of the team and I was so valued as a person. I think that's what makes a job you love: that you can be who you are and you feel you in the right place."

Although most stated the possibility of someone loving their job exists, some had doubts about what love really is and when to call it "love" in the context of work. The wording itself seems to be questionable to some of the respondents. One participant, Amalia, a software consultant, also said,

> "I think I don't want to love my job. For me it is important that I as a person have a certain distance to my professional activity. I consciously don't want to build up such strong emotional ties here and let myself be absorbed by a community (company). Ultimately, it only leads to being exploited."

Others argued there is no need to love a job. A job is there for the money and, additionally, for the status and self-actualization, but to love a job would be too much to ask of them or other employees.

In the focus group, where job love was discussed intensely, the group agreed that there are certain requirements to call feelings job love: A person who loves their job must have a passion for the tasks of the job, positive emotions about the job, a feeling of excitement about work and a setting that fits the persons' needs. Milo, for example, stated:

> "I think to love your job you have to have a total passion for what you are doing. If you don't like what you do, it's not possible."

What are reasons for loving a job?

In a next step, study participants were asked for what reason(s) they love their job, or for what reason they think a person in general might love their job.

Sarah said that to her, especially her colleagues are important when it comes to why she loves her job. She said:

> "I love my job, first, because I am looking forward to my work and I really enjoy going there. Second, because I love to work with my colleagues, which are like a family to me. Third, because my job gives me purpose, because [as a nurse] I can help people get better."

Other study participants were more focused on the task in the job itself rather than on relationships. Ava pointed out the feeling of accomplishment which seemed important to her when thinking about reasons why to love a job:

> "I am happy when I finish a good, complete piece of work of mine and I am proud of the result [...] Then, my work gives me these feelings of happiness. That is why I love my work.

Anna, a marketing manager who participated in the focus group, said that for her,

> "loving your job means that you are excited about going to work on Monday morning."

Others, such as Max, highlighted that his job fulfills him and gives him a sense of purpose:

> "It fulfills me, I enjoy it. I also somehow think that my work gives me purpose because we help the environment and that way I can make a contribution to the world."

Sarah, the nurse, added on why a job can give purpose when saying:

> "What I enjoy most is when I see that a patient who almost died can go home and have a few more years to enjoy. That people get well, or they are fine again and have quality of life again."

For Julia, the singing teacher, love can be expressed in a job through doing something good for other people. She explains it as follows:

> "When you discover something meaningful in your work, because you are doing something good for someone else, or you love your job. And that is again connected with charity [in German, charity is translated as 'love for the next', love for other people]. Because you don't just think about "Hey, how can I get

my paycheck at the end of the month?" but "How can I have a positive impact on my environment with what I do?".

Janine, a teacher, also spoke about doing something good for other people:

"I love that I get to change the lives of people by giving them something on the way. It gives me purpose."

For Sebastian, a kindergarten teacher who was part of the focus group, a job to love is a job that offers 'the whole package':

"I love my job because I can't think of any other alternative where the components money, fun, place, security and human contact are more in harmony with one another."

Others, for example, Mathias, who works as a sales manager, describes his reason to love a job: Money:

"I love it because they keep on paying me more money every year."

What are reasons for not loving a job?

After the study participants had to reflect on what reasons are to love a job, they were also asked about what reasons are, not to love a job, or what factors can hinder people from loving their jobs. In the focus group, participants had to draw a journey of their whole working life and identify the 'highs and the lows', the positive parts of their journey, as well as the negative parts. When reflecting about their working life journey, participants came across some positive events, but also negative events and talked about why they may not have loved their jobs, and why other people might do so too.

Anna, a marketing manager in the focus group, stated that she

"couldn't love my position because there was never any recognition of what I did or any appreciation."

She then said that she quit her job because of the lack of appreciation she got. She also recorded that part of that was bad management and a negative relationship with her supervisor – reasons not to love a job for her.

Also, Mathias told about his supervisor:

"My former supervisor was not a good supervisor, always putting stress on other people, including myself. So, under these circumstances, it was hard to love what you do."

This indicates that relationships at work mattered to the respondents, especially the relationship to one's supervisor. Still, not only relationships with supervisors were discussed by the interviewees. For Ava, customers can get exhausting, especially when she has to hear criticism often during her workday. She expressed:

"I hate the unreflective, unjustified criticism from customers without specialist knowledge, to which I am always exposed in my job."

For Peter, who works as a project manager in a big company, quitting his job was an option, but not because of relationships at work, but because of the lack of impact he has in his role. He stated:

"I can't say that I love my job [...] I almost quit my job because the opportunities in a big corporation are huge, but I didn't see the why in my job. I asked myself what impact does my job have?"

Other respondents highlighted the role of development, which was not mentioned often when asked about why people love their jobs. Anna stated during the focus group that:

"The reason not to love my job for me is that I have the feeling that I can 'do more' and that I would like to develop myself further, although this is only possible to a limited extent in the sense of the "career ladder.""

Adam stated:

"If you do the same thing for too long, you feel stuck. I know everything now, I know my way around. But I don't learn anything new. And sometimes I ask myself: Is that everything now? Or do I have an opportunity to grow and to develop myself?"

1.3.4 Clustered Findings of Study 3

In the focus group, all ideas of reasons why people love their jobs or why people do not their jobs were collected on a board. The board was, since the focus group took place in the private rooms of the study director, a window where participants could pin their ideas. Together with the group, clusters were created that group similar words into overall categories. Those clusters are shown in Figure 20. The green sticky notes indicate an attribute of love for the job, while the orange sticky notes contain a characteristic of a reason not to love a job.

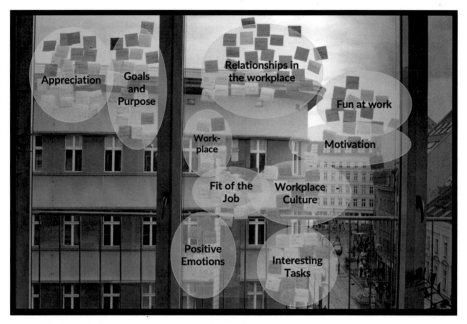

Figure 20. *Final Cluster of Job Love Antecedents*
Note. Photograph taken of the focus group results that were pinned to a window with circles of clusters added.

The results of the cluster are presented in the following two sections. A first section, job love antecedents, discusses all positive factors that lead to job love, according to the study participants. A second section, job love barriers, discusses all negative factors that can hinder people from loving their jobs or are connected to people who do not love their jobs.

Job Love Antecedents

Appreciation and recognition. A trend among interviews and discussions, especially in the focus group, was appreciation and recognition from the job. The participants in the focus group doubted that it was possible to love your job if you never got recognition or appreciation for the work you do. Therefore, they suggested that, in order to be able to love a job, employees need to be appreciated as a person, and their work should be appreciated as well. They also emphasized that good pay is a sign of recognition and that bonuses or presents from the employer can contribute to the feeling of appreciation in the workplace and, therefore, the chances that an individual could develop love for a job.

Goals and purpose. During the discussions about reasons to love a job, many respondents argued that to be able to love a job, the job needs to be fulfilling and purposeful. The participants defined purpose as the fact that people know what and who they work for and why they do what they do. Hence, the goals of the job and the contribution a person makes to the company, to the team or to other stakeholders must be clear. Max, the CEO of a sewage works company, named that one of the reasons he loves his job is that he thinks his company helps the environment, which fulfills him personally. Sarah, a nurse, described that because she helps people, she gets a sense of purpose from her job, which is another reason to love it.

Fit. For job love to manifest, the job must fit the person's personal needs and desires. A job that is too challenging or that does not fit the person's lifestyle regarding pay, working hours, work-life balance is, according to the interviewees, hard to love. Therefore, if a person thinks that the job is exactly what he/she desires, the chances are higher that a person will develop love for their job. Interestingly, one of the interviewees said that the job he chose never was the perfect fit as he imagined it, but it became the perfect fit as he grew in the job, and now he loves it. This leaves the question, whether a job has to be the perfect fit from the beginning or if people grow into a fit.

Positive relationships at work. Good relationships with peers/colleagues and a good relationship with supervisor(s) were also seen as key features of a job a person can love. In that matter, participants of the focus group described it as crucial that colleagues care about each other, help each other when needed and have time for each other to discuss work matters. Two interviewees also said that they loved their job because their colleagues are like family to them.

Positive Emotions. Another factor subjects identified as key antecedents for job love are positive emotions regarding the job. One must have fun at work, like the tasks themselves and have feelings of accomplishment at the job. Also, an individual having passion for the job has been identified as a possible antecedent of job love. One of the respondents said that if one is excited to go to work on Monday, it is a good sign that one may love one's job.

Challenge and growth. The respondents said that being able to grow in the job and having exciting tasks is key to an individual's love of their job. Therefore, the workplace must provide the possibility to grow and develop inside the job.

Job Love Barriers

Lack of purpose. Just as the reasons to love a job included fulfilling and purposeful work, seeing no purpose in the job is, according to the respondents, a big barrier to job love. One of the interviewees did not only name the lack of purpose as the reason why he thinks he does not love his job, but he even claimed it was a reason to quit. When someone does not see the "why" behind the job, it is hard for him/her to love it.

Lack of development opportunities. The participants claimed that a job that is boring and does not provide any possibility to grow is a barrier to an individual loving a job. If there is nothing more to learn or the job is not challenging anymore, participants of the focus group said that it is hard for someone to *stay in love* with a job even though it might have been a loved job.

Work Stress and negative work experiences. Stress and negative experiences at work were also named as main reasons for a lack of individuals' love of their jobs. An organization's culture was discussed as the reason for the high stress level of employees: the presence culture, working-over hours and the lack of a work-life balance lead to negative emotions and demotivation, which are indications that few if any employees in the organization will love their job. This shows that the respondents in the qualitative study mostly thought that love of a job is tied to conditions: Only when all the expectations are met and needs are fulfilled do people think it is possible to love a job. This is a contrary view to love in the interpersonal context: People often stay in relationships that are unfulfilling and even abusive.

Negative work relationships. During the focus group, every participant presented his/her career pathway and the milestones – either positive or negative experiences that shaped the work relationship – were discussed with the group. In the discussion, the supervisor relationship was identified as an especially important workplace relationship with some of the participants indicating that a negative supervisor who places stress on them hindered them from even thinking about loving what they do. Also, annoying colleagues, mobbing, and toxic work environments were all named as barriers to loving one's job.

Negative emotions, criticism and lack of motivation. Negative emotions were identified as a general barrier to job love. If there is always a bad mood at work or everyone is unmotivated to work, people say it is hard to love one's job as love is usually connected to positive emotions. Hence, negative emotions can also destroy a person's joy at work and, hence, their job love. Also, criticism was a factor that was named as a critical factor when it comes to staying motivated for a job and staying in love: constant criticism, according to some of the interviewees, is destructive and hinders people from loving what they do.

1.4 Conclusions on Study 1

The qualitative analysis of social media showed that there are people who state that they love their jobs and some who do state that they do not love their jobs, or they even hate them. People show love, not only by saying "I love my job" out loud, but also by posting on social media about their jobs and why they love what they do (Study 1a). When job love is compared to other possible love objects, like a brand, hobby, or a person, the average score of people's love for their job is not as high as for their loved persons, but can be compared to the level of brand love. Study 1c, interviewing people and discussing job love in a group setting found that people have different views on what love is, and hence, what job love is. Therefore, finding common ground and, e.g. a grounded theory on job love, was hard to build from laypeople's views. Nevertheless, there was some consent on the factors that lead to job love or hinder job love among Study 1c participants: Positive emotions, positive relationships, a sense of purpose at work, growth opportunities and feeling appreciated for what a person does by colleagues, supervisors, clients, or the employer, are factors that respondents felt are positively connected to job love and can, therefore, foster people's love of their jobs. In contrast, a lack of purpose, a lack of growth opportunities, and negative emotions and relationships are seen as barriers to job love and hinder people from loving what they do. To test, which of the factors act as strong predictors of job love, the goal of this research is to test the identified factors in a quantitative study. In order to research the impact of the factors, first, the study object, job love, has to be measured. For being able to measure job love, a measurement instrument, a scale, is needed. The development of this scale will be the focus of Study 2.

2 Study 2: How Can Job Love be Measured?

Developing a measurement of the concept of job love is a difficult, complex task. As the concept of love is psychological in nature and, therefore, not directly measurable like a person's height, weight, or income, it has to be measured indirectly. Still, developing a measurement is an important step in this research. Korman (1974) explains, "The point is not that adequate measurement is 'nice'. It is necessary [...]. Without it we have nothing" (p. 194, cited after Hinkin, 1995), highlighting the importance of a correct measurement of a concept before conducting hypothesis testing. Without a correct measurement, the chances to have inconclusive or even contradicting findings are high (Cook et al., 1981; Schwab, 1980).

Is love too complex to measure? A big question is whether job love can be measured at all. People might argue that the concept is too complex or that the term "love" has a too broad definition to be studied and therefore cannot be measured. In fact, researchers around the globe have hesitated to research the concept of love and had not developed a new measurement scale until the 1970s, when Zick Rubin published his Loving-Liking Scales (1970). Still, Rubin as well as other love researchers, had to face criticism on their research, because others thought "love" was such a holy matter that it should not be touched by science. However, love, like any other psychological variable such as motivation or satisfaction, *can* be measured as extensive literature on those (similar in nature) concepts show. Moreover, although love is indeed a complex concept, it is also such an important topic in people's lives that it cannot be ignored simply because of the awe of the concept and its complexity itself. Putting too much "magic" into the concept has hindered and is still hindering fruitful research as it prevents the mind from evaluating possible beneficial uses of the concept of love in another than the typical interpersonal context. To weaken the argument that love is to be too broad of a concept, the researcher has provided a narrow and distinct definition of job love and its dimensions in Chapter B. On a basis of this distinct operational definition, it is argued that it is indeed possible to develop a measurement scale of job love.

Is love too subjective to measure? Another argument that critics of object-love and other, similar approaches posit that has hindered empirical research of love in the work context is the *subjectivity of love*: everyone has a different opinion of what love is, therefore, as it is too subjective, it cannot be compared among individuals or generalized. This argument is a good one, but the question remains: Does the way people view job love *have to be* objective? Is it important that what one person feels is exactly what another person feels? Of course, the subjective level of love for work – the intensity of how much a person feels they love their job – can differ, so the outcome can also differ. A variable comparable in this context is "well-being," a well-researched variable in the work environment. The level of subjective well-being of a person is significantly connected to various outcomes like work satisfaction, performance, and commitment – although it is highly subjective what "feeling well" means for the single individual. Therefore, it is hypothesized that love also is highly subjective; the outcome of people who report higher or lower levels of job love will differ significantly, so it is rewarding to measure love for work and to compare people with different subjective levels of love for their work.

Is love too volatile to measure? Another question is the question about *when* to measure love. Is love something that is always the same? Or is love something that changes over time, or even every day? Researchers have put extensive thought into this question regarding interpersonal love (e.g. Sternberg, 1970). What research showed: Yes, love changes. Love changes over time, and therefore, it might be important to take into account that any possible measurement of job love only can reflect an employees' level of job love at a distinct time.

In conclusion, one has to admit there are valid arguments on why *not* to measure love as stated above. Nevertheless, arguments against measuring a complex phenomenon can be weakened by providing suitable solutions to the problems. After weighing the arguments that speak for a measurement of love, the researcher concluded that the arguments for measuring the concept of job love prevail over those against it. By avoiding measuring job love in response to the critics of the concept, fruitful and important research in the field of employee engagement and success could be left untouched. Hence, the researcher finds it more valuable to find a proper measurement and will do this with cautiousness towards critiques of the methodology and possible problems.

As the concept of love involves a high degree of abstraction and cannot be directly observed in daily working life, the researcher considers job love as a concept that is not easily quantifiable and therefore not easily measurable (cf. Eisend & Kuss, 2019). Such concepts are also described as latent concepts or variables. To measure a latent variable, one can look at indicators or manifest variables that can be directly measured and, when combined, describe the complex latent concept (Eisend & Kuss, 2019). Those indicators can be questions or statements that are typically evaluated through self-report surveys in which people are asked to evaluate given statements using a numerical scale or a scale with words attached to the different steps (Kalmijn & Veenhoven, 2005). For example, the dimensions that love consists of that are already empirically researched like commitment or passion are measured by asking people how passionate or how committed they are to their job.

2.1 Procedure

The most commonly used method of measuring attitudes, perceptions, or opinions of people is a questionnaire (Stone, 1993). Hundreds of scales have already been developed to examine concepts in the organizational environment, i.e. employee commitment and satisfaction. According to various researchers (Cook et al., 1981; Hinkin, 1995; Schriesheim et al., 1993), there are often problems with those scales when reliability and validity are not tested before using the scales in further studies. Those problems range from measurement inconsistencies to measuring the wrong things to uninterpretable data, all of which should be addressed in order to acquire valid findings from the research (Hinkin et al., 1997). The best way to work around these problems is to follow a systematic process. Hinkin and his colleagues developed a seven-step process that can be used to ensure the development of a reliable and valid scale. All steps that need to be taken to develop a scale are shown in Figure 21.

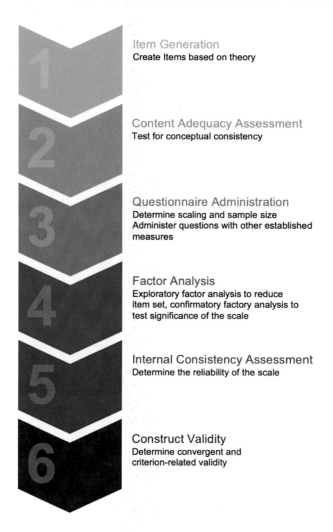

Item Generation
Create Items based on theory

Content Adequacy Assessment
Test for conceptual consistency

Questionnaire Administration
Determine scaling and sample size
Administer questions with other established
measures

Factor Analysis
Exploratory factor analysis to reduce
item set, confirmatory factory analysis to
test significance of the scale

Internal Consistency Assessment
Determine the reliability of the scale

Construct Validity
Determine convergent and
criterion-related validity

Figure 21. *Scale Development Process*
Note. Own illustration adapted from Hinkin et al. (1997)

2.2 Scale Validation Process

2.2.1 Step 1: Item Generation

The first goal of the procedure was to develop a set of items that all adequately represented the researcher's concept of job love. There are two approaches to generating items: the inductive approach and the deductive approach. While the inductive path is taken when exploring new phenomena where no theories exist, the deductive path is usually taken when there is a theory or theories on which item generation can be based (Hinkin et al., 1997). The deductive approach requires extensive literature research and a strong understanding of the phenomenon to be measured. The literature review in Chapter B of this dissertation has shown that Sternberg's Triangular Theory of Love is the most suitable and applicable theory for the concept of love in a work context and hence has been chosen for the deductive item generation approach in Study 2.

To generate items for the questionnaire, the researcher looked at items that have been included in interpersonal love scales that are already determined to be valid by research: Rubin's Liking and Loving Scales (1970), Hatfield and Sprecher's Passionate Love Scale (1986), Hendrick and Hendricks's Love Attitudes Scale (1986) and Sternberg's Triangular Love Scale (1997). Moreover, the researcher looked into brand love research, as researchers there have extensively used Sternberg's Model as a basis for their scales. Bagozzi et al.'s Brand Love Scale (2016) and Carroll and Ahuvia's Brand Love Mini Scale (2006) were examined and investigated whether some items were used in both scales. Finally, the researcher looked at human resources research. As there is yet not a job love scale found in literature, the researcher then looked into the three dimensions of love, passion, commitment, and intimacy/connection, individually. The researcher, therefore, researched scales that measure those three concepts in the work context, such as the Passion for Work Scale (Vallerand, Blanchard, et al., 2003) and the Organizational Commitment Questionnaire (Allen & Meyer, 1990).

From all the items of the original scales, 100 items were collected and consequently used as the basis for building the Job Love Scale. All items were then examined in terms of their transferability to the work context. Some items from the scales were chosen as suitable for a transfer to the work context and therefore adjusted. For example, the item "*I adore Person X*" (Sternberg, 1997) was transferred into "*I adore my work.*" While constantly checking the fit with the selected theoretical model and the operational definitions proposed, the items were then either assigned to one of the three dimensions (e.g. "*I adore my work*" is an indicator of the idealization of the work, hence, this item was assigned to the "passion" dimension) or excluded from further use – either because they did not fit the theoretical model or because they were not applicable to the work context (e.g. "*My relationship with X is very romantic*" from Sternberg's Love Scale was considered as not suitable and therefore discarded).

Finally, 30 items were selected from the item pool for further analysis. Criteria for selection were the fitness to the model, distinctiveness from other indicators, assurance that the indicators measured the concept of job love completely (content validity) and fitness to laypeople (face validity). The 30 items were then assembled into a questionnaire. The items with the originating scale they are adapted from are presented in Table 7.

Table 7. Adjusted Preliminary Item Pool for the Job Love Measurement

Passion

nr	Item (Translated into English)	Aspect	Original Scale
1	*My job is a passion for me.*	Passion	Passion for Work Scale (Vallerand, Blanchard, et al., 2003)
2	*My job is important to me.*	Importance	Passion for Work Scale (Vallerand, Blanchard, et al., 2003)
3	*I can't imagine that any other job would make me as happy as my current one.*	Positive Effect	Passion (Triangular Love Scale, Sternberg, 1997)
4	*I think about work topics beyond my working hours*	Mental Engagement/Rumination	Passion (Triangular Love Scale, Sternberg, 1997)
5	*I am ready to give a lot for my work.*	Willingness to Invest	Passion (Triangular Love Scale, Sternberg, 1997), Passion-Driven Behaviors (Brand Love Scale, Bagozzi et al., 2016)
6	*Losing my job would make me sad.*	Fear of Loss	Passion (Triangular Love Scale, Sternberg, 1997), Anticipated Separation Distress (Brand Love Scale, Bagozzi et al., 2013)
7	*I am excited about my work.*	Excitement	Brand Love Scale (Carroll & Ahuvia, 2006)
8	*There is no better job than the one I have.*	Idealization	Passion (Triangular Love Scale, Sternberg, 1997), Idealization (Brand Love Scale, Bagozzi et al., 2016)
9	*I think I have a wonderful job.*	Excitement	Brand Love Scale (Carroll & Ahuvia, 2006)
10	*I can overlook things in my work that are not positive.*	Willingness to Forgive/Overlook Mistakes	Rubin's Liking-Loving Scale (1970)

Commitment

nr	Item (Translated into English)	Aspect	Original Scale
1	*My job is currently exactly the right job for me.*	Short-term commitment	OCA (Affective Organizational Commitment, Allen & Meyer, 1990), Long-term Commitment (Brand Love Scale, Bagozzi et al., 2016)
2	*I would like to be able to carry out my current job in the future.*	Desire for a long-term relationship	OCA (Affective Organizational Commitment, Allen & Meyer, 1990), Long-term Commitment (Brand Love Scale, Bagozzi et al., 2016)
3	*I am proud of my job.*	Proud	OCA (Affective Organizational Commitment, Allen & Meyer, 1990),
4	*I am sure that I love my job.*	Cognitive Assurance	Commitment (Triangular Love Scale, Sternberg, 1997)
5	*The decision to start this job was the right one.*	Decision	Commitment (Triangular Love Scale, Sternberg, 1997)
6	*My job is an important part of who I am.*	Identity	Commitment (Triangular Love Scale, Sternberg, 1997), OCA (Affective Organizational Commitment, Allen & Meyer, 1990), Identity (Brand Love Scale, Bagozzi et al., 2016)
7	*Even if I had the opportunity to change jobs, I would stick with my current job.*	Loyalty	Commitment (Triangular Love Scale, Sternberg, 1997)
8	*I can identify with my work.*	Identification	OCA (Affective Organizational Commitment, Allen & Meyer, 1990)
9	*My job is of great personal importance to me.*	Identity	OCA (Affective Organizational Commitment, Allen & Meyer, 1990)
10	*Even if it were difficult, I would stay at my current job.*	Forgiveness of Mistakes	Rubin's Liking-Loving Scale (1970)

Connection

nr	Item (Translated into English)	Aspect	Original Scale
1	*I enjoy spending time with my job.*	Wish for Closeness	Intimacy (Triangular Love Scale, Sternberg, 1997)
2	*I feel good about my job.*	Well-being	Intimacy (Triangular Love Scale, Sternberg, 1997)
3	*I trust the people in my work environment*	Trust	Intimacy (Triangular Love Scale, Sternberg, 1997)
4	*I have the feeling that what I give for my job, I get back.*	Desire for reciprocity	Intimacy (Triangular Love Scale, Sternberg, 1997)
5	*I feel emotionally supported by my job.*	Emotional support	Intimacy (Triangular Love Scale, Sternberg, 1997)
6	*I feel connected to my job.*	Connection/closeness	Intimacy (Triangular Love Scale, Sternberg, 1997), Brand Love Scale, Bagozzi et al., 2016
7	*I experience joy at work.*	Positive Emotions	Brand Love Scale, Bagozzi et al., 2016
8	*The concerns of my employer/job are close to my heart.*	Caring	Intimacy (Triangular Love Scale, Sternberg, 1997), OCA (Affective Organizational Commitment, Allen & Meyer, 1990)
9	*I feel that I belong in my work environment.*	Belonging	OCA (Affective Organizational Commitment, Allen & Meyer, 1990)
10	*I look forward to my work in the morning when I get up.*	Positive Emotions	Intimacy (Triangular Love Scale, Sternberg, 1997)

2.2.2 Step 2: Content Adequacy Assessment

The questionnaire items then had to be tested in terms of their content adequacy, also called content validity. Validity in general is defined as the measure of how good something measures what it is actually designed to measure (Field, 2009; Ghauri &

Grønhaug, 2005). There are different types of validity (see Figure 22). While content and face validity are examined before testing a new scale, criterion and construct validity can be examined after conducting the test with a sample. Therefore, in Step 2, only content and face validity were assessed, saving the examination of the other two validity measures for later steps.

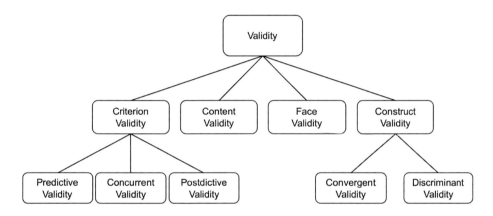

Figure 22. *Different Types of Validity*
Note. Own illustration based on Taherdoost, 2016

Content validity is important as it examines "the degree to which individual items represent the construct being measured and cover the full range of the construct" (Field, 2009, p. 12). It is used to ensure that all indicators that are essential for a construct are included in a measure and that indicators that do not fit the construct are eliminated. Applying this knowledge to our item set, the final items of the measurement of job love have to present all three dimensions and cover aspects of those dimensions completely. To evaluate content validity, two distinct experts, one psychologist and one marketing expert, were asked separately to evaluate the items in terms of their suitability to the theoretical model and the completeness of the measurement items. The items were adjusted following the indications of the experts.

Face validity is described as "the degree to which a measure appears to be related to a specific construct" (Taherdoost, 2016, p. 30) and can be examined by asking laypeople to evaluate if the items describe the construct and its dimensions well. For the development of the questionnaire of this study, five different laypeople from the researcher's workplace and private surroundings were asked to evaluate the items in terms of their comprehensibility and their apparent fit to the previously explained concept of job love. Further improvements of the items selected were made (e.g. irritable items such as "*I would be sad if I wouldn't work at my current job anymore*" were changed into "*Losing my current job would make me sad*").

2.2.3 Step 3: Questionnaire Administration

To develop a questionnaire that can validate the job love measure, there are different items and scales that need to be included beyond the job love measurement. The proposed items need to measure correctly (item properties) and should relate to variables the concept usually is related to (Hinkin, 1995). For example, job love is hypothesized to be strongly related to job satisfaction; hence, the measurement should also be related to a measurement of job satisfaction, providing evidence for a predictive (criterion) validity. Therefore, several other measurements were included in the questionnaire to test criterion validity, convergent validity, as well as discriminant validity.

Item Scaling. The most used scaling in questionnaires today is the Likert-type scale (Cook et al., 1981). The most important factor in the decision of a scaling technique is the ability of the scaling to generate enough variance (Stone, 1978) in order to be used for statistical analyses. The original scale Likert published in 1932 contained five intervals: "*strongly disagree*," "*disagree*," "*neither agree nor disagree*," "*agree*," "*strongly agree*." Studies have shown below five intervals, coefficient alpha reliability decreases, but there is not much increase with more than seven intervals (Lissitz & Green, 1975). For the choice of scale for Study 2, the researcher referred to original love scales other researchers have used and found most researchers have used a 7-point Likert scale (e.g. Passion for Work Scale, Vallerand, Blanchard, et al., 2003). As such, a 7-point Likert scale is used in Study 2 because it was found to be most suitable for the study's goals. Concluding, the job love items were assessed on a 7-point-Likert scale ranging from *1 = strongly agree* to *7 = strongly disagree.*

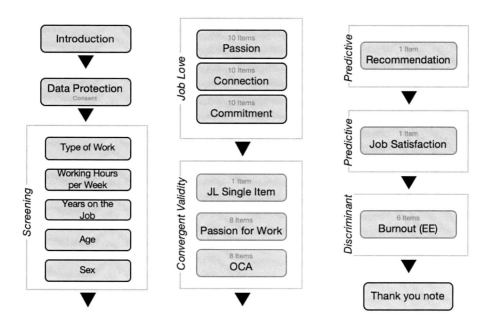

Figure 23. *Overview of Questionnaire Variables of Study 2*

Note. JL = job love, OCA = affective organizational commitment, EE = emotional exhaustion. See Appendix 1 for the full questionnaire.

Data Collection. The final questionnaire was programmed online with Unipark and first pre-tested with a small sample of 20 people. After the pre-test, the questionnaire was presented to an online panel. Data were collected between 20-26th of September in 2019 in Germany. A total of 163 people finished the online questionnaire, providing a sufficient sample size (see Velicer, 1988) for analyzing the Job Love Scale.

Data Cleaning. Before analyzing the data in the data set, the set had to be cleaned from possible disturbing variables. In some cases, the age of the respondent or the time working within the organization they work for were not plausible. Implausible variables were coded as missing or completely excluded from further analysis (see Table 8). The questionnaire also included an attention check item: *"I am reading every question of this questionnaire with caution"* with a possible answer ranging from *1 = I totally agree* to *7 = I do not agree at all.* All cases stating other than "1" were checked individually, excluding two cases from the sample (see Table 8). Moreover, implausible answering patterns were analyzed, such as giving always the same answer to differing items. Therefore, an item was created showing if the plausibility check was positive (e.g. ID 11, see Table 8). In total, 10 cases were excluded from the sample resulting in $n = 153$.

Table 8. *Data Cleaning of Study 2 Sample*

ID	Reason for Exclusion	Description
3	Plausibility + Attention Check	Years working in Organization: years working = 73, age = 35, Attention Check: failed
10	Plausibility Check	Answered with "1" to all questions indicating a "click-through-case"
11	Plausibility Check	Answered with "7" to almost all questions indicating a "click-through-case"
59	Plausibility Check	Answered with "1" to all questions indicating a "click-through-case"
90	Attention + Plausibility Check	Attention Check: failed; answered mostly with the same number indicating a "click-through-case"
97	Plausibility Check	Answered with "1" to all questions indicating a "click-through-case"
110	Plausibility Check	Answered with "7" to almost all questions indicating a "click-through-case"
118	Plausibility Check	Answered with "1" to almost all questions indicating a "click-through-case"
158	Plausibility Check	Answered with "1" to almost all questions indicating a "click-through-case"
159	Plausibility Check	Years working in Organization: Years working = 52 years, age = 47, answered almost all items with "1 = I totally agree" (click-through suspicion)

Sample. The remaining data set ($n = 153$) showed a relatively equal distribution of the sex with 51.5% females and 48.5% males and a mean age of 47.6.

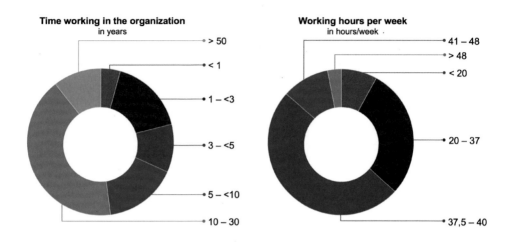

Figure 24. *Demographics of Study 2 Sample*

Most respondents worked for 10-30 years in their organization, and the majority worked the typical (in Germany) 38-40-hour job (see Figure 24).

Item Analysis

The items of the dataset had to be examined in their performance to determine whether each item was suitable for further analysis (Hinkin et al., 1997). Therefore, normal distribution, item selectivity, and homogeneity, as well as discrimination power, were checked. All analyses were conducted using IBM SPSS Statistics Version 26.

Normal distribution. Regarding the normal distribution of the items, many item distributions showed a slightly positive skewness, which means that there was a tendency towards positive answers.

Item selectivity. This indicator measures the degree to which an item differentiates between subjects with a high level and subjects with a low level of the characteristic it measures. German statisticians state that selectivity should be above .50, and all items included in the questionnaire show a selectivity > .50 (criterion Bortz & Döring, 2006).

Homogeneity. This measure checks the correlation between the items to see whether items might measure the same thing. To test for homogeneity, the correlations of each item pair got calculated and items with high correlation were marked as possible exclusion candidates for further factor analysis.

Extreme group comparison. When dividing the sample into two groups (e.g. with high versus low level of a characteristic), the variance between groups should be significant, which can be tested with variance or t-tests. Hence, t-tests were conducted for every item with significant results to make sure that the items were suitable to create enough variance between groups. A small value of variance would indicate that the item creates similar answers across all subjects and therefore is not useful for further analysis.

2.2.4 Step 4: Factor Analysis

In Step 4, the 30 items were tested in their factor structure to see whether the three-factor model of Sternberg's Triangular Theory of Love can be applied as a structure to the researcher's Job Love Scale.

First, the extraction had to be chosen and then which rotation method should be used (Moosbrugger & Kelava, 2012). As the goal is to interpret the latent variable and its underlying factors that explain the correlation between the items, the principal axes factor analysis (PFA) was chosen as the most suitable method for data reduction (Moosbrugger & Kelava, 2012). Regarding the rotation method, the varimax rotation method has been excluded because of the condition of unrelatedness of factors: the researcher assumed that the nature of complex psychological phenomena, such as love, results in the fact that it will always be some kind of related to other constructs. As the three factors – passion, connection and commitment – are, in theory, not completely independent (Sternberg, 1997), a factor extraction method allowing the correlation between factors had to be chosen. The researcher, therefore, selected the *oblique rotation* method as it tolerates the correlation between factors (Field, 2013). To ensure the separability of factors, the *direct quartimax rotation method* was used, as it does allow for correlation between factors.

Due to the relatively small sample size *(n = 153),* the Kaiser-Meyer-Olkin measure of sampling adequacy (KMO, Kaiser, 1974) was calculated before analysis. It sets the sum of partial correlations in relation to the sum of correlations to see whether a factor analysis produces distinct and reliable factors. The KMO can range between 0 and 1. A value close to 0 would produce a very poor result in a factor analysis, and a value close to 1 indicates a sufficient result. Study 2's KMO was 0.963, which indicated that the sample of the study was sufficient for factor analysis.

Exploratory Factor Analysis

In the first iteration of exploratory factor analysis, there were 3 factors extracted, following a three-dimensional structure. To see which items loaded on which factor, the loadings on the factors were analyzed using the pattern matrix shown in Table 9. This first exploratory factor analysis shows that the 30 variables tested loaded on three different factors. There were some vital discoveries made in this first part of the analysis: First, not all variables were loading on the factors they were intended to theoretically. Some of the suggested Passion variables loaded onto the factors Connection and Commitment. For example, commitment-item JL_C06 „*My job is an important part of who I am*" [8] was statistically assigned to another factor: passion.

Concluding the first factor analysis, two items were moved to the passion dimension, while other items with lower loadings or double-loadings were removed from the scale to only leave the most meaningful items in the scale for further testing. In Table 9, items that were assigned to Factor 1 were colored in pink and assigned to the dimension "connection", while items that loaded on Factor 2 were colored purple and assigned to "passion". Items that loaded on Factor 3 were assigned to the dimension "commitment" and colored green.

---

[8] The original item was: "*Mein Job ist ein wichtiger Teil dessen, wer ich bin.*"

Table 9. *Exploratory Factor Analysis*

Items (i.e. statements)	Derived common factors			Communality
	Factor 1	Factor 2	Factor 3	
JL_P01: Job is a passion		0.549		0.668
JL_P02: Job is important		0.564		0.629
JL_P03: Idealization			-0.531	0.628
JL_P04: Rumination		0.671		0.341
JL_P05: Willingness to invest		0.509		0.577
JL_P06: Separation Anxiety			-0.681	0.566
JL_P07: Excitement	0.366		-0.375	0.816
JL_P08: Idealization			-0.459	0.606
JL_P09: Positive Emotion	0.343		-0.354	0.758
JL_P10: Readiness to forgive	0.426			0.293
JL_V01: Happiness	0.650			0.711
JL_V02: Well-being	0.629			0.764
JL_V03: Trust	0.664			0.475
JL_V04: Getting something back	0.740			0.732
JL_V05: Support	0.751			0.793
JL_V06: Connectedness		0.533	-0.336	0.853
JL_V07: Enjoyment	0.692			0.717
JL_V08: Caring	0.522	0.406		0.657
JL_V09: Appreciation	1.047			0.833
JL_V10: Feeling of Belonging	0.400	0.413		0.771
JL_C01: Current commitment			-0.842	0.859
JL_C02: Desire of future relationship			-0.841	0.765
JL_C03: Proud		0.610		0.693
JL_C04: Assurance of Love	0.320	0.372	-0.323	0.793
JL_C05: Awareness of right decision			-0.682	0.754
JL_C06: Identification		0.607		0.612
JL_C07: Resistance to competitors			-0.686	0.75
JL_C08: Refusal to terminate			-0.654	0.362
JL_C09: Personal importance		0.675		0.769
JL_C10: Wish to stay in hard times			-0.905	0.759
Eigenvalue	18.528	1.631	1.138	
Percentage of variation	61.760	5.438	3.793	
Cumulative percentage	61.760	67.197	70.99	

Note. Pattern matrix, Extraction method: principal factor analysis (PFA), rotation method: oblique rotation, explanation of code names in first row: JL = Job Love, P = Passion, V = Verbundenheit (Connection), C = Commitment, loadings below .30 were not shown, loadings can go beyond -1/+1 within the oblique rotation, n = 153

Confirmatory Factor Analysis

For the following confirmatory factor analysis, the items that loaded high on Factor 1, 2, and 3 were included. The other eleven items (colored black in Table 9) were excluded from further analyses as they showed double loadings and could not be safely assigned to a factor. With the remaining nineteen variables, a confirmatory factor analysis was conducted to see whether the variables loaded on three factors (see Table 10).

Table 10. *Confirmatory Factor Analysis*

Items (i.e. statements)	New	Derived common factors			
		Factor 1	Factor 2	Factor 3	Communality
JL_P01: Job is a passion	P01	0.31	0.604		0.668
JL_P02: Job is important	P02		0.584		0.629
JL_P04: Rumination	P03		0.601		0.628
JL_P05: Willingness to invest	P04		0.483		0.341
JL_C06: Identification	P05		0.654		0.577
JL_C09: Personal importance	P06		0.742		0.566
JL_V01: Happiness	V01	0.621	0.371		0.816
JL_V02: Well-being	V02	0.559		0.32	0.606
JL_V03: Trust	V03	0.625			0.758
JL_V04: Getting something back	V04	0.714			0.293
JL_V05: Support	V05	0.692			0.711
JL_V07: Enjoyment	V06	0.657			0.764
JL_V09: Appreciation	V07	0.975			0.475
JL_C01: Current commitment	C01			0.798	0.732
JL_C02: future relationship	C02			0.869	0.793
JL_C05: right decision	C03			0.703	0.853
JL_C07: Resistance to competitors	C04			0.695	0.717
JL_C08: Refusal to terminate	C05			0.649	0.657
JL_C10: Wish to stay in hard times	C06			0.871	0.833
Eigenvalue		11.446	1.453	0.997	
Percentage of variation		60.244	7.646	5.248	
Cumulative percentage		60.244	67.889	73.137	

Note. Extraction Method: principal factor analysis (PFA), rotation method: oblique rotation, explanation of code names in first row: JL = Job Love, P = Passion, V = Verbundenheit (Connection), C = Commitment, loadings < .30 were omitted. n = 153.

Results show reasonable factor loadings (>.50) for almost all variables. As the factors are still highly correlated, and confirmatory factor analysis of the remaining nineteen variables showed that all load onto one factor, it can be assumed that, although they all described different dimensions of love theoretically and conceptually, their levels were interconnected, so the statistical analysis showed high correlations between the factors (see Table 11).

Table 11. *Correlation Matrix of Factors*

Factor	1	2	3
1	1	0.53	0.765
2	0.53	1	0.609
3	0.765	0.609	1

The remaining variables were six items measuring passion, six items measuring commitment and seven items measuring connection. There is no standard number of how many items a measure should have, but under efficiency aspects, a measure should be as long as necessary and as short as possible. A smaller number of items may prevent negative effects, such as respondents getting bored or fatigued and consequently answering the latter items differently than they would if the scale was shorter (Schmitt & Stuits, 1985; Schriesheim & Eisenbach, 1995). Another reason to keep scales short would be that the more items included, the more time is needed to develop them and to assess them (Carmines & Zeller, 1979). Nevertheless, various researchers suggest having at least three items per scale to be able to count adequate internal consistency (Cook et al., 1981). At least four items per scale are needed to test the homogeneity of each scale (Harvey et al., 1985). Cortina (1993) still argues to keep a scale short; Cortina found that with more items in a scale, the internal consistency reliability can still be high although the item intercorrelations are low. These findings suggest that each factor should contain at least three items.

2.2.5 Step 5: Internal Consistency Assessment

Internal consistency is measured to see whether the items of one scale measure the same (Huck, 2007; Robinson, 2017) and if the results of a scale measure stable and consistent results (Carmines & Zeller, 1979). For example, when we test the scale again with the same sample, we expect the same results when we test under constant conditions (Carmines & Zeller, 1979). Especially when using Likert scales for testing, the measure most often used to calculate reliability is Cronbach's Alpha (Robinson, 2017), which can have values between 0 and 1. There are different opinions on how high Cronbach's Alpha should be. Most researchers suggest that a low reliability is any value below 0.5, a moderate reliability is between 0.5-0.7, a good reliability above .70, a *high* reliability between 0.7-0.9 and *excellent* above 0.9 (Robinson, 2017). Based upon previous knowledge, reliability analyses were conducted with each of the dimension scales passion, connection, and commitment (see Table 12).

Job Passion: The reliability analysis of the passion scale showed an overall Cronbach's alpha of 0.884. Only one of the six items (JL_P04[9]) showed an item-scale correlation of less than 0.5, so it was excluded from the scale. The final Job Passion scale, therefore, contained five items with an overall satisfying internal consistency of 0.902 (see Table 12).

Connection to Job: The seven items of the connection scale were analyzed for their reliability. All items showed sufficient item-scale correlations > 0.5, although one item was suspicious as the item-scale correlation was lower than that of the other items. After excluding the item, internal consistency had a sufficient value of $\alpha = 0.941$. The final connection to the job scale included six items.

Job Commitment: When deconstructing the results of the reliability analysis of the commitment dimension only one item stood out: JL_C08 (*"I cannot imagine quitting my job"*). The item showed, compared to the other items in the scale, only a medium item-

---

[9] Item JL_P04 is „*Arbeitsthemen beschäftigen mich auch über meine Arbeitszeit hinaus.*" *(English = "I think about work topics beyond my working hours.")*

scale correlation (see Table 12). By excluding the item from the final scale, the internal consistency could be improved to $\alpha = 0.94$.

Table 12. *Internal Consistency Analyses*

Dimensions/Items	M	SD	Item-total correlation	α, when Item deleted	α-value
Factor 1: Passion					0.884
JL_P01: Job is a passion	3.39	1.561	0.735	0.857	
JL_P02: Job is important	2.44	1.307	0.733	0.860	
JL_P03: Rumination	3.92	1.806	0.488	0.902	
JL_P04: Willingness to invest	3.45	1.720	0.691	0.865	
JL_P05: Identification	3.22	1.578	0.754	0.854	
JL_P06: Personal importance	3.01	1.583	0.827	0.841	
Factor 2: Connection					0.939
JL_V01: Happiness	3.22	1.42	0.764	0.934	
JL_V02: Well-being	2.72	1.393	0.833	0.928	
JL_V03: Trust	2.92	1.423	0.666	0.941	
JL_V04: Getting something back	3.63	1.731	0.829	0.928	
JL_V05: Support	3.24	1.669	0.865	0.924	
JL_V06: Enjoyment	3.56	1.53	0.802	0.93	
JL_V07: Appreciation	3.28	1.756	0.865	0.924	
Factor 3: Commitment					0.922
JL_C01: Current commitment	2.78	1.568	0.863	0.896	
JL_C02: Future relationship	2.53	1.469	0.833	0.902	
JL_C03: Right decision	2.65	1.47	0.811	0.904	
JL_C04: Resistance to competitors	3.48	1.854	0.825	0.901	
JL_C05: Refusal to terminate	3.12	1.985	0.592	0.94	
JL_C06: Wish to stay in hard times	2.90	1.486	0.824	0.902	

Note. Explanation of Code names in first row: JL = Job Love, P = Passion, V = Verbundenheit (Connection), C = Commitment; SD = standard deviation, α = Cronbach's alpha; Grey color: item was excluded because of small item-total correlation.

After reliability analysis, the scale was reduced to 16 items: five items measuring passion, six items measuring connection, and five items measuring commitment.

2.2.6 Step 6: Construct and Criterion Validity Testing

After checking for content and face validity in step two, criterion and construct validity (see Figure 25) could be assessed after conducting the testing of the new scale.

Criterion Validity

Criterion validity is the degree to which a measure is connected to a specific outcome in the past, present and future. This is especially important when a measure is used to predict variables like specific behavior or performance. There are three different types of criterion validity: *Predictive validity* tests if the measurement is accurately predicting behavior in the future and can usually be tested in a long-term validity study (Eisend & Kuß, 2019).

Concurrent validity is the degree to which the results are similar to the testing of another test that measures the construct at the same time (Eisend & Kuß, 2019). To measure concurrent validity, job satisfaction was chosen as a suitable concept to test, because in interpersonal relationships, the level of love is correlated to the level of relationship satisfaction. Hence, in our case, job love should also be correlated to job satisfaction (for an illustration see Figure 26). Job satisfaction was measured using a single item, as supposed by Dolbier et al. (2005).

Postdictive validity is given if the new measurement is providing similar results to tests that have been conducted in the past, for example, if a new intelligence test has similar outcomes compared to tests that had been done before. To summarize, criterion validity must be pursued to support the possibility to interpret the test outcomes and to justify the use of the measurement compared to other measures. For the calculation of postdictive validity, a single item measuring the likelihood to recommend the job to another person, an adaption from Reichheld's idea (2003) of the Net Promoter Score (NPS), was used.

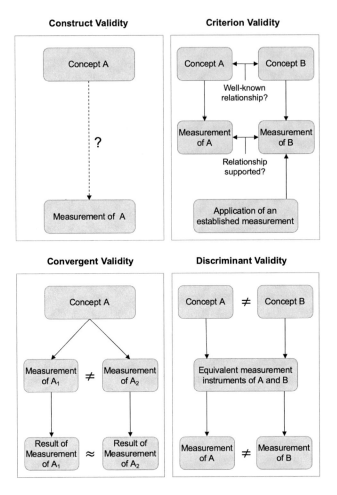

Figure 25. *Construct, Criterion, Convergent and Discriminant Validity*
Note. Own illustration based on Kuß & Eisend (2019, p. 102)

Construct validity

Construct validity is typically the last validity type tested in a validation process. It investigates the causal relationships of a measurement with typical outcomes and related constructs, for example, should love be connected to satisfaction or loyalty. There are two different types of construct validity: discriminant and convergent validity.

Discriminant Validity. Discriminant validity measures the extent to which a variable is discriminant from another variable it should not be related to (Campbell & Fiske, 1959).

Subsequently, variable A (measurement construct, i.e. job love) should not correlate with variable B (unrelated construct, i.e. intelligence). Therefore, one has to identify a concept that is distinct from the concept to be tested. The researcher identified the concept burnout as a distinct concept from job love. Burnout is generally a state of exhaustion caused by prolonged stress. The exhaustion can be emotional, physical, and/or cognitive and occurs when individuals feel overwhelmed and stressed. In the work context, people who experience burnout are not able to face daily job demands. To test burnout for the discriminant validity analysis of this study, the researcher used Maslach's Burnout Inventory (MBI), which was published by Maslach and Jackson in 1981 and is still the most widely used test in studies on burnout. The test consists of three subscales: emotional exhaustion, depersonalization, and reduced personal accomplishment. Study 2 only used the items of one of the subscales, emotional exhaustion.

Convergent validity. Analogous to discriminant validity, convergent validity examines the extent to which the results of a measurement are the same as those of another scale that measures the same. As the love of a job, in this study's model, consists of the three factors – passion, connection, and commitment – the parts of the study's scale should measure the same as other scales that measure the same concepts, i.e. Vallerand, Blanchard et al.'s (2003) Passion for Work Scale already exists to measure passion in the job context. To measure convergent validity, the researcher calculated whether the passion subscale measures the same as the passion for work scale. Likewise, the commitment scale's convergent validity could be tested with Meyer and Allen's (1990) Organizational Commitment Measurement.

An overview of the proposed type of validity testing with the used concept (e.g. convergent validity: Passion for Work Scale) is shown in Figure 26.

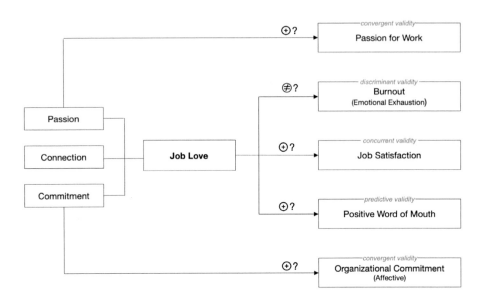

Figure 26. *Conceptual Model of Validity Testing*

Results of Validity Testing

To calculate validity, one can use the correlation coefficient between variable A and variable B. Additionally, for construct validity, one can correct for measurement errors.

The formula for calculating construct validity is:

$$\frac{r_{xy}}{\sqrt{r_{xx} \times r_{yy}}}$$

r_{xy} refers to the correlation between variable x (e.g. job love) and variable y (e.g. discriminant validity: emotional exhaustion). r_{xx} is the reliability of x (e.g. job love scale) and r_{yy} the reliability of y (e.g. emotional exhaustion scale).

There is no standard value for validity, but a result of less than 0.85 is generally seen as a likely result for the non-existence of a highly correlating construct, while a value above 0.85 indicates that the constructs overlap greatly and are likely to measure the same thing. For example, the calculated discriminant validity score for x = *job love average* and y = *emotional exhaustion average* was r = *-0.679 (r_{xy} = -0.642, r_{xx} = 0.964, r_{yy} = .928)* As the score is below 0.85, discriminant validity of the job love scale can be assumed. All other validity types (concurrent, criterion, and convergent validity) are shown in Table 13.

Table 13. *Results of Validity Testing*

Validity Type	Measured by	Correlation		Result
		r	p	
Criterion Validity				
Concurrent Validity	Job Satisfaction: Single Item (Dolbier et al., 2005)	.840	.000	Validity confirmed
Predictive Validity	Positive word of mouth: Single Item "likely to recommend" adapted from Net Promoter Score (Reichheld, 2003)	.682	.000	Validity confirmed
				Construct Validity
Discriminant Validity	Burnout: Emotional Exhaustion Subscale from Maslach Burnout Inventory (Maslach & Jackson, 1981)	-.658	.000	Validity could not be confirmed
Convergent Validity	Passion Scale: Passion for Work Scale (Vallerand et al., 2003)	.958	.000	Validity confirmed
Convergent Validity	Commitment Scale: Organizational Commitment – Affective Subscale (Meyer & Allen, 1990)	.800	.000	Validity confirmed

Note. r = correlation, p = probability

Almost all of the other validity types show sufficient validity values. The only exception is the result of discriminant validity: The result *should be* that there is no relationship between the tested variables. Still, the correlation *was r = -.658 (p < .001)* indicating a high (negative) correlation. The reason for this result might be that there is a high correlation between the love for a job and burnout, and that, therefore, burnout is not suitable to measure discriminant validity. Therefore, it is suggested to test discriminant validity with a concept that fits better that is known to not be unrelated to love.

All other measures show high validity values. The passion scale developed by Vallerand et al. (2003) correlated highly with the job love passion scale *(r = .958, p < .001),* indicating that the scale shows a high convergent validity, as well as the commitment scale *(r = .800, p <001)* that was tested with the Affective subscale of the Organizational

Commitment inventory introduced by Meyer and Allen (1990). Also, concurrent validity was high, measured with a single item of job satisfaction $(r = .840, p < 001)$, as well as predictive validity with $r = .682 \ (p < .001)$, indicating the confirmation of the validity of the Job Love Scale.

2.3 Conclusions on Study 2

In Study 2, a scale of job love was developed and validated that can measure an individual's love of his/her job. The final Job Love Scale (JLS) consists of sixteen items assessing how much an individual experiences job passion, job connection and job commitment. It can be located in the Appendix (Appendix 2). The scale can be used in individual contexts as well as the organizational context. Companies can use the scale to assess whether or not an employee loves his/her job and to compare employees and their love type with each other. Companies can assess why an employee does not love their job – whether it is a lack of passion for their job, a lack of connection or a lack of commitment to the job.

3 Study 3: Assessing possible Antecedents of Job Love

The focus of Study 3 is to answer the question "Why do some people love their jobs and why do other people not?" The aim is to answer the following research questions:

1. What are the central antecedents of job love?
2. Which antecedents are important for people to develop a job love?
3. How do people who love their job differ from those who do not?

Therefore, possible antecedents of job love were explored in a first step. In order to derive suitable antecedents, influencing factors of similar constructs such as passion for work or commitment were analyzed. Insights from Study 1, which included qualitative research, were included as hypotheses as well. As there are many possible antecedents of job love, a selection of the most relevant was made and included in a complex causal model of job love. In order to find out which antecedents are suitable to distinguish people who love their job from those who do not, all antecedents were explored in their correlation to job love.

The result of this study will be a prediction model with factors that can be assessed to predict job love or a lack thereof. Hence, Study 3 of this dissertation:

1. develops hypotheses on factors leading to job love.
2. follows with the empirical testing of these hypotheses.
3. provides a prediction model of job love.
4. provides implications for business practice.

3.1 Development of Hypotheses

In the search for possible influencing factors of job love, different paths were taken. The first was an empirical methodology: the results of the qualitative research carried out in Study 1 were used to derive concrete hypotheses. The second approach was to derive hypotheses from findings in literature or studies conducted in the field of interpersonal love and/or similar concepts (e.g. passion for work, organizational commitment) in order to create hypotheses for factors that may not have been addressed by the respondents in Study 1.

All identified variables were grouped into three different groups: job variables, person variables, and relationship variables. Whether the variables were derived from literature, qualitative research, or both, can be seen in Table 14.

Table 14. *Overview of Job Love Antecedents*

nr	Group	Influence Factor	Derived from
1	**Job**	Purpose	Literature + Qualitative Research
2		Growth Opportunities	Qualitative Research
3		Salary	Literature + Qualitative Research
4		Salary Satisfaction	Literature +Qualitative Research
5	**Person**	Person-Job-Fit	Literature
6		Competence	Literature
7		Autonomy	Literature
8	**Relationships**	Appreciation	Literature + Qualitative Research
9		Supervisor Relationships	Literature + Qualitative Research
10		Peer Relationships	Literature + Qualitative Research
11		Client Relationships	Qualitative Research

3.1.1 Job Variables

The first group of variables is job variables. The term "job variables" was chosen to separate variables that have to do with the job itself from those that come with the relationships in the job and those that depend on the person itself.

Purpose

The first variable identified as an antecedent of job love was 'purpose'. Qualitative research showed that, according to the participants of Study 1c, one of the main reasons to love a job is purpose. People stated they want to know the "why" behind the "what" in the job: they want to know why they do things at work. Purpose refers to what fuels people to get up in the morning and add something of value to the world. According to various researchers, purpose is a human need that is inherent in *all* humans (Alderfer, 1972; Herzberg, Mausner, & Snyderman, 1959; Mausner, & Synderman, 1993; Maslow, 1943; McClelland, 1965, McGregor & Cutcher-Gershenfeld, 1960). The lack of purpose is, according to Maddi (1967), a problem of humankind that rose significantly during the 20th century. Without purpose, people lose the ability to believe in their importance and usefulness, and finally, they lose interest and motivation to work (Maddi, 1967). Therefore, seeing work as purposeful is important. In contrast, if the individual cannot see the purpose of their work, the job will become a meaningless chore that needs to be done. Employees perceive their jobs as meaningful and purposeful is given when employees believe and/or see their job tasks are important both inside and outside the organization. It can be an expression of the creative values of the individual (Frankl, 1970). It includes the employee's perception of the importance and significance of their work and the contribution they make to the organization's goals and mission. The purpose-driven organization describes an organization that takes action on something bigger than just the products and services it provides. Purpose-driven people find purpose in their job and understand how their work adds value to others and to a larger organizational goal. Maslow stated in 1971 that people do not live to their full professional potential when they do not think of their work as purposeful and meaningful. Mihály Csíkszentmihályi, who introduced the concept of flow, states that the level of the individual's happiness depends on how the "mind filters and interprets everyday experiences." So, he advises people to "learn to find enjoyment and purpose, regardless of external circumstances. To become happy, people must strive to become independent of the social environment, i.e. become less sensitive to its rewards and punishments" (Csikszentmihalyi, 1990, p.1).

The Cambridge Dictionary (2020) defines purpose as "why you do something or why something exists" or as "determination or a feeling of having a reason for what you do." In the work context, people who do not know the why behind their work are not likely to perform well. Pradhan et al. (2017) found that purpose has an indirect effect on performance: when workers experience purpose together with a passion for work, these two concepts together drive performance significantly. Passion and purpose seem to have some similarities, yet, their orientation is different: while passion is focused inwardly and motivates people from the inside, purpose is focused outwardly as it is the extent to which people perceive their work to have an impact on other people, organizations, or society itself (Pradhan et al., 2017, p. 4). Subsequently, it is argued that a higher level of perceived purpose will lead to a higher probability that a person experiences love of a job.

Hypothesis₁: *The more highly an individual perceives the purpose of their job, the higher the probability of job love.*

Growth Opportunities

According to the results of the qualitative study (Study 1c), workers need to have the opportunity to grow with the job and develop themselves as an antecedent to job love. Most workers today are looking for more than just economic survival when selecting a job. They want a career that is in line with their interests and personality, and a job that gives them the opportunity to develop themselves and to grow (Ogaboh et al., 2010). The need to grow is a basic human need (Alderfer, 1972). Alderfer describes in his ERG theory that people have three different sets of needs – Existence (E), Relatedness (R), and Growth (G) needs. Growth needs are similar to the esteem and self-actualization needs described by Maslow. According to both researchers, individuals have the desire to grow and are motivated by this desire. Other theorists also see growth opportunities as motivators, such as Herzberg et al. (1959) who developed the concept of job enrichment. Job enrichment is defined as the process of helping employees build achievement, giving them recognition, responsibility, and growth opportunities. The process in which companies can help their employees grow usually includes three steps: (1) forecasting, (2) planning, and (3) counseling. In the first step, analyzing the employee's potential and growth needs helps identify career paths and improvement potential. The second step, planning, structures the growth of an employee and develops the employee's career plan. The third step, counseling, directly helps the employee through interventions, training, or coaching (Alderfer, 1972). Growth can happen on either the personal level or the organizational level. On the personal level, growth opportunities include those that help the individual learn valuable skills that help in both the professional surrounding as well as the personal surrounding of the employee. On the organizational level, there are usually planned programs that are designed to help the employees in a company learn all the skills needed to match and advance organizational goals.

Helping each other grow is a topic already discussed on the individual level. A supportive partner who helps the other and supports them in their growth leads to greater relationship quality (Overall et al., 2010). By showing interest in the growth of one's partner, the partner feels supported and loved. Applying this knowledge from interpersonal love relationships to the workplace, employers who are willing to invest in the growth and development of their employees show them how much they care about them. This feeling of care is especially important for the connection dimension of love and for the feeling of love in general. The commitment dimension of job love might be fostered by growth opportunities as the connection between growth opportunity and organizational commitment has already been shown (Hall, 1976). Hence, empirical research points to the assumption that the more growth opportunities an individual has in his/her job, the higher the chances are that the person develops love for their job. Therefore, the following hypothesis is suggested:

Hypothesis$_2$: *The more positively an individual perceives the growth opportunities within the job, the higher the probability of job love.*

Salary

Salary is a topic that has been studied extensively in workplace literature in the context of various outcomes, such as job satisfaction (Beutell & Wittig-Berman, 1999; Malka & Chatman, 2003; Sanchez & Brock, 1996) and job performance (Akter, & Husain (2016); Hamed, Ramzan, Zubair, et al. (2014); Holt (1993); & Ivancevich & Glueck, 1989). A meta-analysis conducted by Judge et al. (2001) looked at over 90 studies over a time span of 120 years and showed that the relationship between salary and job satisfaction is very weak: how much money employees make only accounted for 2% of the variance of job satisfaction. Surprisingly, in the real world, most employers think that money is an important factor when it comes to reasons to stay in or leave a company; the majority of managers (89%) think that employees who leave a company, leave for more money, while only 11% think of other major reasons for an employee's self-termination (Gallup, 2018). The reality, though, is very different: Only 12% of the employees asked stated that they left former jobs for more money, while 88% stated there were other reasons they left a job for (Gallup, 2018).

Still, Study 1c showed that the salary is not entirely irrelevant when it comes to love of a job. Although studies show that money is not an effective motivator for many people (Chapman & White, 2019; Vallerand, Houlfort, & Forest, 2003), the participants of the qualitative focus group still said that being underpaid is a reason that hinders an individual to even develop love of a job and that the salary and extra bonuses can help individuals feel safe in the working relationship and feel appreciated for their work. In their eyes, a good salary is a requirement for a job that someone can love. Therefore, it is assumed that there is a positive relationship between salary and job love.

Hypothesis$_3$: *The higher the salary an individual receives, the higher the probability of job love.*

Salary Satisfaction

Nevertheless, although the salary itself may not play a key role in the relationship to job love, what may be more important is how satisfied people are with their pay. This is determined by the outcome of the comparison of what a person wants and what a person perceives to get in the work environment (Locke, 1976). Salary satisfaction is connected to the salary itself and found to be one of the core components of overall job satisfaction as described by Smith, Kendall and Hulin (1969) in their Job Descriptive Index. In addition to being connected to satisfaction, the salary can also be considered an expression of appreciation – and underpaid workers may feel unappreciated. Hence, when studying salary as an antecedent of job love, it is important to determine how satisfied people are with their pay. The researcher, therefore, suggests that satisfaction with the pay has a positive relationship with the chances of a person loving their job.

Hypothesis$_4$: *The higher an individual's salary satisfaction is, the higher the probability of job love.*

3.1.2 Person Variables

Person-Job-Fit

There is a pervasive belief that love is found through finding the "right person" or the "right match" (Knee, 1998). This "destiny belief" or "fit mindset" is characterized by the thought that a relationship is either meant to be or not. We see it in movies like "*The Perfect Match*" (Woodruff, 2016): if one just finds the right partner for life, one will live happily ever after. Not surprisingly, this view of love has found its way to the work context. A growing number of books with titles like *How to Find the Job You Love* (Boldt, 2004) and *How to Get a Job you Love* (Lees, 2014) indicate a rising interest in a workplace "fit mindset" in popular job literature. Also, in business practice, love has found its way into the job context. As described in the introduction of this dissertation, in 2011, German job search platform Stepstone launched their nationwide advertising campaign "You too can find a job you love." The campaign is still evolving, and Stepstone keeps the idea of a job one loves as a key topic for advertising their job search services: In an Instagram posting from June 2020, Stepstone showed an image of a unicorn writing "Who you really are" and a donkey below labeled "How you feel right now." The post is captioned: "With Stepstone you find a job, you love. More than 80,000 jobs are waiting for you." The picture's message is clear: if one feels like a donkey even though one is actually a unicorn, one has not found the job one loves yet, but Stepstone will help find it. A broad amount of research has been conducted regarding the question of how much a person fits their job or the job fits the person's need. Everyone has heard the saying "Find a job you love and you will never work a day in your life again," indicating that it is a common belief that people just have to find the job that fits them to find job love. This is sometimes called the *destiny belief* (Knee, 1998): people believe that relationships are either successful or unsuccessful from their start depending on whether partners are compatible or not. If a relationship does not work out in the end, people with the destiny mindset tend to believe that the unsuccessful end was caused by an imperfect fit and that the relationship was just not meant to be (Knee et al., 2003).

There is another distinct belief people commonly hold: the *growth belief* (Knee, 1998). Contrary to the destiny belief, people with the growth belief think that love develops over time, and relationships change, depending on the energy and time people invest into them. Those with the growth mindset are more likely to believe their partners can change, and they are more likely to let a relationship grow over time, instead of giving up quickly (Knee, 1998). Moreover, those with a growth mindset tend to be more realistic and tolerant when their partners show characteristics that do not match their ideal partner characteristics, while people with destiny mindsets are more negatively affected by those undesired characteristics (Knee et al., 2001).

There are different types of fit regarding the job: person-vocation fit, person-organization fit, person-group fit, person-person fit and person-job fit. The broadest type, person-vocation fit, deals with the amount of compatibility of an individuals' interests to a vocation in general. In his Theory of Vocational Choice, Holland (1959, 1985) states that successful people tend to choose work environments that fit their personal needs better than less successful people. Holland divides individuals into different personality types (Realistic, Investigative, Artistic, Social, Enterprising, Conventional) that each correspond with a basic type of work environment. Interestingly, Holland did not only find that it is beneficial for the individual to choose a vocation that fits his/her personality type, but he also found that working with other people with similar personality types and interests creates a work environment that is even more rewarding for the individual (Holland, 1985). *Person-job fit* (P-J Fit) describes the compatibility between the characteristics of a person and those of a job (Kristof-Brown & Guay, 2011).

In brand love research, Carroll and Ahuvia argue that the brand needs to fit the self in order to create brand love among its users (2006, p. 84.). So, in regards to the job, the researcher argues that people who think their jobs fit themselves would be more likely to love their job.

Hypothesis$_5$: *The higher the perceived fit of the job to the person, the higher the probability of job love.*

Perceived Competence

People want to be good at what they do. The need for competence, for being effective in interacting with the environment, is described by Deci and Ryan in their widely recognized self-determination theory (STD) (Deci & Ryan, 1985, 2008, 2012). Being good at one's job is what drives an individual to grow, develop, take on challenging tasks at work. From accomplishing tasks and extending one's capacities, an individual can gain not only satisfaction, but also pleasure (White, 1959). The concept of competence is closely related to the psychological concept of self-efficacy. Self-efficacy, introduced by Bandura in 1986, describes the extent to which a person believes in their own abilities to accomplish a task and to achieve expected outcomes. While self-efficacy is a concept about a person more generally, competence is focused on the person in a specific setting. In the work context, perceived competence stems from experiences of being good at the job, from external feedback, e.g. affirmation from a supervisor or coworker, and the feeling of mastery, i.e. accomplishing a task or project. Deci and Ryan (1985) view competence as a basic need that motivates people intrinsically. Hence, it is suggested that the perception of being good at one's job is an antecedent of job love.

Hypothesis$_6$: *The higher the perceived level of competence of an individual, the higher the probability of job love.*

Perceived Autonomy

People want to make decisions autonomously in order to feel self-determination. This need for autonomy is defined as "individuals' inherent desire to feel volitional and to experience a sense of choice and psychological freedom when carrying out an activity" (Deci & Ryan, 1985). It is intertwined with the psychological concept of control. People want to be in control rather than be controlled by others. Increasing people's options and choices increases intrinsic motivation (Zuckerman et al., 1978).

Slemp and colleagues (2020) found that leaders have a big part in encouraging their workers' sense of autonomy. They call those leaders "autonomy-supportive leaders", which give their workers a sense of choice and encourage autonomy of the individual. Leader autonomy support "refers to a cluster of interpersonal leader behaviors that nurture inner motivational resources in employees" (Slemp et al., 2020). This leadership behavior enhances passion for work in the individual (Slemp et al., 2020). Hence, it is suggested that an increase of autonomy will lead to higher passion for the job, and consequently, will be positively related to the love for a job.

Hypothesis₇: *The higher the perceived autonomy of an individual, the higher the probability of job love.*

3.1.3 Relationship Variables

The people individuals work with can have a strong impact on the overall work experience and, moreover, on the quality of people's lives. People in the workplace, whether supervisors, co-workers, or even the clients people work for, can uplift a worker with a kind word, positive feedback, a nice talk, or they can discourage the worker through negative feedback, mistrust, disrespect or harsh words. Because of the beneficial outcomes of healthy workplace relationships, the topic has received growing interest in research (Ragins & Button, 2007; Dutton & Ragins, 2017).

General Appreciation

According to the Gallup Engagement Index, one of the most stated reasons why people have left a job was the lack of appreciation they experienced (2018). Gallup even found that 65% of employees believed they had not received any words of praise or recognition during the past year. In the workplace, recognition helps employees understand the "how" behind their behavior: How employees contribute to the goals of the organization, how their work makes a difference and how their work is important. Without recognition, people feel a lessened sense of ownership, a decrease in responsibility and, moreover, less pride in their work (Achieve Global, 2003). In contrast, employees who feel recognized are more motivated and experience higher job satisfaction (White, 2016). Recognition is not a costly thing, but it is a highly effective way to motivate employees to perform better at work (Danish, & Usman, 2010).

Sometimes, recognition and appreciation are used interchangeably as if they were the same thing. Theoretically, there are some differences that are important to understand in order to distinguish the concepts theoretically before concluding measurements of them. While recognition is specifically about the behavior of a person, appreciation is more directed to the value of someone as a person. *Recognition* "refers to the act of acknowledging an individual or team's behavior, performance, effort and accomplishment that help the organizational goals and values. Recognition encourages employees to repeat good performances." (Maharjan, 2018). *Appreciation* "is about acknowledging a person's inherent value. The point isn't their accomplishments. It's their worth as a colleague and a human being." (Robins, 2019). When a supervisor gives recognition, it is about improving the performance of a subordinate and focuses on what is good for the company. Appreciation emphasizes what is good for the company and good for the person simultaneously (Chapman & White, 2019). In the qualitative interviews described in Study 1c of this dissertation, appreciation was among the most often named reasons for people to love their jobs as well as a reason for people to not love their jobs. Hence, appreciation is assumed to be a key antecedent to job love. The following hypothesis is proposed.

Hypothesis$_8$: *The higher the level of general appreciation perceived by an individual, the higher the probability of job love.*

Relationships with Supervisors

When it comes to workplace relationships, managers or immediate supervisors play a key role in the work-life of a worker: A supportive relationship between an employee and his/her leader who expresses appreciation for the employee's achievements, milestones and excellent work can enhance the feeling of recognition of the employee significantly. On the other hand, supervisors who treat their employees with no respect, who do not listen or who destroy the confidence of their subordinates can have detrimental effects on employee behavior. The yearly Gallup poll found the number one reason people quit their jobs is a bad boss or immediate supervisor (Gallup, 2018). Nonetheless, not all experts share this opinion. Dr. Jason McPherson, CEO of Culture Amp[10], states that the statement "People quit managers" would be the biggest lie in HR, caused by flawed data and an overly simplistic view of the matter (Elzinga, 2016). The team of Culture Amp looked at data from over 300,000 employees and found that good managers may not be as important to people's intention to stay, as bad managers are motivating people to leave. However, in the end, Culture Amp concluded that managers are not the most important reason for people to stay in or leave a company (Elzinga, 2016).

The most recognized theory explaining supervisor-subordinate relationships is the leader-member exchange (LME) theory, introduced by Graen and Uhl-Bien (1991). It suggests that supervisors and their subordinates form different relationships regarding relationship quality: high-quality relationships are formed with mutual trust, respect, and are accompanied by obligation and internal motivation. Leaders in high-quality relationships are more likely to show support and positive feedback. The outcomes of high-quality relationships are higher motivation and commitment among employees (Wayne et al.,

---

[10] Culture Amp is an employee analytics platform in Melbourne that focuses on surveying and analytics.

1997). Moreover, those positive supervisor-subordinate relationships result in higher job satisfaction and a lower intention to quit (Allen & Meyer, 1996). While those in high-quality LME relations are "going the extra mile," those in low-quality LME relationships are the ones performing routine tasks or doing only what is instructed. When it comes to loving one's job, the participants of the focus group in Study 1 indicated that people need to have a good relationship with their supervisor to love their job. The participants especially remarked how important appreciation, recognition and support (all indicators for a high-quality LMW relationship) would be important for the chances of a person loving their job. Hence, the following hypothesis is proposed:

Hypothesis$_9$: *The more positively an individual perceives the relationships with their supervisors, the higher the probability of job love.*

Relationships with Colleagues

Co-workers can either inspire and motivate each other, or they can hinder each other and obstruct each other's path to success, and potentially job love. According to Meyer and Allen (1997), workplace relationships are crucial to employees' wellbeing, motivation to perform and actual job performance. Employees who are well-connected to their peers are better informed about their work tasks, experience less uncertainty about company goals and perform better (Brown & Mitchell, 1993; Sharda et al., 1999). Therefore, it is crucial for employees to be socially integrated into the circle of co-workers (Connolly & Viswesvaran, 2000). Furthermore, a study by Globoforce (2014) found that people who have friends at work tended to be more committed to their organization compared to people who stated they do not have any friends at work. And as sometimes people spend more time with their colleagues than with their families, work relationships can have a strong impact on employees' quality of life. The qualitative research conducted for this dissertation in Study 1 indicated the importance of co-worker relationships. Participants of the focus group suggested that people who have good relationships at work with their colleagues are also more likely to love their jobs as they experience positive interactions at work, have more fun at work and feel more positive emotions, which were mentioned as important aspects of an individual's love of a job.

Hypothesis$_{10}$: *The more positively an individual perceives the relationships with their colleagues, the higher the probability of job love.*

Relationships with Clients

Also, relationships with clients may play a role in the workplace relationship quality. Especially in some professions, the worker-client relationship may be considered an important relationship in the working life of an individual. There are various formulations of worker-client relationships that have been researched, for example, the relationship of teachers to their students (= their clients): A study conducted by Spilt et al. (2011) looked at the impact students have on the well-being of their teachers. According to the researchers, teachers have a basic need to relate with the students in their class (p. 457). While student misbehavior has a negative effect on the perceived stress level of teachers, positive interactions can enhance teacher well-being and influence the personal and professional self-esteem of teachers. Whether client behavior also plays a role in a person's love of their job is yet unclear. It is suggested, however, that positive client behavior also improves the chances of a person loving their job.

Hypothesis$_{11}$: *The more positively an individual perceives the relationship with their clients, the higher the probability of job love.*

3.1.4 Concluding Hypotheses Model

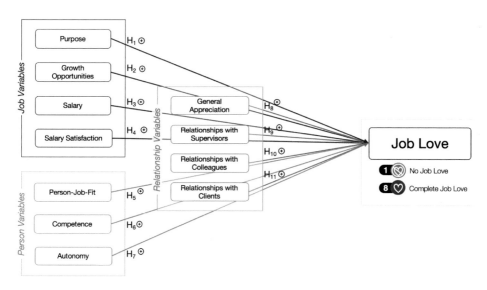

Figure 27. *Hypotheses Model of Study 3*

Note. H = hypothesis, + = suggested positive relationship, job love outcome variable: Non-Job Lovers (Type 1) vs. Job Lovers (Type 8).

Based on previous qualitative studies and literature research, this study developed various hypotheses of which factors can lead to job love. The concluding model of hypotheses includes all variables into one model (see Figure 27).

3.2 Method

The goal of Study 3 was to find out which factors lead to job love and how important different antecedents are for the development of job love. Therefore, job love was measured in each individual and using the data, it was determined whether someone loves his/her job or does not love his/her job. Different hypotheses of possible antecedents of job love were developed and presented in the model of the study in Figure 27. To test the hypotheses, a cross-sectional study design was chosen.[11] Although typically, a

---

[11] To test hypotheses that state a causal relationship between two variables, typically, a longitudinal design is needed to prove that a change in the level of an independent variable (e.g. salary) leads to a change in a dependent variable (in our case: job love). Yet, regarding the high

longitudinal design is needed to prove causal relationships between variables, various reasons can justify the use of the cross-sectional design instead: First, the assumption of causal relationships stems from research that has already been validated by previous research on love and brand love. Second, the influence of different independent variables can be better modeled in an inclusive study measuring all variables at a same point in time than by conducting numerous studies at different points in time, which can also lead to methodological problems, such as comparing different study samples. Third, from an efficiency point of view, a cross-sectional design is the most suitable for the time and resources available for this dissertation project.

3.2.1 Procedure

The study was programmed via Typeform, a cloud-based online survey software that creates an advanced user experience. To recruit participants for the study, the social media platforms Facebook, Instagram, and LinkedIn were used. Information about the study was sent to all suitable contacts including a short description of the study, an overview of how the study works, and a link or QR code with the link to register online for the study.

The study was described as a "Study on the Topic Love of Work." In total, the researcher sent the link with information about the study to around 100 people within her contact lists on the social media platforms. Criteria for participating in the study were stated as being fluent in German and having a regular job with at least 5 working hours per week. Furthermore, the researcher encouraged participants to forward the registration link to interested friends or acquaintances. Some of the respondents gave feedback that they forwarded the link to their colleagues and people in their professional circle.

---

number of hypotheses proposed, various field studies assessing data at different points in time would be needed to test them, which is not possible with the given time and resources available for this dissertation.

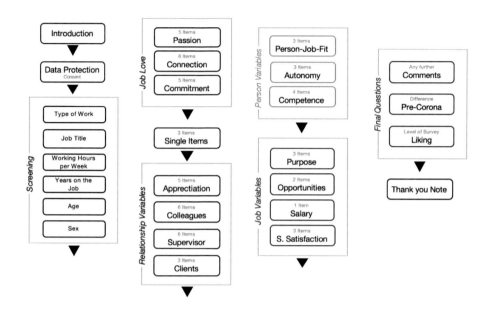

Figure 28. *Overview of Questionnaire Variables of Study 3*
Note. See Appendix 3 for the full questionnaire.

In total, the questionnaire contained 60 items (for an overview see Figure 28). When people clicked on the link, they were presented a landing page that included a brief description of the contents of the study. The data protection page informed participants that study participation was anonymous, confidential, and voluntary. When agreeing to continue and participate, they were directly forwarded to the general screening part of the questionnaire, captured demographic data and questions regarding their employment status and title. After completing the general questionnaire, the Job Love Scale (JLS) developed in Study 2 was included as a measure of the dependent variable job love. All eleven antecedents of job love were included in variable-oriented sections – relationship variables, person variables and job variables. At the end of the questionnaire, the participants had the chance to give feedback and to say anything they wanted to state regarding the topic that did not belong elsewhere in the questionnaire.

Sample. In total, 301 people clicked on the questionnaire with a total sample of 202 people finishing the questionnaire, resulting in a completion rate of 67.1%. Participants took an

average of 17 minutes to complete the questionnaire. An overview of all demographical
and screening data that were assessed can be seen in Figure 29.

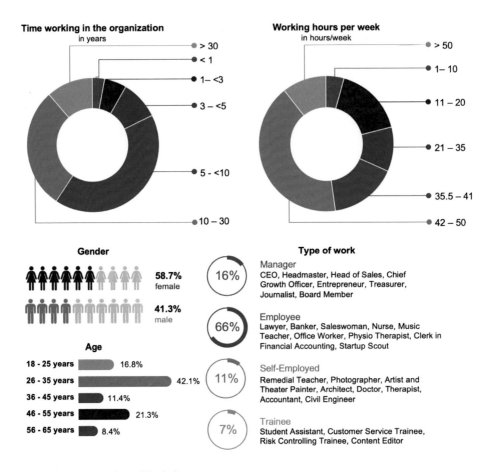

Figure 29. *Demographics of Study 3*

With 58.7% women and 41.3% men, female participants were overrepresented in the
sample. The average age was 36.9 with an excessively large number of younger
participants between 25 and 35. The biggest share of the participants, almost one-third of
the sample, have already worked in the same job in the same company for more than 10
years, and the majority of the sample (82.2%) worked full time at the time of the
questionnaire (more than 35 hours a week). The participants were asked to name their job
titles. The jobs participants had, were diverse: attorney-at-law, teacher, model,

headmaster, nanny, neon sign maker, administrative assistant, police officer, social worker, nurse, theater painter, journalist, curative educator, content marketing manager, CEO, doctor, medical technical assistant, physiotherapist, tax consultant, piano teacher, office worker, groundsman and secretary are some of the job titles, to name only a few.

3.2.2 Measures

Independent Variables

All independent variables were operationalized on a 7-point Likert scale ranging from *0 = do not agree at all* to *6 = completely agree*. The best fit of each item to the scale was then calculated using Cronbach's Alpha measure to ensure that each item selected represented the scale. An overview of all independent variables with the internal consistency measures is presented in Table 16. All scales showed a sufficient $\alpha > 0.70$. Moreover, an ANOVA with Friedman's Chi-Square-Test was calculated showing significant variance between persons to use the scale to differentiate between respondents for all used scales.

Perceived Purpose. Purpose has been referred to as the "why" we do things (Ulrich et al., 2010). Hence, the perceived purpose of work is when an individual knows the why behind their daily tasks and overall work. May et al. (2004) define the meaning of work as "the value of a work goal or purpose, judged to the individual's own ideals or standards" (p. 11). For assessing purpose, three items were included assessing whether individuals thought that their job has a meaning and whether they feel they know what they do the job for.

Growth Opportunities. Growth Opportunities were assessed with two items asking how much an individual is able to develop and grow in a job (e.g. "My job gives me the opportunity to develop myself further") and how satisfied he/she is with the career opportunities of the job.

Salary. The salary (net income) was assessed to see whether the real income can have different correlations to individuals' attitudes towards their jobs. It was assessed on a scale asking the monthly net income with six different steps ranging from *1 = 0-500€/month* to *6 = over 6,000€/month*.

Salary Satisfaction. The satisfaction of an individual with his/her pay was measured using three items, the first described how attractive the salary of the job is, and a second assessed how much money was being paid compared to other companies or jobs (when the respondent works as self-employed). A third item, which assessed whether the respondents thought that a good salary was important to them, was excluded because of a small item-scale correlation.

Person-Job-Fit. Person-Job-Fit is defined as the level of congruence of a person's abilities and the demands of a job (Holland, 1959, 1985, 2011). To calculate person-job-fit, three items were used assessing whether the person thought that the job he or she has fit them and whether they thought they have the abilities and skills that are needed to conduct the job.

Autonomy. To measure autonomy, four items were used that reflect how much the individual felt they are in control and can do their job as they want to do the job (Deci & Ryan, 1985, 2000). One item measuring the possibility to combine work and family was excluded from the scale because of a low item-scale correlation resulting in a three-item scale.

Perceived Appreciation. For the general level of appreciation, four items were included: (1) how much a person felt personally valued as a person by the work environment, (2) whether they got enough appreciation for the work, (3) whether a person thought he or she was needed at work and (4) whether the individual had the feeling of being a valuable employee.

Relationships with Supervisors. Regarding the relationships to supervisor(s), individuals were asked six items including: how much (1) they felt valued by their supervisor(s), (2) whether the supervisor(s) had time for them to discuss their matters, (3) whether they were praised, (4) got support when they need it, (5) felt that they are trusted by the supervisor(s) and (6) whether they heard thank you for their work.

Peer Relationships. Relationships with colleagues were assessed with four items: (1) whether people felt they were valued by their colleagues, (2) they were supported, (3) they felt colleagues liked to spend time with them, and (4) whether the colleagues paid special attention to them on occasions (e.g. their birthday).

Relationships with clients. Relationships with clients were assessed with three items, measuring whether people feel their work is (1) appreciated by clients, (2) the level of criticism is low, and (3) they got a "thank you" for their work from clients.

Dependent Variable

Job Love. According to the model of job love, complete love is only present when all three dimensions of love – passion, commitment, and connection – are present in an individual. To calculate whether a person belonged to the group of people who love their job, the researcher calculated for each participant the love type he/she belonged to. In total, there are eight types that can be identified (see Figure 30).

Individuals belong to type 1, when no connection, passion, or commitment is present. Those people do not love their job. Types 2, 3, and 4 are types where only one of the dimensions is present, e.g. Type 2 with high connection, but no passion or commitment to the job. Types 5, 6, and 7 are mixed types with two of three dimensions present, e.g. a friendship is a relationship with high commitment and connection, but no passion for the job. Finally, Type 8 is what is called the only "real love," which is attained when all three dimensions are present and measure high.

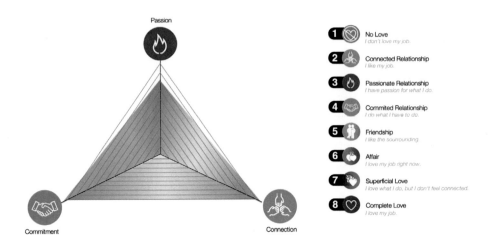

Figure 30. *Overview of Job Love Types*

What is "high"? This is the golden question: Where is a limit expressed when distinguishing between love and non-love? All items were measured on a seven-point Likert scale ranging from *0 = strongly disagree* to *6 = strongly agree*.

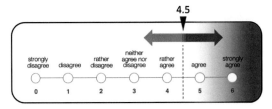

Figure 31. *Job Love Scale – Cut Off Value*

The researcher decided to demarcate a value of 4.5 out of 6 as "high" (see Figure 31), measuring all who do agree to the items of a scale on average. In our sample, the number of people in each group is distributed as follows:

With 27.4 % of people who belong to type 8 *(n = 55),* complete love, Study 3 included a relatively high sample of people who are classified as Job Lovers (see Table 15). Another approximately 30% of the sample are classified as Non-Job Lovers *(n = 59).*

Table 15. Distribution of Job Love Types in Study 3 Sample

	Love Type	n	%
Type 1	No Love (Non-Job Lovers)	59	29.2%
Type 2	Connected Relationship	6	3.0%
Type 3	Passionate Relationship	20	9.9%
Type 4	Committed Relationship	12	5.9%
Type 5	Friendship	10	5.0%
Type 6	Affair	8	4.0%
Type 7	Superficial Love	32	15.8%
Type 8	Complete Love (Job Lovers)	55	27.2%

Note. n = 202.

In Study 3, the researcher wanted to calculate predictions: *How likely is a person with a high sense of purpose to love their job?* (Hypothesis 1). The dependent variable is "Love Type 8 (*Complete Job Love*) versus Love Type 1 (*Non-Job Love*)". As shown in Figure 32, types 2 (Liking) through 7 (fatuous love) were excluded from the analysis. The reason was that, if the whole sample was included, and for example, Love Type 8 was compared with all Types 1-7, there would have been a lot of variance that was unexplainable. Types 2-7 all have some high expression of one or two love dimensions, but not all of them. Hence, if those in the sample who only lack passion (type 5: Utility Relationship) or who have passion but lack commitment (type 6: Romantic Love) were included, there would be too great a variance. Hence, only job non-lovers with job lovers were compared.

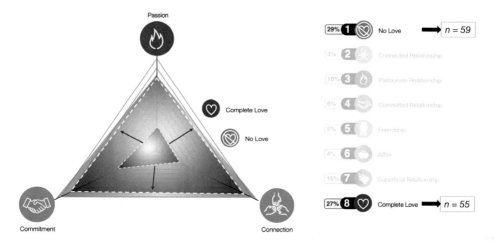

Figure 32. *Illustration of Dependent Variable (Job Lovers vs. Non-Job Lovers)*

Control Variables. Personal characteristics such as age, gender, type of employment (i.e. fully employed, self-employed), and years working on the same job were included in the study as control variables. They were all single item measures.

3.2.3 Data Evaluation Process

For data analysis, the software package SPSS (Version 26) was used and additional analyses were conducted in RStudio with the R package Lavaan (Rosseel, 2012, 2014) to test the overall fit of the models. The data evaluation process was conducted in six different steps as presented in Figure 33:

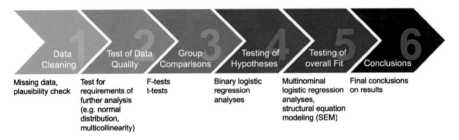

Figure 33. *Data Evaluation Process of Study 3*

Data cleaning. In the first step, the data set was cleaned and processed in SPSS. There were only a few data sets with missing data, as most of the items collected in the online survey were mandatory. Participants could not continue to the next page of the questionnaire without answering every question. Therefore, data was only missing when people were allowed to skip the item. This was true for "unnecessary" qualitative questions such as *Do you have anything else you want to say on the matter?* Also voluntary were the questions regarding the exact net salary. Since especially in Germany, salary is a topic that people generally are hesitant to talk about publicly, the questionnaire was formatted so that it was possible to skip the questions; an option only a few participants did use (4%, 8 out of 202). When people were asked about their relationships with supervisors, colleagues and clients, they were able to skip questions by clicking "I do not have supervisors/colleagues/clients, I work with." Missing answers were coded as missing values in the dataset. All variables were named using a standardized coding system and mean values were calculated.

Test of data quality. In the second step, the data set was checked for data quality. The scales measuring the predictor variables were tested in their reliability. Therefore, Cronbach's Alpha was calculated for each of the scales (see Table 16). Since Cronbach's Alpha cannot be calculated with only two items, the Spearman-Brown coefficient was calculated for scales that only contained two items (e.g. "growth opportunities"), as suggested by Eisinga et al. (2013). Due to the fact that all calculated Cronbach's Alphas and Spearman-Brown coefficients were above .70, all scales proved to be worthy of further analyses.

Table 16. Reliability Analyses of Predictor Scales

Scale Items	Mean (SD)	Item-Scale- Correlation	Cronbach's Alpha
Perceived Purpose			0.837
My work fills me with meaning.	4.28 (1.53)	0.762	
With my work, I am doing something useful for others.	4.46 (1.51)	0.674	
There are rarely moments when I wonder what I'm doing the job for.	4.01 (1.59)	0.664	
Growth Opportunities			0.764**
My job gives me the opportunity to develop myself further.	4.08 (1.66)	0.550	
I am satisfied with the growth opportunities my job provides me.	3.71 (1.77)	0.550	
Salary Satisfaction			0.844**
My employer pays me an attractive salary.	4.17 (1.48)	0.665	
Compared to others, my employer offers more money (including additional benefits).	3.54 (1.82)	0.661	
A good salary is important to me.*	4.97 (1.02)	0.193	
Person-Job-Fit			0.768
I have exactly the skills you need for the job that I do.	4.86 (1.16)	0.546	
My job suits me.	4.76 (1.35)	0.763	
There is no other job that would suit me better than my current job.	3.06 (1.86)	0.588	
Competence			0.840
I am really good at what I do in my work.	4.82 (1.03)	0.702	
In my work, I can show what I can do.	4.56 (1.24)	0.633	
I feel competent in my job.	4.87 (1.07)	0.796	
Autonomy			0.757
At work, I have the freedom to choose how I do my job.	4.71 (1.41)	0.606	
In my work, I rarely feel that others control what I do.	4.19 (1.58)	0.479	
My employer gives me the opportunity to schedule my time freely.	4.39 (1.63)	0.681	
My job enables me to combine work and family*	4.00 (1.53)	0.403	
Perceived Appreciation			0.874
In general, I feel valued as a person in my work environment.	4.45 (1.35)	0.773	
In general, I get enough appreciation for the work I do.	4.00 (1.50)	0.770	
I feel like I'm needed at work.	4.58 (1.37)	0.608	
My employer gives me the feeling that I am a valuable employee.	4.12 (1.55)	0.776	
Supervisor Relationships			0.931
I feel valued by my manager.	4.41 (1.55)	0.849	
When I have a concern, my manager takes the time for me.	4.57 (1.40)	0.801	
When I have done something well, my superior praises me.	4.04 (1.67)	0.775	
I can count on my manager's help when I need it.	4.41 (1.47)	0.762	
I feel like my manager trusts me.	4.85 (1.47)	0.760	
My supervisor makes me feel thankful for my work.	4.26 (1.59)	0.844	
Peer Relationships			0.795
I have the feeling that my colleagues value me as a colleague.	4.94 (1.06)	0.717	
My colleagues support me when I need their help.	5.04 (1.08)	0.612	
My colleagues like to spend time with me (e.g. lunch together).	4.74 (1.31)	0.611	
When there is an occasion, my colleagues try to make me happy.	4.23 (1.55)	0.551	
Client Relationships			0.733
I think most of the people I work for appreciate my work.	4.78 (1.03)	0.625	
It's rare that I get criticism for my work from my customers.	4.75 (1.25)	0.494	
I often get a "thank you" from my customers for my work.	4.22 (1.48)	0.597	

Note. SD = Standard Deviation, *Item was excluded from the scale because of a small item-scale correlation.
**Spearman-Brown-Coefficient was calculated, because there were only two items to conduct reliability analysis.

3.3 Results

Correlation Analysis. Means, standard deviations, and correlations are presented in Table 18.

Analyses of Control Variables

Analysis of the correlation between the control variables and job love level in general, and the distinct dimensions of job love, are shown in Table 17. The results of a single logistic regression analysis of all control variables and two outcome variables (1: Type 8 (Job-Love), 2: Type 1 (Non-Job Love)) are presented in Table 19.

Table 17. Correlation Analyses of Control Variables

	Job Love[c]	Passion	Connection	Commitment
Control Variable	*r*	*r*	*r*	*r*
Gender[a]	.040	.012	.084	.006
Age	.106	.097	.051	.134
Permanent Employee[b]	-.194***	-.165**	-.171**	-.179**
Executive[b]	.162**	.166**	.113	.156**
Self-Employed[b]	.304***	.306***	.229***	.280***
Working Hours/Week	.119	.269***	.007	.078
Years on the Job	.088	.097	.020	.121

Note. r = correlation coefficient; *p < .10; **p < .05; ***p<.01; n = 202; [a]male =0; female =1; [b]vs. others; [c]mean of all 16 variables of the passion/connection/commitment dimensions.

Gender. Regarding the differences between different sexes, regression analyses showed that gender is not correlated with the average of all job love variables, or the dimensions of passion, connection, or commitment (see Table 17).

Age. Single logistic regression analyses showed no power of age to predict whether a person belongs to the group of those who love their jobs or those who do not love their jobs (see Table 19). Also, age was not correlated with average job love, passion, connection, or commitment (see Table 17). Hence, it seems possible to love a job whether one is young or old.

Table 18. *Means, Standard Deviations, and Correlations in Study 3*

Variable/Scale	M	SD	N	1	2	3	4	5	6	7	8	9	10	11	12	13	14	15	16	17	18	19	20
1 Age	36.90	11.82	202																				
2 Sex[a]	0.59	0.49	202	.01																			
3 Type of Employment	2.14	0.90	202	-.22	.11																		
4 Years on the Job	8.51	9.43	202	.73	-.02	-.07																	
5 Working hours	5.22	1.15	202	.07	-.34	-.42	.01																
6 Job Love[b]	4.24	1.11	202	.11	.04	-.12	.09	.12															
7 Passion	4.42	1.12	202	.10	.01	-.15	.10	.27	.82														
8 Connection	4.08	1.21	202	.05	.08	-.06	.02	.01	.90	.58													
9 Commitment	4.24	1.45	202	.13	.01	-.13	.12	.08	.92	.65	.76												
10 Salary Satisfaction	3.86	1.54	202	.17	-.09	-.25	.07	.29	.36	.27	.28	.39											
11 Net Income	4.29	1.49	194	.40	-.36	-.42	.26	.59	.24	.28	.13	.23	.47										
12 Perceived Purpose	4.24	1.34	202	.19	.10	-.07	.18	.07	.73	.66	.63	.66	.17	.21									
13 Growth Opportunities	3.90	1.54	202	-.05	-.16	-.06	-.01	.15	.55	.31	.51	.59	.29	.21	.37								
14 Person-Job Fit	4.23	1.23	202	.19	-.03	-.12	.22	.14	.75	.65	.58	.75	.29	.24	.65	.38							
15 Perceived Autonomy	4.32	1.16	202	.12	-.05	-.10	.06	.04	.47	.35	.46	.42	.25	.20	.36	.37	.38						
16 Perceived Competence	4.75	0.97	202	.09	-.09	-.14	.13	.14	.60	.60	.48	.52	.22	.24	.49	.26	.71	.39					
17 General Appreciation	4.29	1.23	202	.04	.06	-.15	.04	.13	.72	.49	.78	.61	.31	.28	.50	.48	.40	.45	.34				
18 Relationship to Supervisors	4.42	1.31	177	-.15	.07	-.08	-.14	-.07	.51	.25	.60	.44	.17	.06	.26	.40	.15	.40	.17	.69			
19 Relationship to Colleagues	4.61	1.03	106	-.06	.01	.00	.14	-.07	.32	.19	.40	.25	-.01	-.05	.29	.20	.31	.29	.33	.41	.27		
20 Relationship to Clients	4.59	1.02	138	.24	-.01	.07	.16	-.05	.39	.41	.32	.33	.18	.06	.37	.16	.43	.32	.47	.26	.07	.14	

Note. [a]0 = male, 1 = female. [b]average of all 16 items of the Job Love Scale. $r \geq .13$: $p < .05$; $r \geq .17$: $p < .01$; $r \geq .21$: $p < .001$

Table 19. Single Logistic Regression Analyses of Control Variables

Predictor	β	SE	Wald	df	Sig.	Exp(B)
Years on the Job	0.020	0.037	0.301	1	0.583	1.020
Working Hours/Week	0.705	0.307	5.277	1	0.022	2.024
Age	0.018	0.031	0.349	1	0.555	1.018
Sex[a]	0.311	0.533	0.340	1	0.560	1.365
Constant	-6.424	2.434	6.963	1	0.008	0.002

Note. Outcome variables 1: Job Love (Type 8), 0: Non-Job Love (Type 1). β = regression coefficient; Sig = significance; *Exp* = exponent; n = 202; [a]male =0; female =1.

Type of Employment. There are many different types of employment included in this study. Employees tended to love their job less than those with other types of employment[12] *(r = -.194, p <.01)* (see Table 17). Individuals working on the executive level had a higher chance of loving their job compared to others *(r = .162, p < .05),* as they showed a higher passion and commitment to their job (see Table 17). Self-employment was especially strongly related to job love, with *r = .304 (p < .01).*

Years on the Job. Regarding the time, a person already spent in the same company on the same job, there was no correlation to the level of job love or the dimensions of job love (see Table 17) Years on the job cannot predict whether a person belongs to the group of Job Lovers or the group of Non-Job Lovers (see Table 19).

Working hours per week. When analyzing the correlation between weekly working hours to the single job love dimensions, only the correlation to passion was significant: the more working hours a person works, the higher the score of the passion dimension *(r = .269, p <.01).* Also, working hours per week is suited to predict whether a person loves their job as people who work more hours a week are more likely to belong to the group of Job Lovers (see table 19).

3.3.1 Group Comparisons of Job Lovers and Job Non-Lovers

To find out whether people who love their jobs *(Type 8 = Complete Love)* differed from those who do not love their jobs *(Type 1 = Non-Love)* regarding the proposed antecedents, mean value comparisons were carried out. For this purpose, the arithmetic means of the

---

[12] executives, student workers, self-employed

groups were calculated to see how much variance existed between groups (see Table 20). Moreover, the effect size of the identified difference was calculated. For the significance test, t-tests were conducted. To see how big the effect of the difference was, the researcher calculated Cohen's *d* and the correlation coefficient *r*.

Preparatory Analyses

Before conducting any t-tests, certain requirements must be met (Field, 2013, p. 371; Bortz & Schuster, 2010, p. 122): first, both groups that want to be compared must be independent. Second, all test variables must be at least interval scaled. Third, the variables must be normally distributed and fourth, the variances of the samples to be compared should be homogeneous.

Independency of groups. As the individuals in the sample were independent, both groups in the sample were independent.

Scaling of the variable. The test variables were scaled by the use of a 7-point Likert scale suggesting an interval level of the scales.[13]

Test for normal distribution. To test whether the variables of interest were normally distributed, Shapiro-Wilk tests were calculated. A significant value indicates a deviation from normality, and hence a problem for the further calculation of t-tests. The conducted Shapiro-Wilk test showed no significant results (see Table 20), indicating that the differences between the pre-, and post-scores were normally distributed (Glass et al., 1972). Nevertheless, critics indicate that the Shapiro-Wilk test "is notoriously affected by large samples in which small deviations from normality yield significant results" (Field, 2013, p. 883). Some researchers, therefore, argue that sample size can be used as another indicator for normal distribution. From a sample size of approximately 30, it can be assumed that the groups meet the requirements of normal distribution (Bortz & Schuster,

---

[13] Some authors see the use of Likert scales as interval scales critical (e.g. Coombs, 1960; Jamieson, 2004; Vigderhous, 1977), because the intervals between values cannot be presumed equal. They therefore suggest that Likert scales are only ordinal scales. Other authors, on the other hand, presume that Likert scales can be analyzed as interval scaled (e.g. Baggaley & Hull, 1983; Carifio & Perla, 2007; Knapp, 1990). To do this, the number of intervals should be raised (Wu & Leung, 2007). Therefore, in this research, a 7-point scale is used.

2010, p. 126). As the smallest group to be compared contained 38 cases (Type 1: Non-Lovers, variable "client relationships"), normal distribution was assumed.

Another method used to ensure normal distribution was to calculate skewness and kurtosis. *Skewness* measures the symmetry of a deviation, or more precisely, the lack of symmetry. A distribution is symmetric if it looks the same to the left and right of the center point (Field, 2013). *Kurtosis* measures whether data are heavy-tailed or light-tailed relative to a normal distribution. Data sets with high kurtosis measures tend to have outliers, or heavy tails, while low kurtosis measures are a sign of a lack of outliers (Field, 2013). While skewness and kurtosis should be between -1 and 1, other researchers (e.g. West, Finch, & Curran, p. 74) suggest that only from values of $|> 2|$ for the skewness and $|> 7|$ for the kurtosis of a there is a substantial deviation from the normal distribution.

Homogenous variances. In order to examine whether the variances within groups were homogeneous, Levene's F-Test was calculated. The test examines the hypothesis that the variances in different groups are equal by conducting "a one-way ANOVA on the deviations (i.e., the absolute value of the difference between each score and the mean of its group)" (Field, 2013, p. 878). A significant F-test result indicates that "the assumption of homogeneity of variances has been violated" (Field, 2013, p. 878).

Effect sizes. Effect sizes are measured to see whether an effect is important. The best known and most frequently used method for calculating the effect size is Cohen's d, Pearson's correlation coefficient r and the odds ratio (Field, 2009, p. 57). Cohen's d is used to compare the effect across studies, even if the dependent variable was measured in different ways, or when the groups measured have different group sizes (McGrath & Meyer, 2006). Therefore, in this study, Cohen's d was calculated. According to Cohen (1998),

$$|d| = .20 \text{ is a small effect,}$$
$$|d| = .50 \text{ is a medium effect,}$$
$$|d| = .80 \text{ is a large effect.}$$

While Cohen's $d = .50$ is showing one half standard deviation of difference between groups, $d = .75$ represents ¾ of a standard deviation difference between tested groups. Another widely used coefficient is r. Cohen (1988, 1992) suggested that:

$$r = .10 \text{ is a small effect,}$$

$$r = .30 \text{ is a medium effect,}$$

$$r = .50 \text{ is a large effect.}$$

Results of Group Comparisons

People who love their job (Type 8: Complete Job Love) differed in their overall levels of all tested antecedent variables from people who do not love their job (Type 1: Non-Job Love). The overall results of the t-tests are shown in Table 20.

Table 20. T-test Results of Group Comparisons of Job Lovers and Job Non-Lovers

Antecedent	type	Normal Distribution				Variance	Comparison of Mean Values			Effect Sizes	
		Shapiro-Wilk test Sig	Skew-ness Kurtosis	M	SD	Levene F test Sig	T	df	Sig	d	r
Purpose	8	.000	-0.821	5.3	0.7	.000	11.561	87.2	.000	2.122	.740
	1		0.193	3.0	1.3						
Opportunities	8	.000	-0.691	4.8	1.1	.002	7.109	101.8	.000	1.314	.569
	1		-0.057	3.0	1.6						
Salary	8	.000	0.169	4.7	1.5	.089	3.279	108.0	.000	.580	.279
	1		-0.570	3.8	1.6						
Salary Satisfaction	8	.001	-0.472	4.3	1.4	.089	3.897	112.0	.000	0.726	.333
	1		-0.457	3.2	1.7						
Person-Job-Fit	8	.002	-0.724	5.1	0.6	.000	12.019	85.9	.000	2.205	.742
	1		0.082	3.0	1.2						
Competence	8	.001	-1.076	5.4	0.6	.000	7.596	89.1	.000	1.395	.565
	1		2.193	4.1	1.2						
Autonomy	8	.000	-0.867	5.0	0.8	.000	5.743	90.9	.000	1.056	.466
	1		0.659	3.8	1.4						
General Appreciation	8	.000	-0.920	5.3	0.6	.000	11.363	81.4	.000	2.176	.736
	1		0.529	3.3	1.2						
Supervisor Relationships	8	.000	-1.114	5.2	0.8	.000	6.526	89.9	.000	1.221	.529
	1		0.845	3.7	1.5						
Peer Relationships	8	.000	0.033	5.2	0.8	.033	4.939	103.4	.000	.941	.404
	1		-0.968	4.3	1.0						
Client Relationships	8	.000	-0.838	5.0	0.8	.315	4.006	77.0	.000	.902	.404
	1		0.582	4.2	1.0						

Note. M = mean on a scale from 0 to 6; SD = standard deviation; df = degrees of freedom; Sig = significance – shown as one-sided significance; d = Cohen's d; r = correlation coefficient; $n_{Type\,8}$ = 55, $n_{type\,1}$ = 59, except for Supervisor Relationships ($n_{Type\,8}$ = 41, $n_{type\,1}$ = 57), Peer Relationships ($n_{Type\,8}$ = 50, $n_{type\,1}$ = 57), client Relationships ($n_{Type\,8}$ = 41, $n_{type\,1}$ = 38). For a better overview of the single analyses of all antecedents, see Appendix 4.

As all requirements for conducting t-tests were first checked (normal distribution, homogeneity of variance), and t-tests were calculated to test whether the group of people who love their job differed *significantly* from the group of job non-lovers. As there were already hypotheses of the direction of these differences, a one-sided test design was used for the evaluation of the mean value differences – instead of a two-sided (Field, 2013, p. 375). The detailed results are explained in the following paragraphs and shown in Figures 34-44. The significance values are the values calculated in a t-test and shown as one-sided, because there are prior hypotheses the calculations are based on. All detailed values from the analyses can be obtained from the Appendix (Appendix 4).

Purpose. People who love their job have a significantly higher rating of their overall level of purpose *(M = 5.25, SD = 1.317*, see Figure 34). In detail, the highest difference in mean occurred when people were asked whether they have moments when they wonder what they are doing in their jobs *(Δ^{14} = 2.34)*. Out of those who do not love their jobs, 25% stated that they disagreed to rarely have moments when they wonder what they are doing the job for. Among Job Lovers, this share was only 2% (see Appendix 4.1.3). People who are in the group of job lovers also have a significantly higher value in their perception that their jobs fill them with meaning and that they do something useful for other people with 89% agreeing that their job fills them with meaning. Only 10% of Non-Job Lovers could agree to this statement, while nearly one-third (31%) agrees that they do something useful for others with their work (see Appendix 4.1.3).

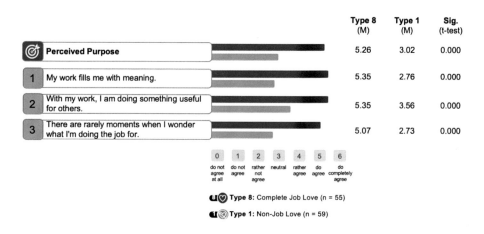

	Type 8 (M)	Type 1 (M)	Sig. (t-test)
Perceived Purpose	5.26	3.02	0.000
1 My work fills me with meaning.	5.35	2.76	0.000
2 With my work, I am doing something useful for others.	5.35	3.56	0.000
3 There are rarely moments when I wonder what I'm doing the job for.	5.07	2.73	0.000

0 1 2 3 4 5 6
do not agree at all / do not agree / rather not agree / neutral / rather agree / do agree / do completely agree

Type 8: Complete Job Love (n = 55)
Type 1: Non-Job Love (n = 59)

Figure 34. *Differences in Purpose of Job Lovers vs. Non-Job Lovers*
Note. For a detailed analysis, see Appendix 4.1.

---

[14] Δ is calculated as the mean of Type 8 subtracted by the mean of Type 1.

Growth Opportunities. In the group of those who love their job, 65% of the respondents stated that they think[15] their job gives them the opportunity to develop themselves further (see Appendix 4.2.3). In the group of those who do not love their job, this share was only half as big (30.5%). Also, when it comes to how satisfied people are with the growth opportunities the job offers, respondents of the job love group showed a significant higher mean compared to those of the non-job love group *($\Delta = 2.02$, $p < .001$*, see Figure 35): While 56% of Job Lovers agreed to being satisfied with their job's growth opportunities, 24% of the Non-Job Lovers did so as well.

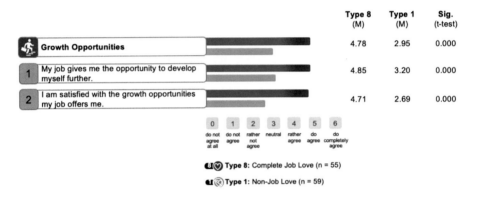

	Type 8 (M)	Type 1 (M)	Sig. (t-test)
Growth Opportunities	4.78	2.95	0.000
1 My job gives me the opportunity to develop myself further.	4.85	3.20	0.000
2 I am satisfied with the growth opportunities my job offers me.	4.71	2.69	0.000

0	1	2	3	4	5	6
do not agree at all	do not agree	rather not agree	neutral	rather agree	do agree	do completely agree

Type 8: Complete Job Love (n = 55)

Type 1: Non-Job Love (n = 59)

Figure 35. *Differences in Growth Opportunities of Job Lovers vs. Non-Job Lovers*
Note. For a detailed analysis, see Appendix 4.2.

---

[15] calculated as sum of the share of those who do agree [5 out of 6] and those who completely agree [6 out of 6].

Salary[16]. People in the group who love their job (Type 8) and those who do not love their job (Type 1) showed differences regarding monthly net salary (see Figure 36). In the group of Job Lovers, no one stated to earn below 500€ a month, while in the Non-Job Lovers group 7% stated to earn this small salary. While the share of people who earn up to 2,000 € a month [17]is almost half in the group of non-lovers, this share among job lovers is only a quarter. In the highest salary groups (4,001-5,000€; above 5,000€), a total share of 34% of the Job Lovers stated to be, compared to 14% of the Non-Job Lovers.

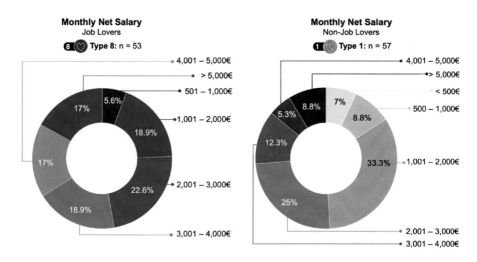

Figure 36. *Differences in Monthly Net Salary of Job Lovers vs. Non-Job Lovers*

---

[16] For salary, there was no t-test calculated, as salary was assessed by group variables (e.g. 1,001 – 2,000€) which is not interval scaled.
[17] Background information: In Germany, the average monthly net salary in 2019 was 2,079€ (Statista, 2000).

Salary Satisfaction. Regarding salary satisfaction, there is a significant difference between Type 8 and Type 1 (see Figure 37): those who love their job have a significant higher satisfaction (mean score = 4.28 out of 6) than those who do not love their job (mean score = 3.16 out of 6). In the group of those who love their job, the share who do not think[18] that their job offers an attractive salary is 0%, while the group of those who do not love their job that share is 10% (see Appendix 4.3.3). Around 60% of Job Lovers think that their employer pays them an attractive salary and around half even think their employer offers more compared to competitors. In the group of Non-Job Lovers, only a third agree that they get paid an attractive salary, and only 29% agree that their employer offers more money than others. When it comes to the importance of pay, 58% of Non-Job Lovers agreed with the statement "A good salary is important to me", compared to 78% of Job Lovers (see Appendix 4.3.3).

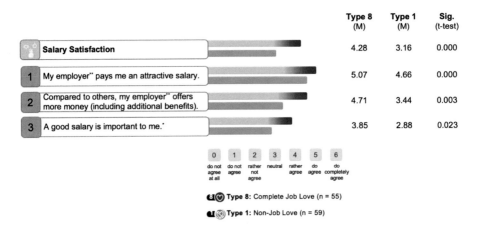

		Type 8 (M)	Type 1 (M)	Sig. (t-test)
	Salary Satisfaction	4.28	3.16	0.000
1	My employer" pays me an attractive salary.	5.07	4.66	0.000
2	Compared to others, my employer" offers more money (including additional benefits).	4.71	3.44	0.003
3	A good salary is important to me.*	3.85	2.88	0.023

0 — do not agree at all
1 — do not agree
2 — rather not agree
3 — neutral
4 — rather agree
5 — do agree
6 — do completely agree

Type 8: Complete Job Love (n = 55)
Type 1: Non-Job Love (n = 59)

Figure 37. *Differences in Salary Satisfaction of Job Lovers vs. Non-Job Lovers*
Note. For a detailed analysis, see Appendix 4.3, *item is not included in the scale because of low item-scale correlation, **"my job offers" for those where 'employer' does not apply.

---

[18] calculated as sum of the share of those who do not agree [1 out of 6] and those who do not agree at all [0 out of 6].

Person-Job-Fit. People in the group of Job Lovers had a significantly higher average rating on the person-job-fit scale *(Δ = 2.08, p < .001,* see Figure 38). Of the Job Lovers, nearly all (95%) thought that the job suits them (answered "do agree" and "do completely agree" to item 2, see Appendix 4.4.3), while of the Non-Job Lovers, 27% thought the job suits them. Also, only half of the Non-Job Lovers thought that they have exactly the skills needed for the job, compared to 91% of the Job Lovers. When asked whether there is no other job that is a better fit than the current one, around half of Job Lovers agreed, with only 3% of the Non-Job Lovers who agreed to this statement (see Appendix 4.4.3).

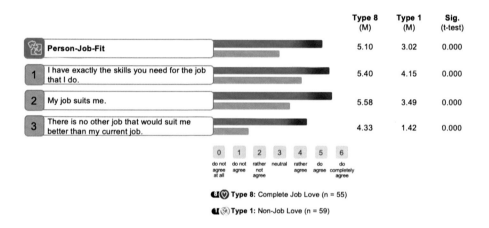

	Type 8 (M)	Type 1 (M)	Sig. (t-test)
Person-Job-Fit	5.10	3.02	0.000
1. I have exactly the skills you need for the job that I do.	5.40	4.15	0.000
2. My job suits me.	5.58	3.49	0.000
3. There is no other job that would suit me better than my current job.	4.33	1.42	0.000

0 — do not agree at all
1 — do not agree
2 — rather not agree
3 — neutral
4 — rather agree
5 — do agree
6 — do completely agree

Type 8: Complete Job Love (n = 55)
Type 1: Non-Job Love (n = 59)

Figure 38. *Differences in Person-Job-Fit of Job Lovers vs. Non-Job Lovers*
Note. For a detailed analysis, see Appendix 4.4.

Competence. When it comes to how competent people think they are in their job, people of Type 8 differed significantly from those of Type 1 (($\Delta = 1.31, p < .001$, see Figure 39). While nearly no one in both groups thought that they are not good at what they do, half of the Non-Job Lovers agreed that they are really good at what they do in their job, and 86% of those in the Job-Love group. Also, nearly no one in both groups disagreed with feeling competent in one's job, but while almost all Job Lovers (93%) feel competent in their jobs, only half of Non-Job Lovers do. Moreover, of those of Type 1, only a third (29%) could agree to the statement "At work, I can show what I can do.", compared to 91% of those of Type 8 (see Appendix 4.5.3).

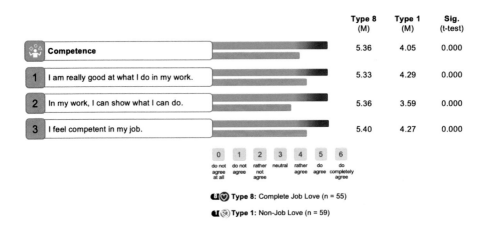

		Type 8 (M)	Type 1 (M)	Sig. (t-test)
	Competence	5.36	4.05	0.000
1	I am really good at what I do in my work.	5.33	4.29	0.000
2	In my work, I can show what I can do.	5.36	3.59	0.000
3	I feel competent in my job.	5.40	4.27	0.000

0	1	2	3	4	5	6
do not agree at all	do not agree	rather not agree	neutral	rather agree	do agree	do completely agree

Type 8: Complete Job Love (n = 55)
Type 1: Non-Job Love (n = 59)

Figure 39. *Differences in Competence of Job Lovers vs. Non-Job Lovers*
Note. For a detailed analysis, see Appendix 4.5.

Autonomy. Regarding autonomy, the overall mean difference between average scores of Type 1 and Type 8 was $\Delta = 1.2$ ($p < .001$, see Figure 40). Most Job Lovers agreed that they have the freedom to decide how they do their jobs (86%), and of the Job Lovers no one did state that they do not agree to this statement (see Appendix 4.6.3). Among Non-Job Lovers, also a very small share of 7% disagreed to have the freedom to decide, with around half agreeing to have the freedom to decide on how to do the job. When it comes to feeling controlled, 20% of the respondents of Type 1 thought they have the feeling of being controlled at work, compared to only 2% of the Job Lovers. Not only having the freedom of deciding on how to do the job, but when, did 78% of the Job Lovers agree. Among Non-Job Lovers, around half (51%) agreed to have the possibility to schedule their time freely and 36% agreed that their job enables them to balance work and family. Among those who love their jobs, that share is slightly higher, as 56% of those of Type 8 agreed that their job enables them to combine work and family (see Appendix 4.6.3).

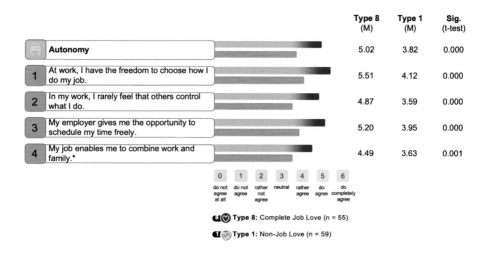

Figure 40. *Differences in Autonomy of Job Lovers vs. Non-Job Lovers*
Note. For a detailed analysis, see Appendix 4.6, *item is not included in the scale because of low item-scale correlation.

General Appreciation. The mean difference in appreciation between Type 1 and Type 8 was $\Delta = 2$ ($p < .001$, see Figure 41). The majority of Job Lovers stated that they feel valued in their working environment (91%). Among Non-Job Lovers, this share was nearly one-third (see Appendix 4.7.3). While no Job Lover did not agree to getting enough appreciation for the work they do, the share among those of Type 1 was almost a quarter (22%). Only 37% of Non-Job Lovers feel that they are needed at work, compared to 91% of Job Lovers. While among Non-Job Lovers, only 17% agreed their employer gives them the feeling of being a valuable employee, and 22% did not agree to have this feeling of being a valuable employee. Among Job Lovers, this share was 0% – with 87% agreeing that they feel their employer gives them the feeling of being a valuable employee (see Appendix 4.7.3).

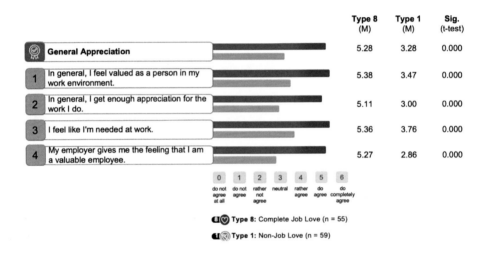

	Type 8 (M)	Type 1 (M)	Sig. (t-test)
General Appreciation	5.28	3.28	0.000
1 — In general, I feel valued as a person in my work environment.	5.38	3.47	0.000
2 — In general, I get enough appreciation for the work I do.	5.11	3.00	0.000
3 — I feel like I'm needed at work.	5.36	3.76	0.000
4 — My employer gives me the feeling that I am a valuable employee.	5.27	2.86	0.000

0 — do not agree at all
1 — do not agree
2 — rather not agree
3 — neutral
4 — rather agree
5 — do agree
6 — do completely agree

Type 8: Complete Job Love (n = 55)
Type 1: Non-Job Love (n = 59)

Figure 41. *Differences in General Appreciation of Job Lovers vs. Non-Job Lovers*
Note. For a detailed analysis, see Appendix 4.7.

Supervisor Relationships. The differences between those who love their job (Type 8) and those who do not (Type 1) are significant with a mean delta of 1.5 (see Figure 42). The majority (80%) of Job Lovers felt valued by their manager (see Appendix 4.8.3). Also, the majority of Type agreed that their manager takes time for them (81%), but only 68% stated that they get praise from their supervisor when they have done something well. Among those of Type 1, this share is only one-third. Also, around one-third (37%) of them felt valued by their manager and agreed that their manager takes time when they need it (35%). Regarding support, 39% of Non-Job Lovers agree that they can count on their manager when they need help, compared to 81% of Job Lovers. When it comes to trust, 10% of the Non-Job Lovers did not feel their manager trusts them, and only 50% did agree that their manager trusts them. Compared to this, the majority (81%) of Job Lovers agreed that their manager trusts them, while no one in this group did not agree to this statement. Also, three third of Job Lovers think their manager gives them a feeling of being thankful for their work, while only one-third of Non-Job Lovers stated the same (see Appendix 4.8.3)

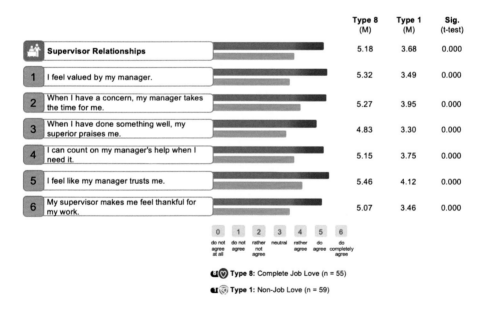

Figure 42. *Differences in Supervisor Relationships of Job Lovers vs. Non-Job Lovers*
Note. For a detailed analysis, see Appendix 4.8.

Peer Relationships. The mean differences in peer relationships were significant ($\Delta = 0.87$, $p < .001$, see Figure 43). In general, more than half of Non-Job Lovers (60%) agreed that their peers value them as a colleague, and also the majority (76%) of Job Lovers did (see Appendix 4.9.3). Most Job Lovers (86%) and Non-Job Lovers (63%) also felt their colleagues support them when they need support. When it comes to spending time, only around 40% of Non-Job Lovers think their peers like to spend time with them, and 76% of Job Lovers stated so. Regarding having someone at work they would call a friend, only 62% of Job Lovers agreed to that, while half of Non-Job Lovers also agreed to having someone at work they call a friend (see Appendix 4.9.3).

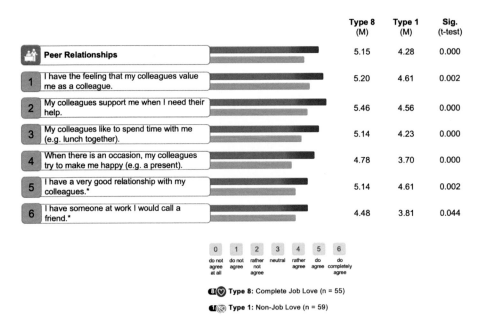

	Type 8 (M)	Type 1 (M)	Sig. (t-test)
Peer Relationships	5.15	4.28	0.000
1 I have the feeling that my colleagues value me as a colleague.	5.20	4.61	0.002
2 My colleagues support me when I need their help.	5.46	4.56	0.000
3 My colleagues like to spend time with me (e.g. lunch together).	5.14	4.23	0.000
4 When there is an occasion, my colleagues try to make me happy (e.g. a present).	4.78	3.70	0.000
5 I have a very good relationship with my colleagues.*	5.14	4.61	0.002
6 I have someone at work I would call a friend.*	4.48	3.81	0.044

0	1	2	3	4	5	6
do not agree at all	do not agree	rather not agree	neutral	rather agree	do agree	do completely agree

8 🤍 Type 8: Complete Job Love (n = 55)

1 🤍 Type 1: Non-Job Love (n = 59)

Figure 43. *Differences in Peer Relationships of Job Lovers vs. Non-Job Lovers*
Note. For a detailed analysis, see Appendix 4.9, *item is not included in the scale because of low item-scale correlation.

Client Relationships. The mean difference between Type 8 and Type 1 regarding client relationships was rather small, but significant ($\Delta = 0.86$, p < .001, see Figure 44). In the group of Job Lovers, 78% agreed that they feel valued by the people they work for, that they rarely get criticism (81%) and that they often get a "thank you" from their customers (68%). Among those who do not love their job those shares are lower: While 55% feel they are valued by their customers, only 40% get to hear a "thank you" often, and around half get rarely criticized (see Appendix 4.10.3).

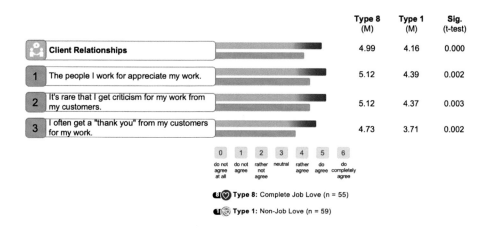

Figure 44. *Differences in Client Relationships of Job Lovers vs. Non-Job Lovers*
Note. For a detailed analysis, see Appendix 4.10.

3.3.2 Hypotheses Testing

This study's objective was to determine which antecedents job love has, subsequently the study also sought to understand which factors lead to love of a job and which factors may not be important for someone to develop job love. To find out, all possible antecedents that have been identified were transferred into hypotheses at the beginning of Study 3 as shown in Figure 45.

All hypotheses were tested by conducting binary logistic regression analyses. Logistic regression belongs to the regression analysis family and is one of the most versatile statistical methods. As it can be used for forecasting as well as examining relationships between variables, the method was chosen as a suitable method for testing Study 3's hypotheses. Linear regression typically examines the relationship between a dependent variable (i.e. job love) and one or more independent variables (e.g. purpose, salary, competence). Regression analysis can also be used for predictions (e.g. how likely is it that a male employee of 53 years with a low perception of purpose and a high salary loves his job?). While within linear regression, the dependent variable needs to be normally distributed; a logistic regression is calculated when the dependent variable is nominally scaled. Binary logistic regression is a special case of regression, in which the dependent variable has a dichotomous expression, that is two categories.

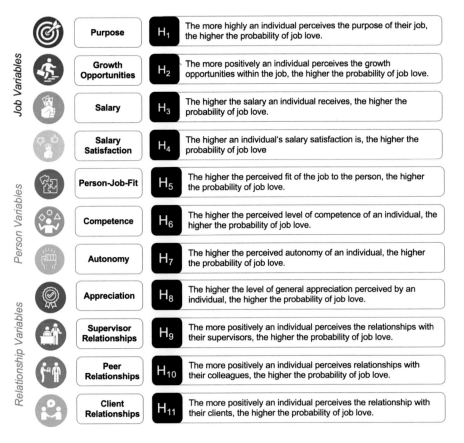

Figure 45. *Hypotheses of Study 3*
Note. H = Hypothesis

Preparatory Analyses

There are several things to consider before conducting logistic regression analysis. First, the predictor variables must be *normally distributed*, which was already shown for this study in the previous section. Second, sample size should be sufficient.

Sample size. To conduct logistic regression analyses, Urban (1993, p. 13) indicates a minimal needed number of 100 cases, while (Backhaus et al., 2008, p. 288) request that each category of the outcome variable should have at least 25 cases in a dataset – the more independent variables are included in the model, the more cases the dataset should have. Hosmer and Lemeshow (2000, p. 346) even suggest having at least ten times as many cases as predictor variables. In this present study, between 38 and 59 people were in each outcome group (Job Lovers, Non-Job Lovers), which was sufficient according to Backhaus et al. (2008) who requested a minimum number of 25 per group.

Omnibus test and Hosmer-Lemeshow test. Omnibus Tests and Hosmer-Lemeshow Tests are calculated to see whether data meets the requirements for subsequent regression analysis. The Omnibus test examines the probability that groups tested in the binary logistic regression do not differ from each other. The test needs to be significant, meaning that the probability that outcome groups do not differ is low. The Hosmer-Lemeshow test is a statistical test of goodness of fit for logistic regression models. The test divides the sample into ten groups maximum and assesses the differences between observed and expected values. The smaller the difference, the better the model adaptation. Therefore, a confirmation of the H_0 (i.e. no significant result) is needed. In conclusion, the result of the Hosmer-Lemeshow test should be non-significant in order to proceed with the calculations. As shown in Table 21, for all binary logistic regression models the Omnibus test showed significant values, and the Hosmer-Lemeshow showed non-significant values, which indicates that the data was suitable for logistic regressions.

Nagelkerke's R^2. R^2 is the so-called coefficient of determination. It describes the proportion of variance that can be explained by the predictor variable. Nagelkerke's R^2 is "a version of the coefficient of determination for logistic regression" (Field, 2013) that can have values between 0 and 1. The nearer Nagelkerke's R^2 is to a value $= 1$, the higher the share of variance that can be explained.

Prediction probability. This measure indicates the probability that one can predict whether a person belongs to group 1 or 2 when the predictor is known.

Regression coefficient B. Regression coefficient B indicates the strength of the relationship between a given predictor and an outcome. In logistic regression, the value cannot be directly interpreted, as first it has to be re-calculated into odds ratios in column Exp (B).

The Wald statistic. This value is "a test statistic with a known probability distribution (a chi-square distribution) that is used to test whether the b coefficient for a predictor in a logistic regression model is significantly different from zero" (Field, 2012, p. 796).

Exp (B). This value shows the logit coefficient de-logarithmized as an odds ratio. The odds ratio is an indicator for the change in odds that results from a change in the predictor. If the odds ratio is greater than 1, it means that an increase in the predictor variable results in an increase of the outcome variable. A value less than 1 indicates the contrary: the probability of the outcome will decrease with an increase of the predictor (Field, 2013, p. 785).

Results of Hypotheses testing

Results of the binary logistic regression analyses are shown in Table 21.

Perceived Purpose (H1). Single binary logistic regression analysis shows that the higher the perceived purpose of the job, the higher the probability that a person loved their job $(Exp(B) = 13.9, p<.001)$. With a high probability of 86.8%, a person can be assigned to group 1 or 2 when the level of purpose in a person is known. Hence, *hypothesis 1 can be confirmed.*

Growth Opportunities (H2). There is an impact of the predictor on the probability of a person to love their job. The chance that a person with a one unit higher value on the growth opportunities scale was 2.5 times as likely to be a Job Lover than to be a Non-Job Lover. *Hypothesis 2 is therefore confirmed.*

Table 21. Single Binary Logistic Regression Analyses of Antecedents of Job Love

Predictor Variable	n	Omni-bus test Sig	Hosmer-Leme-show test Sig	Nagel-kerke's R^2	Prob.	B	Wald	Sig	Exp(B)
Purpose	114	.000	.344	.736	86.8%	2.632	25.166	.000	13.895
Growth Opportunities	114	.000	.613	.401	72.8%	0.929	25.904	.000	2.532
Salary	110	.001	.869	.119	63.6%	0.404	9.259	.002	1.498
Salary Satisfaction	114	.000	.125	.156	68.4%	0.467	12.258	.000	1.596
Person-Job-Fit	114	.000	.909	.734	87.7%	2.589	28.895	.000	13.313
Competence	114	.000	.493	.475	78.1%	1.801	26.233	.000	6.057
Autonomy	114	.000	.611	.308	67.5%	1.045	19.714	.000	2.843
Appreciation	114	.000	.941	.720	86.8%	2.716	26.210	.000	15.121
Supervisor Relationships	98	.000	.108	.408	70.4%	1.335	18.641	.000	3.800
Peer Relationships	107	.000	.945	.250	66.4%	1.078	16.482	.000	2.939
Client Relationships	79	.000	.942	.231	65.8%	1.021	11.259	.001	2.776

Note. Outcome variable: Type 8 (Job Love) vs Type 1 (Non-Job Love); Prob. = prediction probability; Sig = significance, B = regression coefficient B; Exp(B) = exponent of B.

Salary (H3). A higher salary of a person was connected to a slightly higher chance that the person belongs to love-type 8. The Exp(B) had a value of 1.5, which indicates that a person with a change unit on the salary scale had a higher likelihood to belong to the group of Job Lovers than to belong to the Non-Job Lovers. *Hypothesis 3 can be confirmed.*

Salary Satisfaction (H4). When looking at the single regression analysis, the strength of the predictor was slightly higher than the net salary. With an exponent of 1.6, the likelihood of a person with a one-unit higher value on the salary satisfaction to belong to the group of Job Lovers was increased. Hence, *hypothesis 4 can be confirmed.*

Person-Job-Fit (H5). The increasing perception that the job fits the person was connected to a higher likelihood of a person loving their job *(Exp(B) = 13.3, p<.001).* Concluding, the more one thinks the job fits, the higher the chance to love the job. *Hypothesis 5 can therefore be confirmed.*

Competence (H6). The probability of a person to belong to the group of those who love their job (Type 8: Complete love) was higher when the person scored higher on the competence scale. The higher the perceived level of competence, the higher the probability of the person loving their job ($Exp(B)$ = 6.1, $p<.001$). Hypothesis 6 can therefore be confirmed.

Autonomy (H7). A higher perceived level of autonomy of a person was connected to a slightly higher chance that the person belongs to Type 8 ($Exp(B)$ = 2.8, $p<.01$). Hypothesis 7 can be confirmed.

Perceived Appreciation (H8). The feeling of appreciation in the job was strongly connected to the probability of belonging to the group of Job Lovers ($Exp(B)$ = 15.1, $p<.001$). Concluding, the more one feels appreciated in the job, the higher the chances that he/she loves the job. Hypothesis 8 is thereby confirmed.

Supervisor Relationships (H9). Compared to the general appreciation level, the results for the relationship by supervisors were not as strong. If how well a person perceives his/her relationship with their supervisor(s) is known, his/her probability to love the job can be predicted with only a probability of 70%. A person that was one unit higher on the supervisor appreciation scale, had a higher chance ($Exp(B)$ = 3.8, $p<.001$) of belonging to the group of Job Lovers. Hypothesis 9 can be confirmed.

Peer Relationships (H10). Regarding peer relationships, a unit change in the peer relationships scale resulted in a higher likelihood of a person to belong to the group of Job Lovers to the group of Non-Job Lovers ($Exp(B)$ = 2.9, $p<.001$). Hence, hypothesis 10 can be confirmed.

Client Relationships (H11). When the level of perceived client relationships increases by one unit, the probability of a person to belong to the group of Job Lovers is 2.8 times as high as to belong to the group of Non-Job Lovers. Hypothesis 11 can be confirmed.

When all predictor variables are compared with one another, one can recognize differences between them. While three predictors had a very high prediction power, other variables were less suitable to predict job love. Purpose, person-job-fit and appreciation showed tremendous impact on the probability of a person belonging to the group of people who love their jobs. Also, the share of variance those variables can explain is very high (see Nagelkerke's R^2). Salary and salary satisfaction, as well as the relationships to clients and colleagues, played a smaller role when distinguishing between people who love their jobs and those who do not. That does not mean that those variables, e.g. a good relationship to colleagues, cannot lead to a higher level of job love; it may simply indicate that among those who do not love their job, there are some people who have good relationships with their colleagues, and among those who do love their jobs, there might be some who do not have good peer relationships. In contrast, among those who did not love their jobs, it was very unlikely that someone did not perceive their job as not purposeful, since purpose is a very good predictor of job love.

3.3.3 Testing of the Overall Fit of the Model

During the previous sections, the single hypotheses were tested and the prediction power of each of the antecedents of job love was calculated. Now, the overall fit of the model is tested. Because the study is "research from the right," there is a variable that is attempted to explain with different predictor variables, or antecedents, and the researcher must ensure that the "right" predictors were. *"Which are the right predictors?"* is a valid question: in the end, the right ones are those that can explain most variance in the outcome variable "job love." Hence, it is best if all predictors combined can explain the differences between job non-lovers and lovers (Type 1 and Type 8). To do this, the data was analyzed two ways: first, a multiple logistic regression analysis was conducted using SPSS Version 26.0. Following this, structural equation modeling was used to rule out influences by common variances. The analyses were conducted in R Studio (Version 1.3.1073).

Preparatory Analyses

Selection of predictors. First, the suitable predictors of the model need to be selected. In this study, all predictors could not be included into the model because of sample sizes. The variables assessing relationships to supervisor(s), colleagues and clients each had smaller sample sizes (n = 98, 107, 79, respectively) as not all respondents work for supervisors, with colleagues, or for clients. The inclusion of all those variables would have led to a very small sample (sample size would only have been n = 47), because an overall analysis could only have been calculated with those cases who claimed to have a supervisor, colleagues and clients. With only a tiny part of the sample tested, requirements for multiple regression could not have been met anymore, and the analysis would have excluded various cases of the sample. Hence, the three variables relationships to supervisor(s), colleagues and clients were excluded from the overall model.

Table 22. Multicollinearity Analysis in Study 3

Predictor	Tolerance	VIF
Purpose	.399	2.508
Growth Opportunities	.555	1.803
Salary	.706	1.417
Salary Satisfaction	.684	1.463
Person-Job-Fit	.244	4.105
Competence	.377	2.651
Autonomy	.600	1.667
Appreciation	.395	2.530

Note. VIF = variance inflation factor.

Test for multicollinearity. Moreover, one has to rule out that there is collinearity between the variables. Multicollinearity is "a situation in which two or more variables are very closely related" (Field, 2013, p. 879). This is undesirable as the shared variances can cause invalid results. To test for multicollinearity, one must scan the correlation matrix of all predictor variables and identify high correlates (Field, 2013). Correlations above .80 or .90 are generally considered high and, therefore, problematic regarding multicollinearity. Therefore, in a multiple regression, those factors with high multicollinearity should not be included simultaneously. Single correlation analyses (see Table 18) showed no correlations above .80. Another method to rule out multicollinearity is the calculation of tolerance and variance inflation factor (VIF), that checks whether a variable has a linear relationship with another variable. Tolerance and variance inflation factors (VIF) were calculated and are shown in Table 21. In general, tolerance values below 0.1 indicate serious problems (Field, 2013), and some researchers even name 0.2 as a critical value (Menard, 1995, cited after Field, 2013). As all tolerance values were above .244, the analysis of the overall model was continued. For the VIF there are different critical values. Most researchers suggest that the VIF should be below 10 (Field, 2013), while others name a critical value of 3 (Weiber & Mühlhaus, 2014). In this study's model, only person-job-fit showed a higher VIF = 4.105, which will be considered when discussing results.

Results of Multiple Logistic Regression Analysis

Results of the multiple binary logistic regression analysis are shown in Table 23.

Table 23. Multiple Binary Logistic Regression Analysis Testing Overall Fit

Predictor variable	Omnibus Test Sig	Hosmer-Lemeshow test Sig	Nagel-kerke's R^2	Regression coefficient B	Wald	Sig	Exp(B)
Purpose	.000	1.000	.934	2.409	4.682	.030	11.124
Growth Opportunities				-.022	.001	.974	.978
Salary				-.369	.541	.495	.691
Salary Satisfaction				.312	.596	.440	1.366
Person-Job-Fit				2.743	3.764	.052	15.373
Competence				.679	.360	.549	1.972
Autonomy				-.686	.386	.534	.504
Appreciation				2.654	6.270	.012	14.215
(Constant)				-34.166	7.777	.005	.000

Note. Outcome variable: 1: Type 8 (Job Love), 2: Type 1 (Non-Job Love); Prob. = prediction probability; Sig = significance; Exp(B) = exponent of B.

The overall fit of the model can be considered as excellent with a proportion of explained variance of 93.4% (Nagelkerke's R^2). This indicates that the predictor variables chosen in the model are suitable for the calculations. Also, the prediction probability of 97.3% can be considered as high: the value indicates that when all scores of the predictor variables of an individual are known, it can be predicted with a probability of 97% whether the person belongs to the group of those who love their jobs or to the group of those who do not love their jobs. When looking at the single predictors, it stands out that only two of the predictors showed a significant Wald test: Purpose *(Exp(B) = 11.124, p < .05)*, and appreciation *(Exp(B) = 14.215, p < .05)*. Person-job-fit *(Exp(B) = 15.373)* was only significant with a probability of less than 10% *(p = .052)*. The other variables, e.g. competence, growth opportunities, or salary satisfaction did not show significant Wald tests, indicating that the variance was absorbed by purpose, appreciation, and person-job-fit.

Results of Structural Equation Modeling

The results of the structural equation modeling are shown in Table 24. All significant results are presented in Figure 46.

Table 24. Results of Structural Equation Modeling of Study 3

Model Overview

Estimator	ML		
Optimization method	NLMINB		used
Number of free parameters	70	Number of observations	110

Model Test User Model:		**Model Test Baseline Model:**	
Test statistic	2.751	Test statistic	1174.488
Degrees of freedom	8	Degrees of freedom	66
P-value (Chi-square)	0.949	P-value	0.000

User Model versus Baseline Model:		**Root Mean Square Error of Approximation:**	
Comparative Fit Index (CFI)	1.000	RMSEA	0.000
Tucker-Lewis Index (TLI)	1.039	P-value RMSEA <= 0.05	0.978

Regressions	Estimate	SE	z-value	P(>|z|)	Std.lv	Std.all
Job Love~						
Passion	0.113	0.027	4.151	0.000	0.113	0.293
Connection	0.096	0.034	2.800	0.005	0.096	0.278
Commitment	0.114	0.030	3.878	0.000	0.114	0.383
Passion~						
Purpose	0.347	0.067	5.205	0.000	0.347	0.412
Growth Opportunities	-0.084	0.052	-1.602	0.109	-0.084	-0.108
Salary	0.011	0.048	0.224	0.823	0.011	0.013
Salary Satisfaction	0.010	0.048	0.219	0.827	0.010	0.013
Person-Job-Fit	0.160	0.093	1.728	0.084	0.160	0.175
Competence	0.223	0.092	2.440	0.015	0.223	0.199
Autonomy	-0.038	0.066	-0.581	0.561	-0.038	-0.038
Appreciation	0.274	0.074	3.676	0.000	0.274	0.293
Connection~						
Purpose	0.246	0.057	4.296	0.000	0.246	0.262
Growth Opportunities	0.103	0.045	2.285	0.022	0.103	0.118
Salary	-0.135	0.041	-3.267	0.001	-0.135	-0.150
Salary Satisfaction	0.063	0.041	1.523	0.128	0.063	0.071
Person-Job-Fit	0.168	0.080	2.100	0.036	0.168	0.164
Competence	0.105	0.079	1.334	0.182	0.105	0.083
Autonomy	0.039	0.057	0.688	0.491	0.039	0.034
Appreciation	0.485	0.064	7.572	0.000	0.485	0.463
Commitment~						
Purpose	0.223	0.070	3.200	0.001	0.223	0.204
Growth Opportunities	0.168	0.054	3.090	0.002	0.168	0.167
Salary	-0.085	0.050	-1.700	0.089	-0.085	-0.082
Salary Satisfaction	0.103	0.050	2.060	0.039	0.103	0.100
Person-Job-Fit	0.476	0.097	4.918	0.000	0.476	0.402
Competence	0.020	0.096	0.210	0.834	0.020	0.014
Autonomy	-0.052	0.069	-0.765	0.445	-0.052	-0.040
Appreciation	0.363	0.078	4.676	0.000	0.363	0.300

Covariances	Estimate	SE	z-value	P(>|z|)	Std.lv	Std.all
Purpose~~						
Growth Opportunities	1.257	0.272	4.624	0.000	1.257	0.491
Salary	0.742	0.245	3.027	0.002	0.742	0.301
Salary Satisfaction	0.650	0.247	2.632	0.008	0.650	0.259
Person-Job-Fit	1.576	0.526	6.161	0.000	1.576	0.726

	Estimate	Std. Err	z-value	P(>|z|)	Std.lv	Std.all
Competence	0.964	0.192	5.023	0.000	0.964	0.546
Autonomy	0.828	0.202	4.092	0.000	0.828	0.424
Appreciation	1.342	0.239	5.605	0.000	1.342	0.632
Growth Opportunities~~						
Salary	0.646	0.261	2.473	0.013	0.646	0.243
Salary Satisfaction	0.773	0.269	2.871	0.004	0.773	0.285
Person-Job-Fit	1.173	0.251	4.683	0.000	1.173	0.499
Competence	0.596	0.191	3.119	0.002	0.596	0.311
Autonomy	0.894	0.219	4.084	0.000	0.894	0.423
Appreciation	0.797	0.228	3.498	0.000	0.797	0.354
Salary~~						
Salary Satisfaction	1.253	0.276	4.537	0.000	1.253	0.480
Person-Job-Fit	0.918	0.233	3.946	0.000	0.918	0.406
Competence	0.614	0.185	3.318	0.001	0.614	0.333
Autonomy	0.646	0.203	3.177	0.001	0.646	0.318
Appreciation	0.780	0.224	3.491	0.000	0.780	0.353
Salary Satisfaction~~						
Person-Job-Fit	0.931	0.237	3.927	0.000	0.931	0.404
Competence	0.597	0.188	3.181	0.001	0.597	0.318
Autonomy	0.769	0.211	3.647	0.000	0.769	0.371
Appreciation	0.797	0.228	3.498	0.000	0.797	0.354
Person-Job-Fit~~						
Competence	1.245	0.195	6.380	0.000	1.245	0.766
Autonomy	0.872	0.190	4.584	0.000	0.872	0.486
Appreciation	1.143	0.216	5.300	0.000	1.143	0.586
Competence~~						
Autonomy	0.696	0.154	4.510	0.000	0.696	0.476
Appreciation	0.807	0.170	4.571	0.000	0.807	0.508
Autonomy~~						
Appreciation	1.001	0.193	5.196	0.000	1.001	0.570

Variances	Estimate	Std. Err	z-value	P(>|z|)	Std.lv	Std.all
Purpose	2.363	0.319	7.416	0.000	2.363	1.000
Growth Opportunities	2.771	0.374	7.416	0.000	2.771	1.000
Salary	2.562	0.346	7.416	0.000	2.562	1.000
Salary Satisfaction	2.661	0.359	7.416	0.000	2.661	1.000
Person-Job-Fit	1.996	0.269	7.416	0.000	1.996	1.000
Competence	1.321	0.178	7.416	0.000	1.321	1.000
Autonomy	1.614	0.218	7.416	0.000	1.614	1.000
Appreciation	1.908	0.257	7.416	0.000	1.908	1.000
Job Love	0.050	0.007	7.416	0.000	0.050	1.000
Passion	0.460	0.062	7.416	0.000	0.460	1.000
Connection	0.341	0.046	7.416	0.000	0.341	1.000
Commitment	0.501	0.068	7.416	0.000	0.501	1.000

Note. Std. Err = standard error; std.lv = estimate with standardized latent variables; Std.all = estimate with all variables standardized

R-Square	
	Estimate
Job Love	0.799
Passion	0.725
Connection	0.837
Commitment	0.821

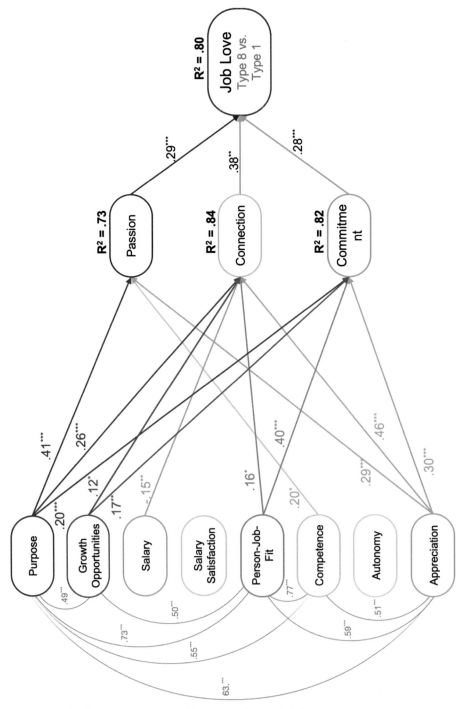

Figure 46. *Graphic Overview of Structural Equation Analysis of Study 3*

Note. *p < .05, ** p < .01, ***p < .001, only covariances > .48 are shown on the left side of the figure.

Goodness-of-fit test. The ratio of Chi square/degrees of freedom was with a value of 0.01 below the cutoff value of $\chi 2/df \leq 3$ (Hornburg & Giering, 1996, p. 13). Root Mean Square Error of Approximation (RMSEA) was 0.0 with a significant value (p < .05), indicating an excellent fit according to Browne and Cudeck (1993, p. 144). The comparative fit index (CFI = 1.000) and Tucker-Lewis Index (TLI = 1.039) both reached values above the cut off criteria value of 0.9 (Homburg & Baumgartner, 1995, p.168) and gave an impression of how much better the fit of the model is compared to a model with no suggested relationships between variables. All those values indicate that all criteria were met for further modeling.

Test of the estimated model. Compared to a multiple linear regression analysis, which suggests that the predictors are unrelated, the structural equation modeling takes into account that there is common variance among the predictor variables. Indeed, as can be seen on the left side of Figure 46, among some variables, there are high covariance values, e.g. between person-job-fit and competence *(cov = .776, p > .001)* and between purpose and growth opportunities *(cov = .491, p < .001).* This indicates shared variance and therefore correlation between study variables as also shown before in correlation analyses.

Passion. In total, approximately 73% of the variance in passion was explained by the included predictors (see table 23). What leads to passion for work, especially, is purpose *(β = .412, p > .001).* Also, the perception of being competent at the job *(β =.119, p > .05)* is a strong predictor of job passion. Third, passion is predicted by the level of person-job-fit *(β = .175, p > .10).* Hence, when companies identify a greater lack of passion among their workers, they can create more purpose and train the competence of people in their organizations. This is usually done by the training and development department of a firm, which can diagnose the need for improvement and learning of an employee and provide training to make the employee feel more competent in his/her job. This then also increases the feeling of person-job-fit, as people who are good at their jobs also experience greater feelings that the job fits them.

Connection. In total, nearly 84% of the variance in connection was explained by the included predictors. What leads to a higher value of the connection dimension is a general feeling of being appreciated *(β = .463, p > .001)*. Hence, to foster connection among employees, employers should make sure their employees feel valued and appreciated. The second strongest predictor of connection was purpose *(β = .262, p > .001)*, followed by person-job-fit *(β = .164, p > .05)*. Salary emerged as a negative predictor of the connection *(β = -.15, p > .001)*. A fifth predictor of connection appeared to be growth opportunities *(β = .118, p > .05)*.

Commitment. In total, around 82% of the variance in passion was explained by the included predictors. The strongest predictor of commitment was the feeling of person-job-fit *(β = .402, p > .001)*. Also, commitment was predicted by general appreciation *(β = .300, p > .001)*, and purpose *(β = .204, p > .001)*. As a fourth and fifth predictor emerged growth opportunities *(β = .167, p > .01)*, and salary satisfaction *(β = .100, p > .05)*.

Job Love. The overall explained variance of the job love indicator (Job Love Type 8 vs. Type 1) was $R^2 = .799$.

3.4 Conclusions on Study 3

In Study 3, different antecedents of job love were identified using two distinct approaches: a literature review approach and a qualitative research approach. For the latter, the insights gained in study 1 were used to identify those antecedents of job love that laypeople suggested. A literature review revealed similar, and different possible antecedents that were added. Based on these insights, a hypothesis model was developed and a quantitative research design chosen to test those hypotheses. In total, eleven antecedents were identified and tested in their impact on job love. All those antecedents (except for salary, which is suggested to be presented in the factor salary satisfaction) are shown in Figure 47.

Figure 47. *Summary of Job Love Antecedents*

In all of the identified antecedents, there were significant differences between those who love their jobs and those who do not love their jobs. Compared to Non-Job Lovers, people who love their job in general feel their job gives them more purpose, offers more growth opportunities, more autonomy and more salary. They are more satisfied with their pay, they feel more appreciated and they feel more competent in what they do. The relationships they have with supervisors, peers, and clients are rated as better, and they overall have a higher feeling that their job fits them.

Out of all antecedents, there were three that stood out showing higher potential to distinguish between Job Lovers and Non-Job Lovers: Especially purpose, person-job-fit and appreciation appeared as significant predictors of Job Love, even when other variables (such as salary satisfaction, or competence) are known.

D   GENERAL DISCUSSION

In this chapter, the central findings of this dissertation are reflected upon and evaluated. Based on these reflections and evaluations, recommendations for company practice are derived. Limitations of the research, as well as implications for further research on the topic, are also discussed.

1   Central Findings of the Research

In Chapter A, the problem was first described: in today's economy, companies are constantly facing the challenge of how to gain talented workers, engage them and keep them in the company. Building strong relationships between employers and employees has been identified as key to increasing the motivation and commitment of a company's workforce. Therefore, new concepts such as work passion and employee engagement have been a growing interest among researchers as well as practitioners in the field.

The strongest form of interpersonal relationship is the love relationship (Langner & Kühn, 2010). Research has shown that a love relationship cannot only be built between two people but between people and products and between people and brands. People who love a brand are extremely loyal to their loved brand, are willing to invest a premium price in the product, and function as brand ambassadors when speaking positively about their loved brands in front of others. Therefore, brand love has become a trending topic in the marketing field. Surprisingly, relationships between employers and employees, or between the "job" as a product and the "employee" as a consumer, have not yet been considered as love relationships – at least not in empirical research. Studies that address the relationship between employees and their jobs as a love relationship and that investigate possible positive outcomes, as well as antecedents of job love are missing from the field of available literature. The goal of this dissertation was to fill this research gap by finding out if there are people who love their job, how job love can be measured, and why people love a job, all in order to provide implications to organizations so that they can create work surroundings where employees can love their jobs.

Chapter B offered a theoretical review of literature on both "job" and "love." The concept "job" was traced through its historical development through contemporary definitions, including what is meant by "job" when it is used today. This history of "job" began with the ancient view of work as punishment from the gods and moved forward to more contemporary definitions that frame a "job" as something that can give people meaning and fulfillment in their lives and provides more than just the possibility to earn money. From here, further implications of the theory of the job were explored.

The second part of Chapter B focused on love and the theories that explain the phenomenon. Literature on both, love from a psychological perspective as well as love from a marketing perspective, was reviewed, and a theoretical model of the love of a job was derived. Sternberg's Triangular Theory of Love (1986) was presented as the most suitable theoretical basis for the development of a job love theory.

Chapter C then provided empirical research on the topic of job love in three empirical studies. Each study answered a different research question. Study 1 answered the question *"Does job love exist?"* through social media research, a quantitative pre-study, and a qualitative study using interviews and a focus group. Study 2 answered *"Can job love be measured?"* by developing and validating a 16-item-measurement scale. Study 3 answered *"Why do some people love their job and others do not?"* by examining the quantitative results of a questionnaire assembled from items built based on the results of Studies 1 and 2 using single and multiple regression analyses, binary logistic regression analyses, and structural equation modeling.

The central findings of the research are:

1. Yes, there are people who say they love their job.

2. Job love is measured from three dimensions: passion, connection, and commitment. A person who loves their job has a high level of passion for the job, feels highly connected to the workplace, and is highly committed to the job in the long run. In this theory of job love, all three dimensions must be present to truly experience job love.

3. People love their jobs because they feel appreciated by their job, both financially and personally (supervisors, colleagues, clients); they are good at what they do and think the job fits them well, and they experience purpose and autonomy and have the opportunities to grow in the job. Three factors especially distinguish Job Lovers from Non-Job Lovers: appreciation, purpose, and person-job-fit.

In this chapter, those findings are discussed in detail. Implications for business practice are discussed in a structured framework. The discussion is then followed by the limitations of the conducted studies, implications for further research, and a final summary.

1.1 Does Job Love Exist?

The qualitative and quantitative studies conducted in Study 1 showed there are people who state they love their jobs. Instagram research showed thousands of people post pictures from their job or themselves at their job with the hashtags *#lovemyjob* or *#ilovemyjob*. Also, when asked to rate how much they love their job on a scale between 1-10, there were people who said *"I love my job"* with a 10 out of 10. Although there are also people who rated very lowly their job love and who stated they did not love their job at all, what is interesting is the variance among people who say they do not love their job and those who say they love it. In qualitative interviews and a focus group, people were asked to name possible reasons for this variance; the results showed that there are a large variety of reasons.

1.2 Can Job Love Be Measured?

Study 2 focused on the question *Can job love be measured?* and if yes, how? In order to measure a latent construct, i.e. a construct that is not directly measurable, distinct indicators for the latent construct have to be identified. Study 2, therefore, followed a fixed procedure to identify indicators that represent job love in an individual. Sternberg's Triangular Love Model was used as a basis to identify factors that describe someone who has love, which were then adapted to the job context. A person who loves their job has a high level of passion for the job, a feeling of connectedness to the workplace, and long-term commitment to the job. A Job Love Scale (JLS) was built and tested for reliability and validity. By measuring the three dimensions, the JLS can identify a "job lover" with high passion, high connection, and high commitment.

In summary, a person who loves their job:

1. **Has a passion for the job:** Passion stems from motivational involvement in the job and comes with high positive emotions about the job, a high identification with the job, and the willingness to invest in it.

2. **Feels connected to the job:** Connection to the job stems from emotional investment into the job and the people someone works with, from feeling cared for and supported, and refers to the feeling of closeness.

3. **Has a commitment to the job:** Commitment stems from cognitive considerations and the decision for a job in the present and the desire to maintain the job for the long-term in the future.

1.3 Why Do Some People Love Their Job and Others Do Not?

In Study 3 of this dissertation, hypotheses were tested in order to predict what leads to an individual's love of a job. The hypotheses were tested and the antecedents were compared with each other in their impact on the probability of a person to be a job lover versus a non-lover. Binary logistic regression analyses were conducted to calculate whether a predictor was suitable to predict whether a person belongs to the type of people who love their job or to the type of people who do not love their job. As mentioned before, only people with high passion, high connection, and high commitment were classified as Job Lovers. Those with low passion, low connection, and low commitment were classified as Non-Job Lovers. Those with combination love styles, e.g. high passion but low commitment and connection *or* high commitment and passion but low connection, were not included in the comparisons to avoid diluting the results. The analyses showed that all eleven influence factors included in the study model have a significant effect on the probability of a person to love their job. Therefore, all eleven hypotheses built with those factors could be confirmed:

1. People love their jobs because **they see purpose in what they do**. Knowing what or who one works for and doing work that is considered useful in some way increases the probability of job love enormously.

2. People love their jobs because **their job gives them the opportunity to grow**. People want to grow in life, develop their abilities and build a career. A job that offers career and development opportunities significantly increases the probability of love of a job.

3. People love their jobs because **they earn a high salary**. The more a person earns, the higher the probability to love the job. Although the relationship is not as high as for other factors, salary might be one of the puzzle pieces that is needed to raise a person's chances to love a job when all other factors (e.g. purpose, appreciation, growth opportunity) are already provided for.

4. People love their jobs because **they are satisfied with their salary.** As the salary itself varies strongly depending on age, education, profession and career, not only is net salary important for people but also whether or not they perceive their net salary as a good salary. Analyses showed that the higher the satisfaction with what people earn, the higher the chances that they love their job.

5. People love their jobs because **they think the job fits** them. High person-job-fit emerged as a strong predictor of the probability of a person to love a job. Hence, people who find that their job matches their skills and their expectations of a job, tend to love their job more than people who do not have the feeling of having a job that fits them.

6. People love their jobs because **they are good at what they do**. The feeling of competence is strongly connected to the concept of self-efficacy or the belief of a person in their abilities to achieve goals and overcome difficulties on the way. People want to perform well at work, and they want to show what they can do. If a person is able to feel

competent in their job, the likelihood that this person will love the job increases significantly.

7. People love their jobs **because they feel autonomous at work.** Autonomy has to do with the individual's desire to feel in control and to what extent this need for control is satisfied. Analyses showed that the more freedom a person feels to have in their job and the more in control a person feels, the more likely it is that a person loves their job.

8. People love their jobs **because they feel appreciated**. People want to be valued – not only for what they do (recognition) but also for who they are (appreciation). Analyses showed that people who feel they are needed and valued in the job they work, are more likely to love their job than people who do not feel appreciated.

9. People love their jobs because **they have good relationships with their supervisors.** People who feel valued by their manager and have the feeling to have supervisor(s) that are there for them, care for them and trust them are more likely to love their jobs than those who do not feel that the relationship with their supervisor is a good one.

10. People love their jobs because **they have good relationships with their colleagues.** People with good relationships with the people they work with are more likely to love their job compared to those who do not have good work relationships.

11. People love their jobs because **they have good relationships with their clients.** Those people that work for clients that are appreciative and thankful for the work they do for them are more likely to love their jobs than people with negative client relationships.

Despite the fact that all of the variables could be confirmed to have some degree of effect on job love, when the variables were compared among each other, there are some factors that have a greater impact on the probability of a person loving their job than other factors. Three factors that emerged as having a higher impact were perceived purpose *(Exp(B)* = *13.895)*, person-job-fit *(Exp(B)* = *13.313)* and appreciation *(Exp(B)* = *15.121)*. Binary logistic regression analyses showed increases in those three factors increased, by a multiple, the likelihood of a person to belong to the group of people who love their job. Also, a factor that is strongly connected to the probability of an individual's likelihood of loving a job is competence *(Exp(B) = 6.057)*, followed by the relationship to the supervisor *(Exp(B) = 3.800)*. Less "important" than the relationships with supervisors were peer relationships *(Exp(B) = 2.939)* and relationships to clients *(Exp(B) = 2.776)*, which both had weaker relationships to a person's probability of loving his/her job. This does not mean that for the individual, colleagues might not be important in their development of love for the job. It simply means that peer relationships are not suitable to predict whether a person does love or does not love their job as other variables, such as purpose or person-job-fit. This may be due to the fact that there are people with good work relationships who love what they do, but others who hate it but love the people with whom they work. The same is true for the factor autonomy: the exponent of *Exp(B) = 2.843* is relatively low, indicating that the feeling of autonomy is not decisive in the question of why people love their jobs. The factors with the lowest power to impact a person's likelihood to love a job, were salary *(Exp(B) = 1.498)* and salary satisfaction *(Exp(B) = 1.596)*, which means that a lack of purpose or appreciation cannot be expiated with a higher salary. But, indeed, participants in Study 1 stated that salary is an expression of the appreciation for the work people do and, hence, a lower salary can be connected to a lack of appreciation, which is a strong predictor of non-job love. Still, knowing the salary of an employee or an employee's satisfaction with the compensation alone is not enough to predict whether the person loves his/her job or does not.

To predict whether a person loves or does not love a job, it is best to know about all eleven factors described. The more that is known about the person, the better the chances are that the Job Love Scale can predict an outcome. A prediction model is best when the prediction probability of a model is high, which means that with all factors measured in a model the result of the test is true with a high probability. To see whether the factors chosen for predicting job love were good factors, a multiple linear regression analysis was calculated. From the starting eleven predictors, eight factors could be included. The inclusion of the three remaining factors (relationship to supervisors, colleagues and clients) would have resulted in a sample size of only n = 47, which would have been too small for multiple regression analysis with many factors. The multiple regression analysis showed the model's prediction probability of 97.3%, which is extremely high. This indicates, that when the level of perceived purpose, competence, person-job-fit, autonomy, appreciation, growth opportunities, salary and salary satisfaction of an individual are known, the Job Love Scale can predict with a probability of 97.3% whether a person belongs to the group of Job Lovers or the group of Non-Job Lovers. The explained variance of the total model resulted in Nagelkerke's R^2 of .934, which is also an extremely high measure.

To make sure that these results stem from the excellent fit of the model, the researcher additionally calculated structural equation modeling. The researcher made this decision because of some suspicious material in the data: some of the predictors showed high correlations, e.g. person-job-fit and competence $(r = .71, p < .001)$ and appreciation and purpose $(r = .50, p < .001)$. Although multicollinearity was tested before and showed sufficient but not excellent values to continue onto the multiple regression model, the researcher also calculated a structural equation model. The structural equation modeling still showed a high coefficient of determination of $R^2 = .80$. Additionally, it shed light on the question of how the different dimensions of job love are influenced by the influence factors. It seems like passion, connection and commitment were each influenced more or less strongly by the suggested eleven factors: while passion is highly predicted by purpose; connection is most strongly predicted by appreciation; and commitment is predicted strongest by person-job-fit. This indicates that the predictors influenced the single dimensions individually, which is important for the implications that are derived for business practice, as will be explained in the next section.

2 Implications for Business Practice

As marketing science does not serve as an end in itself but serves organizations that can apply the knowledge to business practice (Schneider, 2015, p. 10ff.), the question of what to do with the findings of the conducted research is a valuable and needed question. According to Backhaus and Schneider (2020), marketing scientists are not only interested in observing, classifying and explaining competitive exchange processes. Rather, marketing science has the goal to derive implications for action (Backhaus & Schneider, 2020, p. 41). To implement research findings into business practice, companies can follow a systematic process. There are frameworks that help to structure an implementation process. As this dissertation is written in the field of marketing science, these recommendations follow a management process framework that leads to a marketing plan described by Bruhn (2014) and adapted the central steps to the researcher's framework. Figure 48 shows the adaption of the findings to the ideal-typical marketing management process suggested by Bruhn (2014). The process consists of four different phases: analysis, planning, implementation and control. To focus on the results of the study, the framework has been strictly simplified and only the most important steps in the process are mentioned in Figure 48.

Phase 1 Analysis of Status Quo

Measure Job Love levels in the organization using the Job Love Scale (JLS) in order to identify a lack of job love. Assess the level of each of the drivers of job love to see potential for improvement.

Phase 2 Strategic Planning

Deciding on which key levers to adjust that are effective and efficient based on analysis of phase 1.

Phase 3 Implementation

Implementing measures in the company driving change through: Training, coaching, feedback, and communication

Phase 4 Control

Evaluation of the results in three main areas: Evaluation of processes, effectiveness, and efficience

Figure 48. *Framework for the Implementation Process*
Note. Own illustration adapted from the ideal-typical marketing management Process from Bruhn, 2014

Phase 1: Analysis of Status Quo

In the first step, companies should analyze their own situation and find out whether people in the organization love their jobs or not using the Job Love Scale (see on the right in Figure 49). The situation analysis usually is the starting point for any systematic marketing planning, as it captures the specific situation in which the company finds itself (Bruhns, 2014).

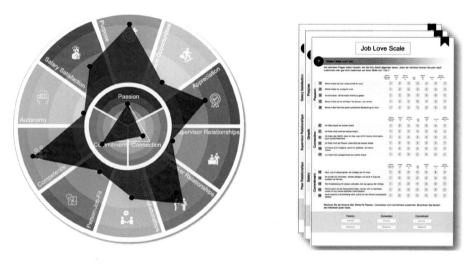

Figure 49. *Phase 1 – Using the Job Love Scale for the Analysis of Status Quo*

For this step, this dissertation provides management practice with a practical validated measurement scale, the Job Love Scale (JLS). With only 16 items, the scale enables companies to assess whether an employee loves their job or not and to compare job love levels among different individuals or groups of employees. As the measurement assesses all three dimensions of job love – job passion, job commitment and job connection – it gives insight into why an employee does not love their job, whether it is a lack of passion, connection, commitment, or a lack of all three of the love dimensions. Also, the key levers of job love, the antecedents identified in this dissertation, should be assessed to see the whole status quo of the organization.

Phase 2: Strategic Planning Phase

After finishing Phase 1, a company knows the share of people in the organization who love their jobs, the share who do not, the share of people who lack passion, the share of people who lack connection and the share of people who lack commitment. What a company does not know yet, is *what* to do. The goal of Phase 2 is therefore to determine a goal and a strategy for reaching this goal. An organization in which everybody already loves their job will have a hard time raising the workplace to an even higher share of Job Lovers, while other companies might identify a lack of passion, a lack of commitment, or a lack of connection among their workforce or varying parts of their workforce.

From the findings of this research, it is clear that there are factors that enhance job love in general; purpose, appreciation and person-job-fit, especially, are highly correlated with the proportion of people who love their jobs. Other factors, such as salary satisfaction or growth opportunities also have an impact but less severe. Hence, some factors are more and others less effective at influencing job love.

In terms of *effectiveness*, the extent to which an intended result (i.e. job love among employees), the Exponent(B) of the single binary regression analyses can be used to measure the effectiveness of a factor. Still, in order to give implications to companies, one also has to think about *efficiency*: the extent to which a manipulation of a factor is using resources like time, money, and energy. Summing up, effectiveness is about doing *the right things*, and efficiency is about *doing things right*. To give an example of what the right things are, and how to do them correctly: person-job-fit is shown to be very effective in predicting job love, hence it scores highly for effectiveness. But if companies cannot do anything to improve it, or it would be extremely expensive to increase person-job-fit, the company would waste a lot of energy and money on the factor, which is not *efficient* and, therefore, not doing things right and other variables should be prioritized.

In order to find out which of the antecedents a company should prioritize, the 2x2 grid with the effectiveness and efficiency in Figure 50 should be considered as a framework. Variables that have high effectiveness and high efficiency should be of top priority (A) in an organization. Variables with high effectiveness but lower efficiency should have second priority (B), and high efficiency with low effectiveness third priority (C). Those variables that have neither efficiency nor effectiveness should be of least priority (D).

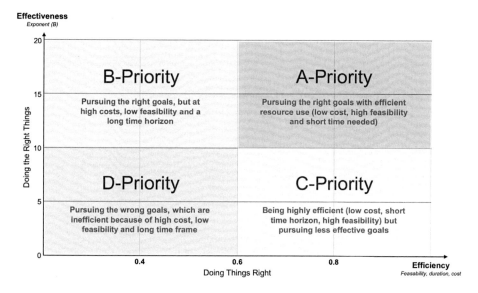

Figure 50. *2x2 Grid of Effectiveness and Efficiency of Implementation Measures*

Effectiveness is already known: to measure to what extent a variable can influence the development of job love, we use the exponent of the single binary logistic regression analysis conducted in Study 3 (see Table 20).

What is unknown is how efficient it would be to change a given variable. In order to determine *efficiency* of the variables examined in Study 3, experts in the field of HR provided their opinions and insights from their own companies, using the following questionnaire with four questions for each variable:

(1) What can companies do to promote X? (open question)

(2) How *easy* would it be for your company to promote X? (rating)

(3) How *expensive* would it be for your company to promote X? (rating)

(4) How *quickly* could measures be implemented that promote X? (rating)

While the first question was an open question, questions two to four asked the respondent to answer on a 7-point Likert scale ranging from *1 = very uneasy/expensive/slow* to *7 =*

*very easy/cheap/fa*st. Efficiency was then calculated as the mean share of the total score of questions two to four. In total, the questionnaire included 40 questions (ten job love antecedents, for each antecedent, four questions were asked). It was programmed in Typeform as an online survey. In total, 18 experts, people who work in HR or in a related field in their company, joined the study. Results are shown in Figure 51. The variable that is easiest to influence, according to the ratings of the experts combined with effectiveness measures, is appreciation followed by purpose.

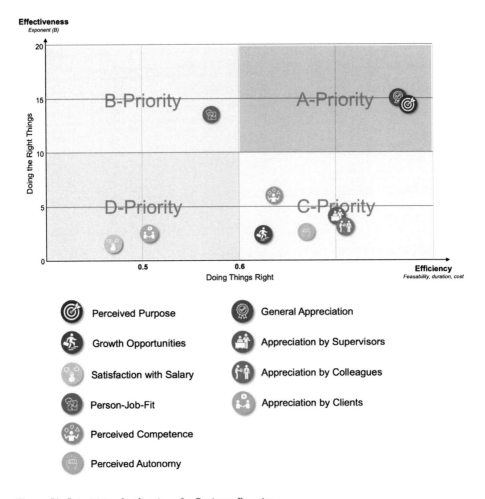

Figure 51. *Prioritizing Implications for Business Practice*

A-Priority. With an odds ratio of *Exp(B)* = *15.121* and an efficiency score of *0.77*, statistical analysis as well as expert opinion shows that organizations should focus on appreciation as an A-priority. Experts suggested different possible actions a company can do to promote general appreciation: some comments focused on feedback and verbal praise as possible ways to promote appreciation. Another A-priority variable is purpose, with a slightly lower effectiveness score (*Exp(B)* = *13.895*), but a slightly higher efficiency score.

B-Priority. The variable with the third-largest odds ratio (Exp(B) = 13.313), person-job-fit, only scored 0.57 on the axis of efficiency. This indicates that experts feel that making a person believe their job is a good fit is not easy (inexpensive, fast).

C-Priority. The variables competence, autonomy, growth opportunities, peer relationships and relationships to supervisors were rated with high efficiency but were lower-rated in their possible effect on job-love.

D-Priority. Relationships to clients, salary, and salary satisfaction were rated as not as easy to promote and improve in the organization. Specifically, to raise salary and salary satisfaction, a company has to invest a lot of money. As salary and salary satisfaction also have a low impact on job love (*Exp(B)* = *1.498; 1.596*), those factors are suggested as the lowest priority when promoting job love.

The follow-up study on the efficiency of the manipulation of factors that lead to job love in a priority matrix was an initial approach to the application of the results in the organization. Still, this is only a single framework that provides one possible way to analyze which variables a company should attempt to change. In practice, the decision-maker in the company has to decide for him- or herself: first, what is not yet developed in the company and, then, whether it is easy/costly/feasible for the company to promote appreciation or focus more on growth opportunities for its employees or improve the fit of people in the organizations to their jobs. Hence, the efficiency axis is not 100 percent resilient, as individual organizational factors play a major role, e.g. for some companies it might be easier to implicate autonomy with home office options, while for other companies, this is not an option because they produce tangible goods.

Phase 3: Implementation Phase

If a company has identified its need in Phase 1 and decided on a course of action in Phase 2, Phase 3 follows the question of *how* to do it. To give implications on how to do it, the answers experts gave in the small questionnaire described in Phase 2 were used, combined with a review of management literature and best practices.

How to promote job love by improving purpose:

People want to know why they do the work they do. Hence, companies should connect their employees with the impact of their work by helping them "connect the dots" and starting with the why. This starts by defining a clear, shared definition of purpose. After defining the company's purpose, it is easier to communicate the why to the workforce. When employees have the feeling that they know why they do things and that the things they do matter, this creates a sense of meaning and purpose in the individual which makes it easier for the individual to love the job. Also, other people around can foster purpose when people in the organization together share the same vision, goals and values. Another strategy to promote a sense of purpose is to give back to society. This can be within the company or outside, i.e. giving employees a day off to get involved in volunteering or using team bonding activities to raise money together for a good cause or to even partner up with non-profit organizations or partners that are supported in their good cause.

How to promote job love by improving growth opportunities:

People want to grow in life. Therefore, it is crucial for organizations to develop a culture of learning and development by providing individuals to learn new skills, improve those they have, and show the career path the individual can take. Employees who engage in learning feel more competent and have higher self-efficacy, a sense of being able to face challenging tasks in life with their own resources. Organizations can develop training programs for their employees and make education and learning part of the annual goals of each employee. Getting feedback from different sources is crucial for identifying the growth potential of the individual. 360 feedback assessments that offer feedback from different sources are often used in organizations to gain those insights into development potential. Supporting people in the organization in their desire to grow does not only help the individual learn things that make work more enjoyable, it also skills people with resources they use on the job and perform better at work.

How to promote job love by improving salary satisfaction:

Paying not enough can create a sense of feeling not appreciated which is a strong predictor of non-job love. Therefore, offering a competitive salary is a requirement for a job-loving workforce. To increase salary satisfaction, companies can expand job benefits, discuss working hours and salary openly with each employee individually and offer bonus payments and promotions. An employee that gets good pay will be more likely to love the job in turn.

How to promote job love by improving person-job-fit:

To increase person-job-fit, it is important to already begin at the start: selecting the right people for a job. Defining the tasks and requirements of a job clearly, and matching the right people with the job is a first way to increase person-job-fit and therewith the share of people who love their job. People who are in a job that does not fit their needs, their skills, or strengths can – in contrast – lead to frustrations. Another way to promote person-job-fit is to train people on the job for a better match: develop people who do not have all the knowledge or skills. Moreover, people should get promoted based on their abilities to do the new job, not based on time in the organization. The Peter principle (Peter, 1969) talks about how people get promoted based on their success in the current position until they rise to their "level of incompetence" where they are no longer successful, resulting in people in positions that do not fit their skill set. To avoid this, organizations should carefully consider who to promote to which position. A last way to promote job love by increasing person-job-fit is to match jobs with the needs of the individual. A job should also fit with the living situation – being flexible about working hours, offering sabbaticals, and career paths raise the sense of fit in the individual and makes it easier to love the job.

How to promote job love by improving competence:

People want to be good at what they do. There are several possibilities to increase perceived competence in the workplace: first, some people need to hear that they are good at what they do. Therefore, fostering a feedback culture in an organization by encouraging employees to offer continuous feedback is a valuable way to provide people with knowledge about what they are good at and where they can improve. Another possibility to develop competence is on the job learning: participating in new projects or work groups helps foster the own sense of competence. Another way to increase competence of employees, is to offer training courses, coaching, seminars, or conferences both, in and outside the company. A study degree accompanying the work can also help increasing competencies and strengthening the sense of being competent in the individual. As results show, individuals who feel good at what they do at work are more likely to love what they do.

How to promote job love by improving autonomy:

Organizations need to be agile in today's economy which is rapidly changing. Therefore, the organization has to become more flexible and faster in order to be able to assert itself successfully in a complex and networked world. For employees, this means more autonomy, more freedom. Especially when hierarchy becomes less, employees must be empowered to make their own decisions and be more independent. Flexible working hours and home office options are possible ways to increase autonomy in organizations and positions where that is possible. But autonomy is not only about working from home, as it is connected to the feeling of control of the individual: letting employees decide themselves, i.e. how to design and equip their workspace, how to dress, how to set their schedules, set goals and deadlines, and, when thinking the bigger picture, even how to plan their individual career path and which development options they want to take, can increase the individual's perception of autonomy enormously. This does not mean that everyone in the organization can act however they want. Rather it is about identifying each individual case where it makes sense to allow the individual for more decision-making and decrease constraints and decisions made by supervisors. Therefore, organizations can think about how to equip leaders in the organization with the ability to lead their subordinates through empowerment, not by control and micromanagement, and thereby break down hierarchy thinking and the need to control which would decrease autonomy.

How to promote job love by improving appreciation:

People want to be seen, they want to feel valued and be recognized. Cultivating appreciation in the workplace starts with the organization itself: appreciative corporate cultures are increasingly becoming a success factor for organizations, especially when companies aim to attract the best talent in the market. Another factor in promoting appreciation is to create recognition programs to make sure people get appreciated for meeting their goals. Recognition can come from the organization as a public recognition via an award, a certificate, a promotion, or more responsibility for the individual to support growth and show trust. It can be a private recognition, i.e. by the supervisor or a customer, or it can be a monetary reward such as a trip, a prize, a pay increase or simply a free meal. Appreciation, moreover, can also come by a simple "thank you". Including saying thank you into the culture of the organization will also increase the feeling of being appreciated and thereby will lead to a higher likelihood of people loving what they do.

How to promote job love by improving relationships with supervisors:

Already selecting supervisors that have the skills to lead and promote good relationships to their subordinates is a first step towards good supervisor-subordinate relationships in the organization. Training managers on how to deal with different employees, how to lead, how to manage can help to equip leaders with the right skill set they need for leadership.

How to promote job love by improving peer relationships:

Promoting good relationships among colleagues already starts by hiring people who fit to each other and have social competencies to act with each other well. By having people in the workforce that are supportive and appreciative to their colleagues, others get encouraged to act the same. Team building events and social events can increase the sense of belonging to a group and thereby the relationships between colleagues. Therefore, companies can encourage get-togethers on a regular basis – whether in person or digital – and foster communication and collaboration. Providing spaces and providing the technological resources and surroundings necessary, encourages employees to hang out with each other. Joint learning programs including mentorship programs can strengthen bonds between colleagues and help improve social skills among the workforce.

How to promote job love by improving relationships with clients:

Providing employees with the resources they need is key for building good relationships with clients. This includes providing technology that helps fast and easy communication, training employees to have all the skills they need to serve the client, and fostering trust among clients by providing knowledge and expertise by the employee. Positive client relationships are a factor that is connected to a higher probability of a person to love their job, therefore investing in good customer care will help promote job love.

Phase 4: Control Phase

After implementing job love-promoting factors, the impact of the implementations should be measured and checked whether they worked. By identifying what worked and what did not work, organizations can learn about the implementation process and rethink the measures.

There are three variables that should be measured: the process, effectiveness and efficiency. First, measuring whether the process worked includes assessing if the implementation process had been accepted in the company. Second, effectiveness is measured by assessing whether the measures were effective: are there more people who love what they do than before? Have some levels of passion, connection, or commitment increased? If so, what do people think improved their situation or attitude the most? What did not work? Besides job love, also other variables can be measured that are suggested to be connected to job love, e.g. job satisfaction, loyalty, or productivity and performance. Therewith the organization can measure the financial impact the implementation had on company goals. Third, efficiency is measured by assessing the real cost of the project, how easy it was to implement the measures in the organization, and how long the real timeframe of the implementation process was in the end. After evaluating, a company can improve the implementation process – even for similar projects and may start the process again with Phase 1 to implement different activities in a different way.

In conclusion, promoting job love is not an easy task for HR managers and executives, as it involves many steps before measuring results. The possibilities to promote job love in the organization, though, are so diverse that for every employer there should be something that deals with manageable realization effort. Whether or not, and to what extent organizations want to implement these measures is not a question of options, but rather of willingness, competency and the level of suffering a company feels. A company that loses good talent constantly to competition and has low motivation and performance among those that stay, needs to take action to improve. In the end, companies that manage to make their employees love their jobs will experience more loyal, satisfied, and highly motivated employees, making it worth going through the described implementation process.

3   Limitations and Implications for Future Research

This research is not without limitations. Research is always a way to try to fit the reality in the best possible way. Still, science always underlies efficiency and efficacy restrictions. Therefore, the findings of this dissertation should be considered in light of its limitations.

Research Design. When deciding on a specific research design, not always is the design chosen the best way to research a question. The first problem regarding design is the problem of *causality*: Typically, the research of causal questions such as "What leads to X?" or "Does a higher amount of X (e.g. appreciation) lead to a higher amount of Y (e.g. job love)?", are researched in an experimental design measuring an independent variable and measuring the change of the dependent outcome variable. Only then we can be sure of a causal relationship between X and Y. Still, in our study, we measured both – independent and dependent variables – at the same point in a cross-sectional research design. As we researched a broad set of hypotheses which would have led to an enormous number of experiments to be researched, which would have not been efficient for the given time of a dissertation process. That is why we theoretically founded our hypotheses based on previously validated findings from love or brand love research. Hence, from an efficiency viewpoint, this was the best research design fit in our sight. Further research could and should address this problem of causality by underpinning the theoretical foundation of the hypotheses with empirical arguments through experimental designs. A second problem that can occur when assessing independent and dependent variables at the same time is a *common method variance*. Common method variance is the error that may occur when the measured relationship between variables is measured due to the fact that both measures come from the same source, rather than a substantial relationship between them. But, because in this dissertation, the opinion and perception of individuals about their jobs and how they feel is important, it was important to ask them about all variables combined. Therefore, special effort was put into developing a proper scale measuring job love with validated and reliable multiple item scales (Hinkin, 1995). A third consideration when using cross-sectional designs can be the *time of the research*. By only assessing variables at one point in time, we can only explain the variance between persons, not within persons: We can see why person X differs from person Y. What we do not know is, whether person X differs in their level of a certain variable over time. Especially interesting is the question of how job love changes over time and why. Hence, by using a longitudinal study design, further research could bring light on why people fall in and out of love of a job and how the love of a job develops over time.

Sample. All three studies had relatively small *sample sizes*[19]. For this reason, the researcher cannot make reliable statements about how many people love their job, for example. To give concrete numbers, a study would need to test a representative sample which is suggested to consider for following research on this topic. A second problem regarding the sample is a *selection bias*. This is relevant especially in Study 1 and Study 3, where participants were recruited via snowball sampling. This recruitment method could have led to the fact that more people who love their job participated in the studies as they are more interested in participating in a study with this topic. Further research should address this sampling problem by providing a less biased recruiting method. A third limitation of the samples used was *sample heterogeneity*: in our samples, the range of jobs, professions, and companies, was high – police officers, teachers, managers, nurses, artists, and many more participated in the studies. While this variety in subjects' careers led to a broad picture across all types of jobs, the results do not demonstrate whether job love, or its dimensions, varies among different jobs or professions. For example, nurses may feel more need for appreciation in their jobs compared to bankers, or person-job-fit could be a more important factor for teachers than cashiers in terms of the probability that they will love their jobs. Hence, when conducting further research, limiting a sample to a specific type of job or company is suggested to shed light on the question of differences in predictors between types of jobs.

Job Love Measurement. A scale measuring a latent variable like job love that cannot be directly measured cannot be a completely perfect measure, as it is subject to measurement error. It can only give an insight into where an individual stands at a point in time and place. Similar to other concepts in personnel marketing, e.g.

---

[19] Study 1b: Love of Job compared to other Love Objects: n = 69; Study 1c – Focus Group: n = 6; Study 2 – Scale Validation: n = 155; Study 3: Influence Factors: n = 202

motivation or satisfaction, love can change over time. Hence, the job love scale proposed in this study can only measure what an individual feels at a certain time. However, this can be seen as an advantage as companies want to know how an employee feels *now* in order to improve the workplace and the proposed job love predictors *in the future*. Another limitation of the job love scale is the theory it is based on. As the present Job Love Scale is built on Sternberg's Triangular Theory of Love, the scale measures what job love is according to the theory. A scale based on other theories of love could be different, as different theories argue different, distinct definitions of love. For example, Aron and Aron's theory (see chapter B) sees love as an extension of the self in the other (only), highlighting the identity component of love. Sternberg's love dimensions like commitment or passion do not play a role in their theory, so a scale based on their theory would be constructed differently. However, since the theory for the Job Love Scale was selected very carefully, it is suggested that the theory and, thus, the scale based on it is the most suitable for this study, which seeks to measure what individuals experience when they love their job.

Applicability. Our studies' insights are limited to an empirical test of hypotheses, while the applicability of the insights in "real life" still needs to be examined. A question in this context would be "Can we increase the share of people who love their jobs by increasing the sense of purpose of work among employees?". For further research, it is recommended to conduct intervention studies focusing on research in real-life settings and therewith add to interventions on how to make people love their job.

4 Overall Conclusions

The current study has added to our understanding of what fosters the love of a job, offering both, a theoretical foundation of a theory of job love as well as implications for business practice on how to increase job love among the workforce. A measurement of job love, the Job Love Scale, was provided and validated. The scale can be used by organizations and individuals to measure whether or whether not they love their job. Factors that lead to or foster job love were identified and tested in their power to predict the love of a job. Especially three factors seem to be strong indicators for people's job love: appreciation, purpose, and person-job-fit. Therefore, companies are advised to look first into those three factors when finding ways to increase job love in their employees. Overall, the concept of job love seems a promising concept for both – scientific research as well as business practice.

Your work is going to fill a large part of your life,

and the only way to be truly satisfied is to do

what you believe is great work.

And the only way to do great work is to

love what you do.

Steve Jobs

References

Ahuvia, A., Batra, R., & Bagozzi, R. (2008). Brand love: Towards an integrative model. *Journal of Marketing, 76*(2), 1-16. https://doi.org/10.1509%2Fjm.09.0339

Akter, N., & Husain, M. (2016). Effect of compensation on job performance: An empirical study. *International Journal of Engineering Technology, Management and Applied Sciences, 4*(8), 108-116.

Albrecht, S. & Leiter, M. (2011). Work engagement: Further reflections on the state of play. *European Journal of Work & Organizational Psychology*, 20, 74-88. https://doi.org/10.1080/1359432X.2010.546711

Alderfer, C. P. (1972). *Existence, relatedness, and growth: Human needs in organizational settings*. Cambridge: Academic Press.

Allen, N. J., & Meyer, J. P. (1990). The measurement and antecedents of affective, continuance and normative commitment to the organization. *Journal of Occupational Psychology, 63*(1), 1-18. https://doi.org/10.1111/j.2044-8325.1990.tb00506.x

Allen, N. J., & Meyer, J. P. (1996). Affective, continuance, and normative commitment to the organization: An examination of construct validity. *Journal of Vocational behavior, 49*(3), 252-276. https://doi.org/10.1006/jvbe.1996.0043

Andersson, M.-L. (1992). The meaning of work and job. *International Journal of Value-Based Management, 5*(1), 89-106.

Aron, A., & Aron, E. N. (1991). Love and sexuality. In K. McKinney & S. Sprecher (Eds.), *Sexuality in close relationships* (25-48). Hove: Psychology Press.

Aron, A., Aron, E. N., & Smollan, D. (1992). Inclusion of other in the self scale and the structure of interpersonal closeness. *Journal of Personality and Social Psychology, 63*(4), 596-612. https://psycnet.apa.org/doi/10.1037/0022-3514.63.4.596

Backhaus, K., Erichson, B., Plinke, W., & Weiber, R. (2008). *Multivariate Analysemethoden: Eine anwendungsorientierte Einführung*. Wiesbaden: Springer Gabler.

Backhaus, K., & Schneider, H. (2020). *Strategisches Marketing* (3rd Ed.). Stuttgart: Schäffer-Poeschl.

Baggaley, A., & Hull, A. (1983). The effect of nonlinear transformations on a Likert scale. *Evaluation & the Health Professions, 6,* 483-491.

Bagozzi, R., Batra, R., & Ahuvia, A. (2016). Brand love: Development and validation of a practical scale. *Marketing Letters, 28*, 1-14. https://doi.org/10.1007/s11002-016-9406-1

Bakker, A. B., Albrecht, S. L., & Leiter, M. P. (2011). Key questions regarding work engagement. *European Journal of Work and Organizational Psychology*, *20*(1), 4-28.

Bakker, A. B., & Demerouti, E. (2008). Towards a model of work engagement. *Career Development International, 13*(3), 209-223. https://doi.org/10.1108/13620430810870476

Bandura, A. (1986). The explanatory and predictive scope of self-efficacy theory. *Journal of Social and Clinical Psychology, 4*(3), 359-373. https://doi.org/10.1521/jscp.1986.4.3.359

Bartlett, C. A., & Ghoshal, S. (2002). Building competitive advantage through people. *MIT Sloan Management Review, 43*(2), 34-41. https://sloanreview.mit.edu/article/building-competitive-advantage-through-people/

Baumeister, R. F., & Bratslavsky, E. (1999). Passion, intimacy, and time: Passionate love as a function of change in intimacy. *Personality and Social Psychology Review, 3*(1), 49-67. https://doi.org/10.1207%2Fs15327957pspr0301_3

Baumeister, R. F., & Wilson, B. (1996). Life stories and the four needs for meaning. *Psychological Inquiry, 7*(4), 322-325. https://doi.org/10.1207/s15327965pli0704_2

Bedeian, A. G., & Wren, D. A. (2001). Most influential management books of the 20th century. *Organizational Dynamics, 29*(3), 221-225. https://doi.org/10.1016/S0090-2616(01)00022-5

Bergmann, F. (1990). Neue Arbeit (New Work): Das Konzept und seine Umsetzung in der Praxis. In W. Fricke (Ed.), *Jahrbuch Arbeit und Technik* (pp. 71-80). Bonn: J.H.W. Dietz.

Bergmann, F., & Schumacher, S. (2005). *Neue Arbeit, neue Kultur.* Freiburg: Arbor.

Berl, R., Williamson, N., & Powell, T. (2013). Industrial salesforce motivation: A critique and test of Maslow's hierarchy of needs. *Journal of Personal Selling & Sales Management, 4*(1), 32-39.

Berscheid, E., & Walster, E. H. (1978). *Interpersonal attraction* (2nd ed.). Boston: Addison-Wesley.

Beutell, N. J., & Wittig-Berman, U. (1999). Predictors of work–family conflict and satisfaction with family, job, career, and life. *Psychological Reports, 85*(3), 893−903.

Birnbaum, G. E., Reis, H. T., Mizrahi, M., Kanat-Maymon, Y., Sass, O., & Granovski-Milner, C. (2016). Intimately connected: The importance of partner responsiveness for experiencing sexual desire. *Journal of Personality and Social Psychology, 111*(4), 530-546. https://doi.apa.org/doi/10.1037/pspi0000069

Boldt, L. G. (2004). *How to find the work you love.* London: Penguin.

Bortz, J., & Döring, N. (2006). *Forschungsmethoden und Evaluation* (pp. 137-293). Berlin: Springer.

Bortz, J., & Schuster, C. (2010). *Statistik für Human-und Sozialwissenschaftler.* Berlin: Springer.

Brown, K. A., & Mitchell, T. R. (1993). Organizational obstacles: Links with financial performance, customer satisfaction, and job satisfaction in a service environment. *Human Relations, 46*(6), 725-757. https://doi.org/10.1177%2F001872679304600603

Brown, T., & Wyatt, J. (2010). Design thinking for social innovation. *Development Outreach, 12*(1), 29-43.

Browne, M. W., & Cudeck, R. (1992). Alternative ways of assessing model fit. *Sociological Methods & Research, 21*(2), 230-258. https://doi.org/10.1177%2F0049124192021002005

Bruhn, M. (2014). *Marketing: Grundlagen für Studium und Praxis* (12th ed.). Wiesbaden: Springer Fachmedien.

Buck, R. (2002). The genetics and biology of true love: Prosocial biological affects and the left hemisphere. *Psychological Review, 109*(4), 739-744. https://doi.org/10.1037/0033-295X.109.4.739

Burkett, J., & Young, L. (2012). The behavioral, anatomical and pharmacological parallels between social attachment, love and addiction. *Psychopharmacology, 224*(1), 1-26. https://doi.org/10.1007%2Fs00213-012-2794-x

Caldwell, R. S. (1987). *Hesiod's theogony*. Cambridge: Focus Information Group.

Cambridge Dictionary (2020). *Definition of purpose.* Retrieved June 2, 2020, from https://dictionary.cambridge.org/de/worterbuch/englisch/purpose

Campbell, D. T., & Fiske, D. W. (1959). Convergent and discriminant validation by the multitrait-multimethod matrix. *Psychological Bulletin, 56*(2), 81-105. https://psycnet.apa.org/doi/10.1037/h0046016

Caplow, T. (1954). *The sociology of work*. Minneapolis: University of Minnesota Press.

Carifio, J., & Perla, R. J. (2007). Ten common misunderstandings, misconceptions, persistent myths and urban legends about Likert scales and likert response formats and their antidotes. *Journal of Social Sciences, 3*(3), 106-116.

Carmines, E. G., & Zeller, R. A. (1979). *Reliability and validity assessment*. Thousand Oaks: Sage Publications.

Carroll, B. A., & Ahuvia, A. C. (2006). Some antecedents and outcomes of brand love. *Marketing Letters, 17*(2), 79-89.

Chalofsky, N., & Krishna, V. (2009). Meaningfulness, commitment, and engagement: The intersection of a deeper level of intrinsic motivation. *Advances in Developing Human Resources, 11*(2). https://doi.org/10.1177/2F1523422309333147

Chapman, G., & White, P. (2019). *The 5 languages of appreciation in the workplace: Empowering organizations by encouraging people*. Chicago: Moody Publishers.

Cherrington, D. J. (1994). *Organizational behavior: The management of individual and organizational performance*. Boston: Allyn and Bacon.

Chojnacki, J. T., & Walsh, W. B. (1990). Reliability and concurrent validity of the Sternberg triangular love scale. *Psychological Reports, 67*(1), 219-224. https://doi.org/10.2466%2Fpr0.1990.67.1.219

Clark, M. S., & Mills, J. (1979). Interpersonal attraction in exchange and communal relationships. *Journal of Personality and Social Psychology, 37*(1), 12-24. https://doi.org/10.1037/0022-3514.37.1.12

Cohen, J. (1988). *Statistical power analysis for the behavioural sciences* (2nd ed.). New York: Academic Press.

Cohen, J. (1990). Things I have learned (so far). *American Psychologist, 45*(12), 1304–1312.

Cohen, J. (1992). A power primer. *Psychological Bulletin, 112*(1), 155–159.

Connolly, J., & Viswesvaran, C. (2000). The role of affectivity in job satisfaction: A meta-analysis. *Personality and Individual Differences, 29*(2), 265-281. https://doi.org/10.1016/S0191-8869(99)00192-0

Cook, J., Hepworth, S. J., Wall, T. D., & Warr, P. B. (1981). *A compendium and review of 249 work review measures and their use.* Cambridge: Academic Press.

Coombs, C. H. (1960). A theory of data. *Psychological Review, 67,* 143-159.

Cortina, J. M. (1993). What is coefficient alpha? An examination of theory and applications. *Journal of Applied Psychology, 78*(1), 98-104. https://doi.org/10.1037/0021-9010.78.1.98

Csikszentmihalyi, M. (1990). *Flow: The psychology of optimal experience.* New York City: Harper & Row.

Danish, R. Q., & Usman, A. (2010). Impact of reward and recognition on job satisfaction and motivation: An empirical study from Pakistan. *International Journal of Business and Management, 5*(2), 159-167. https://doi.org/10.5539/ijbm.v5n2p159

Deci, E. L., & Ryan, R. M. (1985). The general causality orientations scale: Self-determination in personality. *Journal of Research in Personality, 19*(2), 109-134. https://doi.org/10.1016/0092-6566(85)90023-6

Deci, E. L., & Ryan, R. M. (2008). Self-determination theory: A macrotheory of human motivation, development, and health. *Canadian Psychology, 49*(3), 182-185. https://doi.org/10.1037/a0012801

Deci, E. L., & Ryan, R. M. (2012). *Self-determination theory.* In P. A. M. van Lange, A. W. Kruglanski & E. T. Higgins (Eds.). *Handbook of theories of social psychology* (pp. 416–436). Thousand Oaks: Sage Publications. https://doi.org/10.4135/9781446249215.n21

Dik, B. J., & Duffy, R. D. (2013). *Make your job a calling: How the psychology of vocation can change your life at work.* West Conshohocken: Templeton Press.

Dolbier, C. L., Webster, J. A., McCalister, K. T., Mallon, M. W., & Steinhardt, M. A. (2005). Reliability and validity of a single-item measure of job satisfaction. *American Journal of Health Promotion, 19*(3), 194-198. https://doi.org/10.4278%2F0890-1171-19.3.194

Drucker, P. F. (1959). *Landmarks of Tomorrow.* New York: Harper.

Dutton, J., & Ragins, B. (2017). Moving forward: Positive relationships at work as a research frontier. In J. Dutton & B. Ragins (Eds.), *Building a theoretical and research foundation* (pp. 387-400). Hove: Psychology Press.

Eells, R., & Walton, C. (1974). *Conceptual foundations of business* (3rd ed.). Homewood: Richard D. Irwin.

Eisend, M., & Kuss, A. (2019). *Research methodology in marketing: Theory development, empirical approaches and philosophy of science considerations.* Basel: Springer International Publishing.

Eisinga, R., te Grotenhuis, M., & Pelzer, B. (2013). The reliability of a two-item scale: Pearson, Cronbach, or Spearman-Brown? *International Journal of Public Health, 58*(4), 637-642. https://doi.org/10.1007/s00038-012-0416-3

Ekman, P., & Cordaro, D. (2011). What is meant by calling emotions basic. *Emotion Review, 3*(4), 364-370.

Elzinga, D. (2016). *The biggest lie in HR – People leave managers not companies.* Retrieved March 20, 2020, from https://www.cultureamp.com/blog/the-biggest-lie-in-hr-people-quit-managers/

Eppler, M. J., & Hoffmann, F. (2012). Does method matter? An experiment on collaborative business model idea generation in teams. *Innovation: Organization & Management, 14*(3), 388-403. https://doi.org/10.5172/impp.2012.14.3.388

Fetscherin, M., & Heinrich, D. (2014). Consumer brand relationships: A research landscape. *Journal of Brand Management, 21*, 366-371. https://doi.org/10.1057/bm.2014.22

Field, A. (2009). *Discovering statistics using SPSS statistics: (And sex and drugs and rock'n'roll) (3rd Ed.).* Thousand Oaks: Sage Publishing.

Field, A. (2013). *Discovering statistics using SPSS statistics: (And sex and drugs and rock'n'roll) (4th Ed.).* Thousand Oaks: Sage Publishing.

Firestone, S. (1983). *The dialectic of sex: The case for feminist revolution.* New York: Farrar Straus Giroux.

Fisher, H. E. (1992). *Anatomy of love: The natural history of monogamy, adultery, and divorce.* New York: Simon & Schuster.

Fournier, S. (1998). Consumers and their brands: Developing relationship theory in consumer research. *Journal of Consumer Research, 24*(4), 343-373. https://doi.org/10.1086/209515

Fournier, S., & Yao, J. L. (1997). Reviving brand loyalty: A reconceptualization within the framework of consumer-brand relationships. *International Journal of Research in Marketing, 14*(5), 451-472. https://doi.org/10.1016/S0167-8116(97)00021-9

Frankl, V. E. (1970). *The will to meaning: Foundations and applications of logotherapy.* New York: Penguin Books.

Furnham, A. (1988). *Lay theories: Everyday understanding of problems in the social sciences.* Oxford: Pergamon Press.

Gallup (2017). *Driving Employee Engagement: Understanding, measuring and creating employee engagement.* Washington, D.C.: Gallup.

Gallup (2019). *Engagement Index.* Retrieved June 2, 2020, from https://www.gallup.com/de/engagement-index-deutschland.aspx

Ghauri, P., & Grønhaug, K. (2005). *Research methods in business studies: A practical guide (3rd ed.).* Cambridge University Press.

Glass, G. V., Peckham, P. D., & Sanders, J. R. (1972). Consequences of failure to meet assumptions underlying the fixed effects analyses of variance and covariance. *Review of Educational Research, 42*(3), 237-288. https://doi.org/10.3102%2F00346543042003237

Globoforce. (2014). *Workforce Mood Tracker fall 2014 report: The effect of work relationships on organizational culture and commitment.* Retrieved March 10, 2020, from http://go.globoforce.com/rs/globoforce/images/Fall_2014_Mood_Tracker.pdf

Graen, G., & Uhl-Bien, M. (1991). Leadership-making applies equally well to sponsors, competence networks, and teammates. *Journal of management Systems, 3*, 375-380.

Guion, R. M., & Landy, F. J. (1972). The meaning of work and the motivation to work. *Organizational Behavior and Human Performance, 7*(2), 308-339. https://doi.org/10.1016/0030-5073(72)90020-7

Hackl, B., Wagner, M., Attmer, L., & Baumann, D. (2017). *New Work: auf dem Weg zur neuen Arbeitswelt: Management-impulse, Praxisbeispiele, Studien.* Berlin: Springer.

Hamed, A., Ramzan, M., Zubair, H. M. K., Ali, G., Arslan, M. (2014). Impact of compensation on employee performance: Empirical evidence from banking sector of Pakistan. *International Journal of Business and Social Science, 5*(2), 302-209.

Haggbloom, S. J., Warnick, R., Warnick, J. E., Jones, V. K., Yarbrough, G. L., Russell, T. M., . . . Beavers, J. (2002). The 100 most eminent psychologists of the 20th century. *Review of General Psychology, 6*(2), 139-152.

Hall, D. T. (1976). *Careers in organizations.* Santa Monica: Goodyear Pub. Co.

Hall, R. H. (1975). *Occupations and the social structure.* Upper Saddle River: Prentice Hall.

Harlow, H. F. (1958). The nature of love. *American Psychologist, 13*(12), 673-685. https://psycnet.apa.org/doi/10.1037/h0047884

Harvey, R. J., Billings, R. S., & Nilan, K. J. (1985). Confirmatory factor analysis of the Job Diagnostic Survey: Good news and bad news. *Journal of Applied Psychology, 70*(3), 461-468. https://psycnet.apa.org/doi/10.1037/0021-9010.70.3.461

Hatfield, E. (1982). Passionate love, companionate love, and intimacy. In M. Fischer & G. Stricker (Eds.), *Intimacy* (pp. 267-292). Springer.

Hatfield, E., Pillemer, J., O'Brien, M., & Le, Y.-C. (2008). The endurance of love: Passionate and companionate love in newlywed and long-term marriages. *Interpersona: An International Journal on Personal Relationships, 2*(1), 35-64. https://doi.org/10.5964/ijpr.v2i1.17

Hatfield, E., & Rapson, R. L. (1990). Passionate love in intimate relationships. *Affect and Social Behavior*, 126-152.

Hatfield, E., & Sprecher, S. (1986). Measuring passionate love in intimate relationships. *Journal of Adolescence, 9*(4), 383-410. https://doi.org/10.1016/S0140-1971(86)80043-4

Hatfield, E., & Walster, G. W. (1978). *A new look at love*. Boston: Addison-Wesley.

Heider, F. (1958). *The psychology of interpersonal relations*. Hoboken: John Wiley and Sons.

Heinrich, D., Albrecht, C.-M., & Bauer, H. H. (2012). Love actually? Measuring and exploring consumers' brand love. In S. Fournier, M. Breazeale, & M. Fetscherin (Eds.), *Consumer-brand relationships: Theory and practice* (pp. 137-150). Abingdon: Routledge.

Hendrick, C., & Hendrick, S. (1986). A theory and method of love. *Journal of Personality and Social Psychology, 50*(2), 392.

Hendrick, C., & Hendrick, S. S. (1989). Research on love: Does it measure up? *Journal of personality and social psychology, 56*(5), 784-794. https://doi.org/10.1037/0022-3514.56.5.784

Herzberg, F., Mausner, B., & Snyderman, B. (1959). *The Motivation to Work*. New York: Wiley.

Hinkin, T. R. (1995). A review of scale development practices in the study of organizations. *Journal of Management, 21*(5), 967-988. https://doi.org/10.1016/0149-2063(95)90050-0

Hinkin, T. R., Tracey, J. B., & Enz, C. A. (1997). Scale construction: Developing reliable and valid measurement instruments. *Journal of Hospitality & Tourism Research, 21*(1), 100-120. https://doi.org/10.1177%2F109634809702100108

Holland, J. L. (1985). *Making vocational choices: A theory of vocational personalities and work environments*. Englewood Cliffs: Prentice Hall.

Holland, J. L. (1959). A theory of vocational choice. *Journal of Counseling Psychology, 6*(1), 35-45. https://doi.org/10.1037/h0040767

Hollingworth, M. (2013). *Saint Augustine of Hippo: An intellectual biography*. Oxford University Press.

Holt, Davis H. (1993). *Management: Concept and Practices*. New Jersey: Prentice Hall, Englewood Cliffs.

Holy Bible (2011). *New International Version (NIV)*. Colorado Springs: International Bible Society.

Homburg, C., & Baumgartner, H. (1995). Beurteilung von Kausalmodellen. Bestandsaufnahme und Anwendungsempfehlungen. *Marketing: ZFP – Journal of Research and Management, 17*(3), 162-176.

Hornburg, C., & Giering, A. (1996). Konzeptualisierung und Operationalisierung komplexer Konstrukte. Ein Leitfaden für die Marketingforschung. *Marketing: ZFP – Journal of Research and Management, 18*(1), 5-24.

Hosmer, D. W., & Lemeshow, S. (2000). *Applied logistic regression* (2nd ed.). Hoboken: John Wiley & Sons.

Huck, S. W. (2007). *Reading statistics and research* (5th ed.). Boston: Allyn & Bacon.

Illgen, D. R., & Hollenbeck, J. R. (1992). The structure of work: Job design and roles. In M. D. Dunnette & L. M. Hough (Eds.), *Handbook of industrial and organizational psychology* (3rd Ed., pp. 165-207). Sunnyvale: Consulting Psychologists Press.

Ivancevich, J. M., & Glueck, W. F. (1989). *Foundations of personnel/human resource management.* Homewood: Irwin.

Izard, C. E. (1992). Basic emotions, relations among emotions, and emotion-cognition relations. *The Psychological Review, 99*(3), 561-565. https://doi.org/10.1037/0033-295X.99.3.561

Jamieson, S. (2004). Likert scales: How to (ab)use them. *Medical Education, 38,* 1212-1218.

Jobs, S. (2005). Speech held at Stanford University at the University's 114th Commencement [Video]. Retrieved Feb 2, 2020 from https://www.youtube.com/watch?v=UF8uR6Z6KLc

Jones, T. O., & Sasser, W. E. (1995). Why satisfied customers defect. *Harvard Business Review, 73*(6), 88-99.

Judge, T. A., Thoresen, C. J., Bono, J. E., & Patton, G. K. (2001). The job satisfaction–job performance relationship: A qualitative and quantitative review. *Psychological Bulletin, 127*(3), 376-407. https://doi.org/10.1037/0033-2909.127.3.376

Kaiser, H. F. (1974). An index of factorial simplicity. *Psychometrika, 39*(1), 31-36. https://doi.org/10.1007/BF02291575

Kalmijn, W., & Veenhoven, R. (2005). Measuring inequality of happiness in nations: In search for proper statistics. *Journal of Happiness Studies, 6*(4), 357-396. https://doi.org/10.1007/s10902-005-8855-7

Kelley, H. H., Berscheid, E., Christensen, A., Harvey, J. H., Huston, T. L., Levinger, G., . . . Peterson, D. R. (1983). *Close relationships.* New York: Freeman.

Kirchgeorg, M., & Günther, E. (2006). Ist Ihr Unternehmen fit für den "War for Talent?": Unternehmen müssen in Zukunft High Potential Segmente identifizieren und gezielt ansprechen können. *OSCAR.trends, 3,* 1-11.

Kirchgeorg, M., & Müller, J. (2013). Personalmarketing als Schlüssel zur Gewinnung, Bindung und Wiedergewinnung von Mitarbeitern. In: R. Stock-Homburg (Ed.), *Handbuch Strategisches Personalmanagement* (pp. 73-90). Wiesbaden: Springer Gabler.

Knapp, T. R. (1990). Treating ordinal scales as interval scales: An attempt to resolve the controversy. *Nursing Research, 39,* 121-123.

Knee, C., Patrick, H., & Lonsbary, C. (2003). Implicit theories of relationships: Orientations toward evaluation and cultivation. *Personality and Social Psychology Review, 7*(1), 41-55. https://doi.org/10.1207%2FS15327957PSPR0701_3

Knee, C. R. (1998). Implicit theories of relationships: Assessment and prediction of romantic relationship initiation, coping, and longevity. *Journal of personality and social psychology, 74*(2), 360-370. https://doi.org/10.1037/0022-3514.74.2.360

Knee, C. R., Nanayakkara, A., Vietor, N. A., Neighbors, C., & Patrick, H. (2001). Implicit theories of relationships: Who cares if romantic partners are less than ideal? *Personality and Social Psychology Bulletin, 27*(7), 808-819. https://doi.org/10.1177%2F0146167201277004

Korman, A. K. (1974). Contingency approaches to leadership: An overview. In J. G. Hund & L. L. Larson (Eds.), *Contingency Approaches to Leadership* (pp. 189-195). Carbondale: Southern Illinois University Press.

Köthemann, D. (2013). *Macht und Leistung als Werte in Europa: Über gesellschaftliche und individuelle Einflüsse auf Wertprioritäten*. Berlin: Springer.

Kristof-Brown, A., & Guay, R. P. (2011). Person–environment fit. In S. Zedeck (Ed.), *APA handbook of industrial and organizational psychology: Maintaining, expanding, and contracting the organization* (pp. 3-50). Washington, D.C.: American Psychological Association. https://doi.org/10.1037/12171-001

Langhorne, M. C., & Secord, P. F. (1955). Variations in marital needs with age, sex, marital status, and regional location. *The Journal of Social Psychology, 41*(1), 19-37. https://doi.org/10.1080/00224545.1955.9714250

Langner, T., & Kühn, J. (2010). Markenliebe: Vom Wesen der intensivsten aller Markenbeziehungen. In W. Baumann, U. Braukmann & W. Matthes (Eds.), *Innovation und Internationalisierung: Festschrift für Norbert Koubek* (pp. 589-612). Wiesbaden: Gabler.

Lazarus, R. S. (1991). Cognition and motivation in emotion. *American Psychologist, 46*(4), 352-367. https://doi.org/10.1037/0003-066X.46.4.352

Lee, J. A. (1973). *The colors of love: An exploration of the ways of loving*. New York City: New Press.

Lee, J. A. (1977). A typology of styles of loving. *Personality and Social Psychology Bulletin, 3*(2), 173-182. https://doi.org/10.1177%2F014616727700300204

Lee, J. A. (1988). Love-styles. In R. J. Sternberg & M. L. Barnes (Eds.), *The psychology of love* (pp. 38-67). Yale University Press.

Lees, J. (2014). *How to get a job you love* (7th Ed.) London: McGraw-Hill Education.

Lees, J. (2018). *How to get a job you love* (8th Ed.). London: McGraw-Hill Education.

Lemieux, R., & Hale, J. L. (2000). Intimacy, passion, and commitment among married individuals: Further testing of the triangular theory of love. *Psychological Reports, 87*(3), 941-948. https://doi.org/10.2466%2Fpr0.2000.87.3.941

Levenstein, A. (1964). *Why people work*. Springfield: Collier Books.

Liedtka, J. (2014). Innovative ways companies are using design thinking. *Strategy and Leadership, 42*(2), 40-45. https://doi.org/10.1108/SL-01-2014-0004

Likert, R. (1932). A technique for the measurement of attitudes. *Archives of psychology, 22*(140), 5-55.

Lissitz, R. W., & Green, S. B. (1975). Effect of the number of scale points on reliability: A Monte Carlo approach. *Journal of Applied Psychology, 60*(1), 10-13. https://psycnet.apa.org/doi/10.1037/h0076268

Locke, E. A. (1976). The nature and causes of job satisfaction. In: M.D. Dunnette (Ed.), *Handbook of industrial and organizational psychology*. Chicago: Rand-McNally.

Maddi, S. (1967). The existential neurosis. *Journal of Abnormal Psychology, 72*, 311-325. https:// doi.org/10.1037/h0020103

Maharjan, P. (2018, March 24). *What is employee recognition? Why is it important?* Retrieved June 2, 2020, from https://www.businesstopia.net/human-resource/employee-recognition-meaning-types-examples-importance

Malka, A., & Chatman, J. A. (2003). Intrinsic and extrinsic orientations as moderators of the effect of annual income on subjective well-being: A longitudinal study. *Personality and Social Psychology Bulletin, 29*, 737−746.

Manstead, A. S., Frijda, N., & Fischer, A. (Eds.). (2004). *Feelings and emotions: The Amsterdam symposium*. Cambridge University Press.

Marx, K. (1988). *Economic and philosophic manuscripts of 1844*. Buffalo: Prometheus Books. (1844).

Marx, K. (1887). *Capital: A critical analysis of capitalist production.* London: Swan Sonnenschein, Lowrey & Co.

Maslach, C., & Jackson, S. E. (1981). The measurement of experienced burnout. *Journal of Organizational Behavior, 2*(2), 99-113. https://doi.org/10.1002/job.4030020205

Maslow, A. (1943). A theory of human motivation. *Psychological Review, 50*(4), 370-396. https://psycnet.apa.org/doi/10.1037/h0054346

Masuda, M. (2003). Meta-analyses of love scales: Do various love scales measure the same psychological constructs? *Japanese Psychological Research*, *45*(1), 25-37. https://doi.org/10.1111/1468-5884.00030

Mausner, B., & Snyderman, B. B. (1993). *The motivation to work*. Piscataway Township: Transaction Publishers.

May, D. R., Gilson, R. L., & Harter, L. M. (2004). The psychological conditions of meaningfulness, safety and availability and the engagement of the human spirit at work. *Journal of Occupational and Organizational Psychology*, *77*(1), 11-37. https://doi.org/10.1348/096317904322915892

McClelland, D. C. (1965). Toward a theory of motive acquisition. *American Psychologist*, *20*(5), 321-333. https://doi.org/10.1037/h0022225

McGregor, D., & Cutcher-Gershenfeld, J. (1960). *The human side of enterprise* (Vol. 21, pp. 166-171). New York: McGraw-Hill.

Meyer, J. P., Allen, N. J., & Gellatly, I. R. (1990). Affective and continuance commitment to the organization: Evaluation of measures and analysis of concurrent and time-lagged relations. *Journal of applied psychology*, *75*(6), 710.

Meyer, J. P., & Allen, N. J. (1997). *Commitment in the workplace: Theory, research, and application*. Washington, D. C.: Sage Publications.

Moosbrugger, H., & Kelava, A. (2012). Testtheorie und Fragebogenkonstruktion. Berlin: Springer.

Murray, H. A. (1938). *Explorations in personality: A clinical and experimental study of fifty men of college age*. Oxford University Press.

Neff, W. (2017). *Work and human behavior*. Abingdon: Routledge.

O'Leary, K. D., Acevedo, B. P., Aron, A., Huddy, L., & Mashek, D. (2012). Is long-term love more than a rare phenomenon? If so, what are its correlates? *Social Psychological and Personality Science*, *3*(2), 241-249. https://doi.org/10.1177/1948550611417015

Ogaboh, A., Nkpoyen, F., & Ushie, E. (2010). Career development and employee commitment in industrial organisations in Calabar, Nigeria. *American Journal of Scientific and Industrial Research*, *1*(2), 105-114.

Overall, N. C., Fletcher, G. J. O., & Simpson, J. A. (2010). Helping each other grow: Romantic partner support, self-improvement, and relationship quality. *Personality and Social Psychology Bulletin*, *36*(11), 1496-1513. https://doi.org/10.1177%2F0146167210383045

Oxford English Dictionary (2020). *Love, n.1.* Retrieved June 2, 2020, from https://www.oed.com/viewdictionaryentry/Entry/110566

Panksepp, J. (1998). *Affective neuroscience: The foundations of human and animal emotions*. Oxford University Press.

Parsons, T. (1959). The social structure of the family. In R. N. Anshen (Ed.), *The family: Its function and destiny* (pp. 241-274). New York: HarperCollins.

Parsons, T., & Bales, R. F. (1960). *Family socialization, and interaction process*. New York City: The Free Press.

Peter, L. J., & Hull, R. (1969): *The Peter Principle: Why things always go wrong.* New York: William Morrow & Co.

Plattner, H., Meinel, C., & Weinberg, U. (2009). *Design Thinking. Innovation lernen, Ideenwelten öffnen.* München: mi-Wirtschaftsbuch.

Pradhan, R., Panda, P., & Jena, L. (2017). Purpose, passion and performance at the workplace: Exploring the nature, structure and relationship. *The Psychologist-Manager Journal, 20*(4), 222-245. https://doi.org/10.1037/mgr0000059

Ragins, B. R., & Button, J. E. (2007). Positive relationships at work: an introduction and invitation. In J.E. Button & B. R. Ragins (Eds.), *Exploring positive relationships at work: Building a theoretical research foundation* (pp. 3-25). New Jersey: Lawrence Erlbaum Associates Publishers.

Raibley, J. R. (2012). Happiness is not well-being. *Journal of Happiness Studies*, *13*(6), 1105-1129.

Ratelle, C. F., Carbonneau, N., Vallerand, R. J., & Mageau, G. (2013). Passion in the romantic sphere: A look at relational outcomes. *Motivation and Emotion, 37*(1), 106-120. https://doi.org/10.1007/s11031-012-9286-5

Reed, J., & Stoltz, P. G. (2013). *Put your mindset to work: The one asset you really need to win and keep the job you love.* London: Portfolio Trade.

Reichheld, F. F. (2003). The one number you need to grow. *Harvard Business Review, 81*(12), 46-55.

Reik, T. (1944). *A psychologist looks at love.* New York City: Farrar & Reinhart.

Reissman, C., Aron, A., & Bergen, M. R. (1993). Shared activities and marital satisfaction: Causal direction and self-expansion versus boredom. *Journal of Social and Personal Relationships, 10*(2), 243-254. https://doi.org/10.1177/026540759301000205

Roberts, K. (2005). *Lovemarks: The future beyond brands.* New York: powerHouse Books.

Roberts, K. (2006). *The lovemarks effect: Winning in the consumer revolution.* Seattle: Mountaineers Books.

Robins, M. (2019, November 12). *Why employees need both recognition and appreciation.* Retrieved June 2, 2020, from https://hbr.org/2019/11/why-employees-need-both-recognition-and-appreciation#:~:text=Appreciation%2C%20on%20the%20other%20hand,is%20about%20who%20they%20are.

Robinson, M. (2017). Using multi-item psychometric scales for research and practice in human resource management. *Human Resource Management,* *57*(3), 739–750. https://doi.org/10.1002/hrm.21852

Robinson, P., & Kates, S. M. (2005). Children and their brand relationships. *Advances in Consumer Research, 32,* 578-559.

Rosseel, Y. (2012). Lavaan: An R package for structural equation modeling and more. Version 0.5–12 (BETA). *Journal of Statistical Software, 48*(2), 1-36.

Rosseel, Y. (2014). *The Lavaan tutorial.* Department of Data Analysis: Ghent University.

Rubin, Z. (1970). Measurement of romantic love. *Journal of Personality and Social Psychology, 16*(2), 265-273. https://doi.org/10.1037/h0029841

Rubin, Z., Hill, C. T., Peplau, L. A., & Dunkel-Schetter, C. (1980). Self-disclosure in dating couples: Sex roles and the ethic of openness. *Journal of Marriage and the Family*, 305-317. https://doi.org/10.2307/351228

Russell, B. (1932). *In praise of idleness.* Queensland Braille Writing Association. Retrieved March 20, 2020, from http://theanarchistlibrary.org/library/bertrand-russell-in-praise-of-idleness-11-02-05-22-00-46

Sanchez, J. I., & Brock, P. (1996). Outcomes of perceived discrimination among Hispanic employees: Is diversity management a luxury or a necessity? *Academy of Management Journal, 39*, 704–719.

Schallmo, D. R., & Lang, K. (2017). *Design Thinking erfolgreich anwenden.* Wiesbaden: Springer Fachmedien.

Scheier, C., & Held, D. (2006). *Wie Werbung wirkt: Erkenntnisse des Neuromarketing.* Freiburg: Haufe Lexware.

Schmitt, N., & Stuits, D. M. (1985). Factors defined by negatively keyed items: The result of careless respondents? *Applied Psychological Measurement, 9*(4), 367-373. https://doi.org/10.1177/014662168500900405

Schneider, H., & Gerold, M. (2017). *Zwischen Eigensinn und Indienstnahme – Zur Wahrnehmung von Fremdbestimmung im freiwilligen Engagement und dessen Folgen.* Retrieved March 20, 2020, from https://www.bertelsmann-stiftung.de/fileadmin/files/Projekte/90_Synergien_vor_Ort/Studie_Indienstnahme_Gesamt_online.pdf

Schriesheim, C. A., & Eisenbach, R. J. (1995). An exploratory and confirmatory factor-analytic investigation of item wording effects on the obtained factor structures of survey questionnaire measures. *Journal of Management, 21*(6), 1177-1193. https://doi.org/10.1177/014920639502100609

Schriesheim, C. A., Powers, K. J., Scandura, T. A., Gardiner, C. C., & Lankau, M. J. (1993). Improving construct measurement in management research: Comments and a quantitative approach for assessing the theoretical content adequacy of paper-and-pencil survey-type instruments. *Journal of Management, 19*(2), 385-417. https://doi.org/10.1016/0149-2063(93)90058-U

Schwab, D. P. (1980). Construct validity in organizational behavior. *Research in Organizational Behavior, 2,* 3-43.

Schwartz, B. (2015). *Why we work*. New York: Simon and Schuster.

Sharda, R., Frankwick, G. L., & Turetken, O. (1999). Group knowledge networks: A framework and an implementation. *Information Systems Frontiers, 1*(3), 221-239. https://doi.org/10.1023/A:1010098227671

Shaver, P. R., & Hazan, C. (1988). A biased overview of the study of love. *Journal of Social and Personal Relationships, 5*(4), 473-501. https://doi.org/10.1177/0265407588054005

Sheldon, K. M., & Lyubomirsky, S. (2004). Achieving sustainable new happiness: Prospects, practices, and prescriptions. *Positive Psychology in Practice*, 127-145.

Singh, S. & Aggarwal, Y. (2017). Happiness at work scale: Construction and psychometric validation of a measure using mixed method approach. *Journal of Happiness Studies, 19,* 1439–1463.

Shimp, T. A., & Madden, T. J. (1988). Consumer-object relations: A conceptual framework based analogously on Sternberg's triangular theory of love. *Advances in Consumer Research Volume, 15, 163-168.*

Smith, P., Kendall, L., & Hulin, C. (1969). *The measurement of satisfaction in work and retirement: A strategy for the study of attitudes.* Chicago: Rand McNally.

Spilt, J. L., Koomen, H. M. Y., & Thijs, J. T. (2011). Teacher wellbeing: The importance of teacher–student relationships. *Educational Psychology Review, 23*(4), 457-477. https://doi.org/10.1007/s10648-011-9170-y

Standford. (2008, March 7). Steve Jobs' speech at 114th Commencement on June 12 [Video]. Retrieved Feb 2, 2020 from https://www.youtube.com/watch?v=UF8uR6Z6KLc

Statista (2000). *Durchschnittsgehalt in Deutschland.* Retrieved May 7, 2020, from https://de.statista.com/themen/293/durchschnittseinkommen/#:~:text=3.994%20Euro%20brutto.,betrug%20monatlich%202.079%20Euro%20netto.

Sternberg, R. J. (1986). A triangular theory of love. *Psychological Review, 93*(2), 119-135. https://doi.org/10.1037/0033-295X.93.2.119

Sternberg, R. J. (1997). Construct validation of a triangular love scale. *European Journal of Social Psychology, 27*(3), 313–335. https://doi.org/10.1002/(SICI)1099-0992(199705)27:3<313::AID-EJSP824>3.0.CO;2-4

Sternberg, R. J., & Sternberg, K. (Eds.). (2018). *The new psychology of love.* Cambridge University Press.

Stone, D. H. (1993). Design a questionnaire. *British Medical Journal, 307*(6914), 1264-1266. https://doi.org/10.1136/bmj.307.6914.1264

Stone, E. F. (1978). *Research methods in organizational behavior.* Chicago: Scott Foresman.

Stotz, W. (2007). *Employee Relationship Management: Der Weg zu engagierten und effizienten Mitarbeitern.* München: De Gruyter Oldenbourg.

Taherdoost, H. (2016). Validity and reliability of the research instrument: How to test the validation of a questionnaire/survey in a research. *International Journal of Academic Research in Management, 5*, 28-36.

Taylor, F. W. (1911). *The principles of scientific management.* New York City: Harper & Brothers.

Team, M. O. W. I. R. (1987). *The meaning of working.* Cambridge: Academic Press.

Thoring, K., & Müller, R. M. (2011). Understanding design thinking: A process model based on method engineering. *13th International Conference on Engineering and Product Design Education.* London, UK.

Tilgher, A. (1962). *Work through the ages: Man, work and society.* New York: Basic Books.

Todd, B. (2016). *80,000 Hours: Find a fulfilling career that does good.* Oxford: Createspace Independent Publishing Platform.

Ulrich, D., Ulrich, W., & Goldsmith, M. (2010). *The why of work: How great leaders build abundant organizations that win.* New York City: McGraw-Hill Education.

Urban, D. (1993). *Logit Analyse: Statistische Verfahren zur Analyse von Modellen mit qualitativen Response-Variablen.* Stuttgart, Jena, New York: Gustav Fischer Verlag.

Vallerand, R. J., Blanchard, C., Mageau, G. A., Koestner, R., Ratelle, C., Léonard, M., Gagné, M., & Marsolais, J. (2003). Les passions de l'âme: On obsessive and harmonious passion. *Journal of Personality and Social Psychology, 85*(4), 756-767. https://doi.org/10.1037/0022-3514.85.4.756

Vallerand, R. J., Houlfort, N., & Forest, J. (2003). Passion at work: Toward a New Conceptualization. In S. W. Gilliland, D. D. Steiner, & D. P. Skarlicki (Eds.), *Emerging perspectives on values in organizations* (pp. 175-204). Charlotte: Information Age Publishing.

Vallerand, R. J., & Houlfort, N. (Eds.). (2019). *Passion for work: Theory, research, and applications.* Oxford University Press.

Velicer, E. G. W. F. (1988). Relation of sample size to the stability of component patterns. *Psychological Bulletin, 103*(2), 265-275. https://doi.org/10.1037/0033-2909.103.2.265

Vigderhous, G. (1977). The level of measurement and 'permissible' statistical analysis in social research. *Pacific Sociological Review, 20* (1), 61-72.

Wayne, S., Shore, L., & Liden, R. (1997). Perceived organizational support and leader-member exchange: A social exchange perspective. *Academy of Management Journal, 40*(1), 82-111. https://doi.org/10.2307/257021

Weber, M. (1930). *The Protestant Ethic and the Spirit of Capitalism.* London: George Allen & Unwin Ltd.

Weiber, R., & Mühlhaus, D. (2014). *Strukturgleichungsmodellierung: Eine anwendungsorientierte Einführung in die Kausalanalyse mit Hilfe von AMOS, SmartPLS und SPSS.* Berlin: Springer.

West, S. G., Finch, J. F., & Curran, P. J. (1995). Structural equation models with nonnormal variables: Problems and remedies. In R. H. Hoyle (Hrsg.), *Structural equation modeling* (p. 56–75). London: Sage.

White, R. W. (1959). Motivation reconsidered: The concept of competence. *Psychological Review, 66*(5), 297-333. https://doi.org/10.1037/h0040934.

Woodruff, B. (director). (2016). *The Perfect Match.* CodeBlack Films, Jorva Entertainment Productions, Flavor Unit Entertainment.

Wu, H., & Leung, S.-O. (2017). Can Likert scales be treated as interval scales? A simulation study. *Journal of Social Service Research, 43(*4), 527-532.

Zuckerman, M., Porac, J., Lathin, D., Smith, R., 6 Deci, E. L. (1978). On the importance of self-determination for intrinsically motivated behavior. *Personality and Social Psychology Bulletin, 4*(39), 443–446. doi:10.1177/014616727800400317.

1

Questionnaire of Study II
Scale Development

Willkommen zu diesem Fragebogen zu Einstellungen zur eigenen Arbeit.
Danke, dass Sie sich die Zeit nehmen, diesen Fragebogen auszufüllen.

Der Fragebogen ist Teil einer Doktorarbeit an der Steinbeis-Hochschule Berlin - das heißt, Ihre Antworten sind wichtig! Das Ausfüllen wird etwa 5-10 Minuten in Anspruch nehmen. Bitte beantworten Sie alle Fragen zügig und vertrauen Sie Ihrem spontanen Urteil. Wenn dennoch eine Aussage für Sie schwierig einzuschätzen erscheint, versuchen Sie diese bitte trotzdem zu beantworten. Ihre Daten werden mit Sorgfalt behandelt und nur zu Forschungszwecken verwendet.

Viel Freude beim Ausfüllen!

A Screening-Fragen

2 Üben Sie eine regelmäßige Tätigkeit aus? Wählen Sie bitte eine Tätigkeit aus:

- Führungskraft
- Fachkraft, fest angestellt
- Selbstständig/FreiberuflerIn
- WerkstudentIn, Trainee, Azubi
- Minijob
- StudentIn
- SchülerIn, in Ausbildung (ohne Tätigkeit im Unternehmen)
- Hausfrau/Hausmann
- In Rente
- arbeitssuchend
- Keine der oben genannten

3 Wie lange sind Sie in dem Unternehmen, in dem Sie derzeit arbeiten, tätig?

Jahre | Monate

4 Wie viele Stunden gehen Sie dieser Tätigkeit **pro Woche** nach?

Stunden

5 Bitte geben Sie Ihr Geschlecht an:

A männlich | B weiblich

6 Bitte geben Sie Ihr Alter an:

Stunden

B Liebe zum Job

Lesen Sie die folgenden Aussagen genau durch und tragen Sie dann auf der Skala ein, wie sehr Sie dieser Aussage zustimmen oder nicht zustimmen. Beziehen Sie Ihre Antwort auf Ihre aktuelle Arbeit.

		stimme überhaupt nicht zu	stimme nicht zu	stimme eher nicht zu	teils/ teils	stimme eher zu	stimme zu	stimme vollkommen zu
7	Meine Arbeit ist eine Leidenschaft für mich.	1	2	3	4	5	6	7
8	Meine Arbeit ist wichtig für mich.	1	2	3	4	5	6	7
9	Ich kann mir nicht vorstellen, dass mich eine andere Arbeit so glücklich machen würde wie meine aktuelle.	1	2	3	4	5	6	7
10	Arbeitsthemen beschäftigen mich auch über meine Arbeitszeit hinaus.	1	2	3	4	5	6	7
11	Ich bin bereit, viel für meine Arbeit zu geben.	1	2	3	4	5	6	7
12	Meine Arbeit zu verlieren, würde mich traurig machen.	1	2	3	4	5	6	7
13	Ich bin begeistert von meiner Arbeit.	1	2	3	4	5	6	7
14	Es gibt keine Arbeit, die besser zu mir passt.	1	2	3	4	5	6	7
15	Ich habe eine wundervolle Arbeit.	1	2	3	4	5	6	7
16	Ich kann bei meiner Arbeit über Dinge hinwegsehen, die nicht positiv sind.	1	2	3	4	5	6	7

Passion

Appendix 1. Questionnaire Study 2 (1/4)

2

Questionnaire of Study II
Scale Development

Lesen Sie die folgenden Aussagen genau durch und tragen Sie dann auf der Skala ein, wie sehr Sie dieser Aussage zustimmen oder nicht zustimmen. Beziehen Sie Ihre Antwort auf Ihre aktuelle Arbeit.

		stimme überhaupt nicht zu	stimme nicht zu	stimme eher nicht zu	teils/ teils	stimme eher zu	stimme zu	stimme vollkommen zu
17	Ich fühle mich glücklich, wenn ich arbeite.	1	2	3	4	5	6	7
18	Ich fühle mich wohl bei meiner Arbeit.	1	2	3	4	5	6	7
19	Ich vertraue den Menschen in meinem Arbeitsumfeld.	1	2	3	4	5	6	7
20	Ich habe das Gefühl, dass ich das, was ich für meine Arbeit gebe, auch zurück bekomme.	1	2	3	4	5	6	7
21	Ich fühle mich als Person unterstützt bei meiner Arbeit.	1	2	3	4	5	6	7
22	Ich fühle mich mit meiner Arbeit verbunden.	1	2	3	4	5	6	7
23	Ich erlebe Freude bei der Arbeit.	1	2	3	4	5	6	7
24	Die Anliegen meines Arbeitgebers liegen mir am Herzen.	1	2	3	4	5	6	7
25	Ich fühle mich wertgeschätzt bei meiner Arbeit.	1	2	3	4	5	6	7
26	Ich empfinde ein starkes Zugehörigkeitsgefühl zu meiner Arbeit.	1	2	3	4	5	6	7

(Connection)

		stimme überhaupt nicht zu	stimme nicht zu	stimme eher nicht zu	teils/ teils	stimme eher zu	stimme zu	stimme vollkommen zu
27	Meine Arbeit ist aktuell genau die richtige Arbeit für mich.	1	2	3	4	5	6	7
28	Ich würde mir wünschen, meine jetzige Arbeit auch in Zukunft ausüben zu können.	1	2	3	4	5	6	7
29	Ich bin stolz, wenn ich anderen von meiner Arbeit erzähle.	1	2	3	4	5	6	7
30	Ich bin mir sicher, dass ich meine Arbeit liebe.	1	2	3	4	5	6	7
31	Die Entscheidung für meine aktuelle Arbeit war genau die richtige.	1	2	3	4	5	6	7
32	Meine Arbeit ist ein wichtiger Teil dessen, wer ich bin.	1	2	3	4	5	6	7
33	Selbst wenn ich die Gelegenheit hätte, meine Arbeit zu wechseln, würde ich bei meiner aktuellen Arbeit bleiben.	1	2	3	4	5	6	7
34	Ich kann mir nicht vorstellen, meine Arbeit zu kündigen.	1	2	3	4	5	6	7
35	Meine Arbeit hat eine große persönliche Bedeutung für mich.	1	2	3	4	5	6	7
36	Auch wenn es mal schwierig wäre, würde ich bei meiner Arbeitsstelle bleiben.	1	2	3	4	5	6	7

(Commitment)

C   Konvergenz- und Kriteriumsvalidität: Single Item Measures

37	Auf einer Skala von 1 bis 10, wie sehr lieben Sie Ihre Arbeit?

1 = ich liebe meine Arbeit überhaupt nicht bis
10 = Ich liebe meine Arbeit über alles.

1 2 3 4 5 6 7 8 9 10

38	Wie wahrscheinlich ist es, dass Sie Ihre Arbeitsstelle einem Freund oder Kollegen weiterempfehlen?

1 = sehr unwahrscheinlich bis
10 = sehr wahrscheinlich.

0 1 2 3 4 5 6 7 8 9 10

Appendix 1. Questionnaire Study 2 (2/4)

3

Questionnaire of Study II
Scale Development

39 Wenn Sie Ihre Arbeit insgesamt betrachten: Wie zufrieden sind Sie generell?

1 = extrem unzufrieden bis
7 = extrem zufrieden.

1 2 3 4 5 6 7

D **Konvergenzvalidität I**: Passion for Work

Wenn Sie an Ihre Arbeit denken, geben Sie an, inwieweit Sie den folgenden Aussagen zustimmen.

		stimme überhaupt nicht zu	stimme nicht zu	stimme eher nicht zu	teils/ teils	stimme eher zu	stimme zu	stimme vollkommen zu
40	Meine Arbeit ist mir wichtig.	1	2	3	4	5	6	7
41	Meine Arbeit ist eine Leidenschaft für mich.	1	2	3	4	5	6	7
42	Ich mag meine Arbeit sehr.	1	2	3	4	5	6	7
43	Ich verbringe viel Zeit mit meiner Arbeit.	1	2	3	4	5	6	7
44	Meine Arbeit steht in Harmonie zu anderen Aktivitäten in meinem Leben.	1	2	3	4	5	6	7
45	Die neuen Dinge, die ich durch meine Arbeit entdecke, erlauben mir, meine Arbeit noch mehr zu schätzen.	1	2	3	4	5	6	7
46	Meine Arbeit zeigt mir Qualitäten auf, die ich an mir mag.	1	2	3	4	5	6	7
47	Meine Arbeit ermöglicht mir, eine Vielfalt an Erfahrungen zu erleben.	1	2	3	4	5	6	7
48	Meine Arbeit ist sehr gut in mein Leben integriert.	1	2	3	4	5	6	7
49	Meine Arbeit ist in Harmonie mit anderen Dingen, die ein Teil von mir sind.	1	2	3	4	5	6	7

Passion for Work

E **Konvergenzvalidität II**: Affektives Organisationales Commitment

Anhand der folgenden Aussagen möchten wir erfahren, wie sehr Sie sich der Organisation, für die Sie arbeiten, verbunden fühlen. Schätzen Sie bitte ein, wie zutreffend die einzelnen Aussagen für Sie sind.

		stimme überhaupt nicht zu	stimme nicht zu	stimme eher nicht zu	teils/ teils	stimme eher zu	stimme zu	stimme vollkommen zu
50	Ich wäre sehr froh, mein weiteres Arbeitsleben bei meinem Arbeitgeber verbringen zu können.	1	2	3	4	5	6	7
51	Ich rede gerne mit anderen Menschen über meinen Arbeitgeber.	1	2	3	4	5	6	7
52	Ich habe das Gefühl, dass die Probleme meines Arbeitgebers auch meine Probleme sind.	1	2	3	4	5	6	7
53	Ich denke nicht, dass ich mich genauso gut an einen anderen Arbeitgeber binden kann wie an diesen.	1	2	3	4	5	6	7
54	Ich fühle mich bei meinem Arbeitgeber als Teil der Familie.	1	2	3	4	5	6	7
55	Ich fühle mich mit meinem Arbeitgeber emotional verbunden.	1	2	3	4	5	6	7
56	Mein Arbeitgeber hat eine große persönliche Bedeutung für mich.	1	2	3	4	5	6	7
57	Ich empfinde ein starkes Zugehörigkeitsgefühl zu meinem Arbeitgeber.	1	2	3	4	5	6	7

Affective Organizational Commitment

Appendix 1. Questionnaire Study 2 (3/4)

Questionnaire of Study II
Scale Development

F   **Diskriminanzvalidität:** Burnout – Emotionale Erschöpfung

Wenn Sie an Ihre Arbeit denken, geben Sie an, inwieweit Sie den folgenden Aussagen zustimmen.

		nie	mindestens ein paar Mal im Jahr	mindestens ein paar Mal im Monat	einige Male im Monat	ein Mal pro Woche	mehrmals pro Woche	jeden Tag
58	Ich fühle mich durch meine Arbeit emotional erschöpft.	1	2	3	4	5	6	7
59	Ich fühle mich am Ende eines Arbeitstages verbraucht.	1	2	3	4	5	6	7
60	Ich fühle mich bereits ermüdet, wenn ich morgens aufstehe und einen neuen Arbeitstag vor mir liegen sehe.	1	2	3	4	5	6	7
61	Den ganzen Tag mit Menschen zu arbeiten, strengt mich an.	1	2	3	4	5	6	7
62	Ich fühle mich durch meine Arbeit ausgebrannt.	1	2	3	4	5	6	7
63	Ich fühle mich durch meine Arbeit frustriert.	1	2	3	4	5	6	7
64	Ich habe das Gefühl, zu verbissen zu arbeiten.	1	2	3	4	5	6	7
65	Bei der Arbeit in direktem Kontakt zu Menschen zu stehen, stresst mich zu sehr.	1	2	3	4	5	6	7
66	Ich habe das Gefühl, am Ende meiner Kräfte zu sein.	1	2	3	4	5	6	7

Emotional Exhaustion

Vielen Dank für Ihre Zeit.

Appendix 1. Questionnaire Study 2 (4/4)

Final Scale
Job Love Scale (JLS)

? Skala Liebe zum Job

Die nächsten Fragen sollen messen, wie Sie Ihre Arbeit allgemein sehen. Jeder der nächsten können Sie sehr stark zustimmen oder gar nicht zustimmen auf einer Skala von 1 bis 7:

		stimme überhaupt nicht zu	stimme nicht zu	stimme eher nicht zu	teils/ teils	stimme eher zu	stimme zu	stimme vollkommen zu
Passion								
1	Meine Arbeit ist eine Leidenschaft für mich.	1	2	3	4	5	6	7
2	Meine Arbeit ist wichtig für mich.	1	2	3	4	5	6	7
3	Ich bin bereit, viel für meine Arbeit zu geben.	1	2	3	4	5	6	7
4	Meine Arbeit ist ein wichtiger Teil dessen, wer ich bin.	1	2	3	4	5	6	7
5	Meine Arbeit hat eine große persönliche Bedeutung für mich.	1	2	3	4	5	6	7

		stimme überhaupt nicht zu	stimme nicht zu	stimme eher nicht zu	teils/ teils	stimme eher zu	stimme zu	stimme vollkommen zu
Connection								
6	Ich habe Spaß bei meiner Arbeit.	1	2	3	4	5	6	7
7	Ich fühle mich wohl bei meiner Arbeit.	1	2	3	4	5	6	7
8	Ich habe das Gefühl, dass ich das, was ich für meine Arbeit gebe, auch zurück bekomme.	1	2	3	4	5	6	7
9	Ich fühle mich als Person unterstützt bei meiner Arbeit.	1	2	3	4	5	6	7
10	Ich freue mich morgens, wenn ich aufstehe, auf meine Arbeit.	1	2	3	4	5	6	7
11	Ich fühle mich wertgeschätzt bei meiner Arbeit.	1	2	3	4	5	6	7

		stimme überhaupt nicht zu	stimme nicht zu	stimme eher nicht zu	teils/ teils	stimme eher zu	stimme zu	stimme vollkommen zu
Commitment								
12	Mein Job ist aktuell genau der richtige Job für mich.	1	2	3	4	5	6	7
13	Ich würde mir wünschen, meinen jetzigen Job auch in Zukunft ausüben zu können.	1	2	3	4	5	6	7
14	Die Entscheidung für meinen aktuellen Job war genau die richtige.	1	2	3	4	5	6	7
15	Selbst wenn ich die Gelegenheit hätte, meinen Job zu wechseln, würde ich bei meiner aktuellen Arbeit bleiben.	1	2	3	4	5	6	7
16	Auch wenn es mal schwierig wäre, würde ich bei meiner Arbeitsstelle bleiben.	1	2	3	4	5	6	7

Rechnen Sie die Summe aller Werte für Passion, Connection und Commitment zusammen. Berechnen Sie danach den Mittelwert jeder Skala.

Passion	Connection	Commitment
Summe	Summe	Summe
Mittelwert	Mittelwert	Mittelwert

Appendix 2. Job Love Scale (JLS)

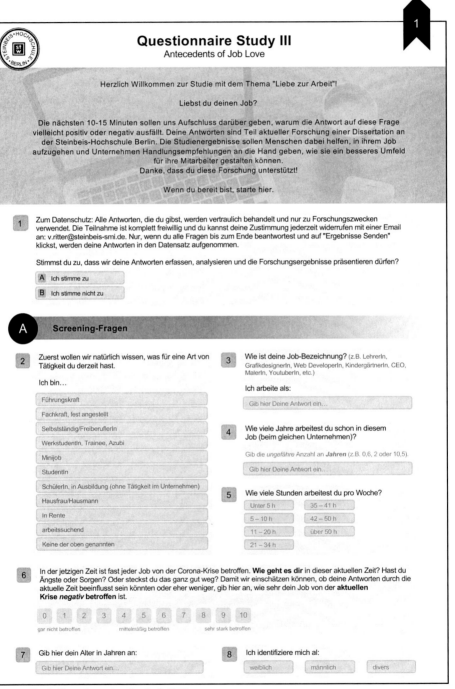

Questionnaire Study III
Antecedents of Job Love

Herzlich Willkommen zur Studie mit dem Thema "Liebe zur Arbeit"!

Liebst du deinen Job?

Die nächsten 10-15 Minuten sollen uns Aufschluss darüber geben, warum die Antwort auf diese Frage vielleicht positiv oder negativ ausfällt. Deine Antworten sind Teil aktueller Forschung einer Dissertation an der Steinbeis-Hochschule Berlin. Die Studienergebnisse sollen Menschen dabei helfen, in ihrem Job aufzugehen und Unternehmen Handlungsempfehlungen an die Hand geben, wie sie ein besseres Umfeld für ihre Mitarbeiter gestalten können.
Danke, dass du diese Forschung unterstützt!

Wenn du bereit bist, starte hier.

1 Zum Datenschutz: Alle Antworten, die du gibst, werden vertraulich behandelt und nur zu Forschungszwecken verwendet. Die Teilnahme ist komplett freiwillig und du kannst deine Zustimmung jederzeit widerrufen mit einer Email an: v.ritter@steinbeis-smi.de. Nur, wenn du alle Fragen bis zum Ende beantwortest und auf "Ergebnisse Senden" klickst, werden deine Antworten in den Datensatz aufgenommen.

Stimmst du zu, dass wir deine Antworten erfassen, analysieren und die Forschungsergebnisse präsentieren dürfen?

A Ich stimme zu

B Ich stimme nicht zu

A Screening-Fragen

2 Zuerst wollen wir natürlich wissen, was für eine Art von Tätigkeit du derzeit hast.

Ich bin...

- Führungskraft
- Fachkraft, fest angestellt
- Selbstständig/FreiberuflerIn
- WerkstudentIn, Trainee, Azubi
- Minijob
- StudentIn
- SchülerIn, in Ausbildung (ohne Tätigkeit im Unternehmen)
- Hausfrau/Hausmann
- In Rente
- arbeitssuchend
- Keine der oben genannten

3 Wie ist deine Job-Bezeichnung? (z.B. LehrerIn, GrafikdesignerIn, Web DeveloperIn, KindergärtnerIn, CEO, MalerIn, YoutuberIn, etc.)

Ich arbeite als:

Gib hier Deine Antwort ein...

4 Wie viele Jahre arbeitest du schon in diesem Job (beim gleichen Unternehmen)?

Gib die *ungefähre* Anzahl an *Jahren* (z.B. 0,6, 2 oder 10,5).

Gib hier Deine Antwort ein...

5 Wie viele Stunden arbeitest du pro Woche?

Unter 5 h	35 – 41 h
5 – 10 h	42 – 50 h
11 – 20 h	über 50 h
21 – 34 h	

6 In der jetzigen Zeit ist fast jeder Job von der Corona-Krise betroffen. **Wie geht es dir** in dieser aktuellen Zeit? Hast du Ängste oder Sorgen? Oder steckst du das ganz gut weg? Damit wir einschätzen können, ob deine Antworten durch die aktuelle Zeit beeinflusst sein könnten oder eher weniger, gib hier an, wie sehr dein Job von der **aktuellen Krise *negativ* betroffen** ist.

0	1	2	3	4	5	6	7	8	9	10

gar nicht betroffen   mittelmäßig betroffen   sehr stark betroffen

7 Gib hier dein Alter in Jahren an:

Gib hier Deine Antwort ein...

8 Ich identifiziere mich al:

weiblich   männlich   divers

Appendix 3. Questionnaire Study 3 (1/5)

Questionnaire Study III
Antecedents of Job Love

B   **Liebe zum Job**

9   Starten wir nun mit den Fragen zur Liebe zum Job: Es gibt verschiedene Meinungen dazu, ob man überhaupt seine Arbeit lieben kann. Was ist deine Meinung?

Kannst du dir vorstellen, dass man seinen Job lieben kann?

- Ja, auf jeden Fall
- Kann ich mir schon vorstellen
- Weiß ich nicht
- Kann ich mir eher nicht vorstellen
- Nein, auf keinen Fall

10   Es gibt verschiedene Thesen dazu, wie Liebe entstehen kann. Schau dir beide Thesen an und entscheide dich für die Version, die dir am Besten zusagen würde:

A „Ich glaube, dass es für jeden den perfekten Job gibt, der zu einem passt. Man muss den perfekten Job nur finden. Wenn man seinen Job nicht liebt, hat man noch nicht den richtigen Job gefunden."

B „Ich glaube, dass man die Liebe für jeden Job entwickeln kann. Das entsteht aber erst nach und nach. Liebe ist ein Prozess. Wenn man seinen Job nicht liebt, hat man sich nicht genügend Mühe oder Zeit gegeben."

11   Auf einer Skala von 1 bis 10: Wie sehr, wenn überhaupt, liebst du deinen Job?

1 = ich liebe meinen Job überhaupt nicht bis
10 = Ich liebe meinen Job über alles.

1   2   3   4   5   6   7   8   9   10

12   Wie wahrscheinlich ist es, dass du deinen Job einem Freund empfehlen würdest?

1 = sehr unwahrscheinlich bis
10 = sehr wahrscheinlich.

1   2   3   4   5   6   7   8   9   10

13   Die nächsten Fragen sollen messen, wie du deine Arbeit im Allgemeinen siehst. Jeder der nächsten Aussagen kannst du zustimmen oder ablehnen. Klicke auf die am besten zutreffende Antwort.

Bitte antworte ehrlich und gewissenhaft. Nur so können wir die Daten später auswerten. Falls du dir die Fragen aus Interesse nur mal durchklicken möchtest, ohne sie zu beantworten, ist das auch Okay. Klicke dies bitte mit Antwort "B" an - dann können wir deine Daten aus der Auswertung ausschließen.

A Ich möchte die folgenden Fragen beantworten

B Ich klicke einfach nur durch, ohne auf die Antwort zu achten

Passion

		stimme überhaupt nicht zu	stimme nicht zu	stimme eher nicht zu	teils/ teils	stimme eher zu	stimme zu	stimme vollkommen zu
14	Meine Arbeit ist eine Leidenschaft für mich.	0	1	2	3	4	5	6
15	Meine Arbeit ist wichtig für mich.	0	1	2	3	4	5	6
16	Ich bin bereit, viel für meine Arbeit zu geben.	0	1	2	3	4	5	6
17	Meine Arbeit ist ein wichtiger Teil dessen, wer ich bin.	0	1	2	3	4	5	6
18	Meine Arbeit hat eine große persönliche Bedeutung für mich.	0	1	2	3	4	5	6

Connection

		stimme überhaupt nicht zu	stimme nicht zu	stimme eher nicht zu	teils/ teils	stimme eher zu	stimme zu	stimme vollkommen zu
19	Ich fühle mich glücklich, wenn ich arbeite.	0	1	2	3	4	5	6
20	Ich fühle mich wohl bei meiner Arbeit.	0	1	2	3	4	5	6
21	Ich habe das Gefühl, dass ich das, was ich für meine Arbeit gebe, auch zurück bekomme.	0	1	2	3	4	5	6
22	Ich fühle mich als Person unterstützt bei meiner Arbeit.	0	1	2	3	4	5	6

Appendix 3. Questionnaire Study 3 (2/5)

Questionnaire Study III
Antecedents of Job Love

		stimme überhaupt nicht zu	stimme nicht zu	stimme eher nicht zu	teils/ teils	stimme eher zu	stimme zu	stimme vollkommen zu
Connection	23	Ich freue mich morgens, wenn ich aufstehe, auf meine Arbeit.	0	1	2	3	4	5	6
	24	Ich fühle mich wertgeschätzt bei meiner Arbeit.	0	1	2	3	4	5	6

		stimme überhaupt nicht zu	stimme nicht zu	stimme eher nicht zu	teils/ teils	stimme eher zu	stimme zu	stimme vollkommen zu
Commitment	25	Mein Job ist aktuell genau der richtige Job für mich.	0	1	2	3	4	5	6
	26	Ich würde mir wünschen, meinen jetzigen Job auch in Zukunft ausüben zu können.	0	1	2	3	4	5	6
	27	Die Entscheidung für meinen aktuellen Job war genau die richtige.	0	1	2	3	4	5	6
	28	Selbst wenn ich die Gelegenheit hätte, meinen Job zu wechseln, würde ich bei meiner aktuellen Arbeit bleiben.	0	1	2	3	4	5	6
	29	Auch wenn es mal schwierig wäre, würde ich bei meiner Arbeitsstelle bleiben.	0	1	2	3	4	5	6

30 Wie zufrieden bist du mit deinem Job insgesamt?

1 = extrem unzufrieden bis
7 = extrem zufrieden.

1 2 3 4 5 6 7

C Einflussfaktoren

31 Im Folgenden geht es um das Thema Wertschätzung und Anerkennung. Anerkennung ist meist bezogen auf die Leistung, die du bringst - wird diese honoriert? Bei Wertschätzung geht es eher um dich als Menschen, wirst du gebraucht und als Person wahrgenommen in deinem Arbeitsumfeld?

Antworte auf die Folgenden Fragen, wie du dich *im Allgemeinen* fühlst.

		stimme überhaupt nicht zu	stimme nicht zu	stimme eher nicht zu	teils/ teils	stimme eher zu	stimme zu	stimme vollkommen zu
Wertschätzung	32	Im Allgemeinen fühle ich mich in meinem Arbeitsumfeld als Person wertgeschätzt.	0	1	2	3	4	5	6
	33	Im Allgemeinen bekomme ich genügend Anerkennung für die Arbeit, die ich mache.	0	1	2	3	4	5	6
	34	Ich habe das Gefühl, dass ich bei der Arbeit gebraucht werde.	0	1	2	3	4	5	6
	35	Mein Arbeitgeber gibt mir das Gefühl, dass ich ein wertvoller Mitarbeiter für mein Unternehmen bin.	0	1	2	3	4	5	6

36 Zuerst geht dabei um vorgesetzte Personen*. Es steht immer wieder im Raum, wie viel Einfluss die Vorgesetzten auf ihre Mitarbeiter haben. Darum ist es wichtig zu verstehen, wie dein Verhältnis mit dem oder denen ist, die über dir stehen. Das kann deine Chefin sein, oder auch ein Kollege, der dir übergestellt ist. Falls du niemanden über dir hast, überspringe die Folgenden Fragen mit Klick auf Antwort "B".

*Der Einfachheit halber wurde auf die Verwendung beider Geschlechter verzichtet - so kannst du die Fragen besser lesen. Vorgesetzter bezieht sich also genauso auf deine Vorgesetzte oder, bei mehreren, auf diese.

A Ich habe jemanden, der mir vorgesetzt ist

B Ich habe niemanden, der mir vorgesetzt ist

		stimme überhaupt nicht zu	stimme nicht zu	stimme eher nicht zu	teils/ teils	stimme eher zu	stimme zu	stimme vollkommen zu
Vorgesetzte	37	Ich fühle mich wertgeschätzt von meinem Vorgesetzten.	0	1	2	3	4	5	6
	38	Wenn ich ein Anliegen habe, nimmt sich mein Vorgesetzter Zeit für mich.	0	1	2	3	4	5	6

Appendix 3. Questionnaire Study 3 (3/5)

4

Questionnaire Study III
Antecedents of Job Love

		stimme überhaupt nicht zu	stimme nicht zu	stimme eher nicht zu	teils/ teils	stimme eher zu	stimme zu	stimme vollkommen zu
Vorgesetzte	39	Wenn ich etwas gut gemacht habe, lobt mich mein Vorgesetzter.	0	1	2	3	4	5	6
	40	Ich kann auf die Hilfe meines Vorgesetzten zählen, wenn ich sie brauche.	0	1	2	3	4	5	6
	41	Ich habe das Gefühl, dass mir mein Vorgesetzter vertraut.	0	1	2	3	4	5	6
	42	Mein Vorgesetzter gibt mir das Gefühl, dass er dankbar für meine Arbeit ist.	0	1	2	3	4	5	6

43 Nun geht es um das Verhältnis zu deinen Kollegen. Ist es ein positives Verhältnis? Verbringst du gerne Zeit mit den Menschen, mit denen du arbeitest? Wie siehst du das?

Falls du keine Kollegen hast, klicke auf Antwort "B", um die Fragen zu überspringen.

A Ich arbeite mit Kollegen zusammen.

B Ich habe keine Kollegen.

		stimme überhaupt nicht zu	stimme nicht zu	stimme eher nicht zu	teils/ teils	stimme eher zu	stimme zu	stimme vollkommen zu
Kollegen	44	Ich habe ein sehr gutes Verhältnis zu meinen Kollegen.	0	1	2	3	4	5	6
	45	Ich habe das Gefühl, dass meine Kollegen mich als Kollegen/in wertschätzen.	0	1	2	3	4	5	6
	46	Meine Kollegen unterstützen mich, wenn ich ihre Hilfe brauche.	0	1	2	3	4	5	6
	47	Meine Kollegen verbringen gerne Zeit mit mir (z.B. zusammen Mittagessen).	0	1	2	3	4	5	6
	48	Ich habe bei der Arbeit jemanden, den ich als Freund bezeichnen würde.	0	1	2	3	4	5	6
	49	Wenn es einen Anlass gibt, bemühen sich meine Kollegen, mir eine Freude zu machen (z.B. mit einem kleinen Geschenk).	0	1	2	3	4	5	6

50 Manche Menschen arbeiten weniger mit Kollegen oder Vorgesetzten, sondern haben viel Kundenkontakt: Für Lehrer sind es die Schüler, für eine Fotografin die Menschen, die sie fotografiert und für einen Krankenpfleger die Patienten, die er betreut.

Falls das nicht auf dich zutrifft, kannst du diese Fragen mit Klick auf Antwort "B" überspringen.

A Ich habe Kunden, für die ich arbeite.

B Ich arbeite nicht mit Kunden zusammen.

		stimme überhaupt nicht zu	stimme nicht zu	stimme eher nicht zu	teils/ teils	stimme eher zu	stimme zu	stimme vollkommen zu
Kunden	51	Ich denke, dass meisten Menschen für die ich arbeite, meine Arbeit wertschätzen.	0	1	2	3	4	5	6
	52	Es ist eher selten, dass ich Kritik für meine Arbeit von meinen Kunden zu hören bekomme.	0	1	2	3	4	5	6
	53	Ich bekomme oft ein "Dankeschön" von meinen Kunden für meine Arbeit zu hören.	0	1	2	3	4	5	6

Die folgenden Fragen beschäftigen sich damit, wie du deinen Job findest. Vielen ist z.B. wichtig, wie viel sie verdienen. Es gibt aber auch andere Faktoren, die wichtig sein können. Wie das genau bei dir aussieht, werden wir mit den nächsten Fragen abfragen.

		stimme überhaupt nicht zu	stimme nicht zu	stimme eher nicht zu	teils/ teils	stimme eher zu	stimme zu	stimme vollkommen zu
Purpose	54	Meine Arbeit erfüllt mich persönlich mit Sinn.	0	1	2	3	4	5	6
	55	Ich denke, dass ich mit meiner Arbeit etwas Sinnvolles für Andere tue.	0	1	2	3	4	5	6
	56	Es gibt selten Momente, wo ich mich frage, wozu ich den Job überhaupt mache.	0	1	2	3	4	5	6

Appendix 3. Questionnaire Study 3 (4/5)

5

Questionnaire Study III
Antecedents of Job Love

			stimme überhaupt nicht zu	stimme nicht zu	stimme eher nicht zu	teils/ teils	stimme eher zu	stimme zu	stimme vollkommen zu
Person-Job-Fit	57	Ich habe genau die Fähigkeiten, die man für den Job braucht, den ich mache.	0	1	2	3	4	5	6
	58	Mein Job passt zu mir.	0	1	2	3	4	5	6
	59	Es gibt keinen anderen Job, der besser zu mir passen würde, als mein aktueller Job.	0	1	2	3	4	5	6

			stimme überhaupt nicht zu	stimme nicht zu	stimme eher nicht zu	teils/ teils	stimme eher zu	stimme zu	stimme vollkommen zu
Kompetenz	60	Ich bin richtig gut in dem, was ich bei meiner Arbeit tue.	0	1	2	3	4	5	6
	61	Bei meiner Arbeit kann ich zeigen, was ich kann.	0	1	2	3	4	5	6
	62	Ich fühle mich kompetent in meinem Job.	0	1	2	3	4	5	6

			stimme überhaupt nicht zu	stimme nicht zu	stimme eher nicht zu	teils/ teils	stimme eher zu	stimme zu	stimme vollkommen zu
Autonomie	63	Bei meiner Arbeit habe ich die Freiheit, zu entscheiden, wie ich meine Arbeit mache.	0	1	2	3	4	5	6
	64	Ich habe bei meiner Arbeit selten das Gefühl, dass andere das kontrollieren würden, was ich tue.	0	1	2	3	4	5	6
	65	Mein Arbeitgeber gibt mir die Möglichkeit, meine Zeit frei einzuteilen.	0	1	2	3	4	5	6
	66	Mein Job ermöglicht es mir, Beruf und Familie* gut miteinander zu vereinbaren. *bzw. dein Privatleben	0	1	2	3	4	5	6

			stimme überhaupt nicht zu	stimme nicht zu	stimme eher nicht zu	teils/ teils	stimme eher zu	stimme zu	stimme vollkommen zu
Entwicklung	67	Mein Job bietet mir die Möglichkeit, mich noch weiter zu entwickeln.	0	1	2	3	4	5	6
	68	Ich bin zufrieden mit den Karriere- und Aufstiegsmöglichkeiten bei meinem Arbeitgeber.	0	1	2	3	4	5	6

D Abschluss

69 Möchtest du noch etwas zum Thema sagen? Zum Beispiel, warum du deine Arbeit liebst oder nicht liebst? Oder Feedback zum Fragebogen?

Hier hast du die Möglichkeit, noch etwas dazu schreiben, wenn du möchtest. Sonst swipe einfach weiter.

Gib hier Deine Antwort ein…

Vielen, vielen Dank für das Beantworten!

Bitte Klicke unten auf ERGEBNISSE SENDEN, um deine Antworten abzusenden.
Wir wissen - es waren viele Fragen!! Aber deine Antworten sind super wichtig für neue Erkenntnisse darüber, wie Menschen sich bei ihrer Arbeit wohl fühlen können und aufblühen. Mit deiner Teilnahme bist du Teil dieser Forschung und leistest damit auch einen Beitrag für den Forschungsoutput der Steinbeis-Hochschule. Falls du Fragen hast, kannst du uns gerne kontaktieren:
v.ritter@steinbeis-smi.de.

Gerne kannst du den Fragebogen auch mit Kollegen oder Freunden teilen, wenn er dir gefallen hat.

Viktoria

Appendix 3. Questionnaire Study 3 (5/5)

Appendix 4. Detailed Tables of Group Comparisons

Appendix 4.1 Detailed Analyses of Purpose

Appendix 4.1.1 Group Statistics

	Item	Job Love Type	n	M	SD	SE
Purpose	Scale Average	Type 1	59	3,02	1,32	0,17
		Type 8	55	5,26	0,67	0,09
Item 1	My work fills me with meaning.	Type 1	59	2,76	1,51	0,20
		Type 8	55	5,35	0,73	0,10
Item 2	With my work, I am doing something useful for others.	Type 1	59	3,56	1,70	0,22
		Type 8	55	5,35	0,84	0,11
Item 3	There are rarely moments when I wonder what I'm doing the job for.	Type 1	59	2,73	1,60	0,21
		Type 8	55	5,07	0,98	0,13

Appendix 4.1.2 Test of Group Mean Difference

	Variances are	Levene's Test for Homogeneity of Variance		t-test for Mean Difference				
		F	Sig.	T	df	Sig. one-sided	95% Confidence Interval	
							Upper Value	Lower Value
Purpose	equal	27,097	0,000	-11,322	112,000	0,000	-2,629	-1,846
	not equal			-11,561	87,199	0,000	-2,622	-1,853
Item 1	equal	24,738	0,000	-11,489	112,000	0,000	-3,028	-2,137
	not equal			-11,746	84,639	0,000	-3,020	-2,146
Item 2	equal	19,126	0,000	-7,044	112,000	0,000	-2,289	-1,284
	not equal			-7,196	86,386	0,000	-2,280	-1,293
Item 3	equal	16,335	0,000	-9,373	112,000	0,000	-2,839	-1,848
	not equal			-9,525	97,243	0,000	-2,832	-1,856

Appendix 4.1.3 Detailed Analyses of Scale Items (1/2)

Item:	My work fills me with meaning.											
	do not agree at all	do not agree	do rather not agree	neutral	do rather agree	do agree	do completely agree	Total	Share of People who do agree (Answer: 5, 6)		Share of People who do not agree (Answer: 0, 1)	
	0	1	2	3	4	5	6	Total				
Type 1	6	7	10	15	15	5	1	59	Share of People who do agree (Answer: 5, 6)		Share of People who do not agree (Answer: 0, 1)	
Type 8	0	0	0	1	5	23	26	55				
Total	6	7	10	16	20	28	27	114				
Type 1 %	10,2	11,9	16,9	25,4	25,4	8,5	1,7		Type 1 %	10,2	Type 1 %	22,0
Type 8 %	0,0	0,0	0,0	1,8	9,1	41,8	47,3		Type 8 %	89,1	Type 8 %	0,0

Appendix 4.1.3 Detailed Analyses of Scale Items (2/2)

Item:	With my work, I am doing something useful for others.											
	do not agree at all	do not agree	do rather not agree	neutral	do rather agree	do agree	do completely agree	Total				
	0	1	2	3	4	5	6	Total				
Type 1	4	6	2	13	16	11	7	59	Share of People who do agree (Answer: 5, 6)		Share of People who do not agree (Answer: 0, 1)	
Type 8	0	0	0	2	7	16	30	55				
Total	4	6	2	15	23	27	37	114				
Type 1 %	6,8	10,2	3,4	22,0	27,1	18,6	11,9		Type 1 %	30,5	Type 1 %	16,9
Type 8 %	0,0	0,0	0,0	3,6	12,7	29,1	54,5		Type 8 %	83,6	Type 8 %	0,0

Item:	There are rarely moments when I wonder what I'm doing the job for.											
	do not agree at all	do not agree	do rather not agree	neutral	do rather agree	do agree	do completely agree	Total				
	0	1	2	3	4	5	6	Total				
Type 1	5	10	10	16	10	5	3	59	Share of People who do agree (Answer: 5, 6)		Share of People who do not agree (Answer: 0, 1)	
Type 8	0	1	0	2	8	24	20	55				
Total	5	11	10	18	18	29	23	114				
Type 1 %	8,5	16,9	16,9	27,1	16,9	8,5	5,1		Type 1 %	13,6	Type 1 %	25,4
Type 8 %	0,0	1,8	0,0	3,6	14,5	43,6	36,4		Type 8 %	80,0	Type 8 %	1,8

Appendix 4.2 Detailed Analyses of Growth Opportunities

Appendix 4.2.1 Group Statistics

	Item	Job Love Type	n	M	SD	SE
Growth Opportunities	Scale Average	Type 1	59	2,95	1,63	0,21
		Type 8	55	4,78	1,09	0,15
Item 1	My job gives me the opportunity to develop myself further.	Type 1	59	3,20	1,70	0,22
		Type 8	55	4,85	1,42	0,19
Item 2	I am satisfied with the career and career opportunities at my employer	Type 1	59	2,69	1,91	0,25
		Type 8	55	4,71	1,17	0,16

Appendix 4.2.2 Test of Group Mean Difference

	Levene's Test for Homogeneity of Variance			t-test for Mean Difference				
	Variances are	F	Sig.	T	df	Sig. one-sided	95% Confidence Interval	
							Upper Value	Lower Value
Growth Opportunities	equal	9,585	0,002	-7,013	112,000	0,000	-2,350	-1,315
	not equal			-7,109	101,756	0,000	-2,344	-1,321
Item 1	equal	2,337	0,129	-5,608	112,000	0,000	-2,235	-1,068
	not equal			-5,643	110,702	0,000	-2,231	-1,071
Item 2	equal	14,085	0,000	-6,750	112,000	0,000	-2,605	-1,423
	not equal			-6,860	97,106	0,000	-2,597	-1,431

Appendix 4.2.3 Detailed Analyses of Scale Items

Item:	My job gives me the opportunity to develop myself further.											
	do not agree at all	do not agree	do rather not agree	neutral	do rather agree	do agree	do completely agree	Total				
	0	1	2	3	4	5	6	Total				
Type 1	4	7	8	16	6	14	4	59	Share of People who do agree (Answer: 5, 6)		Share of People who do not agree (Answer: 0, 1)	
Type 8	1	1	1	6	10	10	26	55				
Total	5	8	9	22	16	24	30	114				
Type 1 %	6,8	11,9	13,6	27,1	10,2	23,7	6,8		Type 1 %	30,5	Type 1 %	18,6
Type 8 %	1,8	1,8	1,8	10,9	18,2	18,2	47,3		Type 8 %	65,5	Type 8 %	3,6

Item:	I am satisfied with the career and career opportunities at my employer											
	do not agree at all	do not agree	do rather not agree	neutral	do rather agree	do agree	do completely agree	Total				
	0	1	2	3	4	5	6	Total				
Type 1	9	9	11	11	6	7	6	55	Share of People who do agree (Answer: 5, 6)		Share of People who do not agree (Answer: 0, 1)	
Type 8	0	0	1	9	14	12	19	55				
Total	9	9	12	20	20	19	25	114				
Type 1 %	16,4	16,4	20,0	20,0	10,9	12,7	10,9		Type 1 %	23,6	Type 1 %	32,7
Type 8 %	0,0	0,0	1,8	16,4	25,5	21,8	34,5		Type 8 %	56,4	Type 8 %	0,0

Appendix 4.3 Detailed Analyses of Salary Satisfaction

Appendix 4.3.1 Group Statistics

	Item	Job Love Type	n	M	SD	SE
Salary Satisfaction	Scale Average	Type 1	59	3,16	1,67	0,22
		Type 8	55	4,28	1,39	0,19
Item 1	My employer pays me an attractive salary.	Type 1	59	4,66	1,23	0,16
		Type 8	55	5,07	0,90	0,12
Item 2	Compared to others, my employer offers more money (including additional benefits).	Type 1	59	3,44	1,64	0,21
		Type 8	55	4,71	1,18	0,16
Item 3	A good salary is important to me.	Type 1	59	2,88	1,90	0,25
		Type 8	55	3,85	1,83	0,25

Appendix 4.3.2 Test of Group Mean Difference

| | Variances are | Levene's Test for Homogeneity of Variance | | | t-test for Mean Difference | | | | |
| | | F | Sig. | T | df | Sig. one-sided | 95% Confidence Interval | | |
							Upper Value	Lower Value
Salary Satisfaction	equal	2,946	0,089	-3,872	112,000	0,000	-1,694	-0,547
	not equal			-3,897	110,648	0,000	-1,691	-0,551
Item 1	equal	9,687	0,002	-2,032	112,000	0,023	-0,813	-0,010
	not equal			-2,053	106,264	0,021	-0,809	-0,014
Item 2	equal	6,081	0,015	-4,703	112,000	0,000	-1,803	-0,734
	not equal			-4,756	105,363	0,000	-1,797	-0,740
Item 3	equal	0,591	0,444	-2,779	112,000	0,003	-1,667	-0,279
	not equal			-2,783	111,890	0,003	-1,666	-0,280

Appendix 4.3.3 Detailed Analyses of Scale Items

Item:	My employer pays me an attractive salary.							
	do not agree at all	do not agree	do rather not agree	neutral	do rather agree	do agree	do completely agree	Total
	0	1	2	3	4	5	6	
Type 1	5	1	10	13	12	13	5	59
Type 8	0	0	3	6	12	17	17	55
Total	5	1	13	19	24	30	22	114
Type 1 %	8,5	1,7	16,9	22,0	20,3	22,0	8,5	
Type 8 %	0,0	0,0	5,5	10,9	21,8	30,9	30,9	

	Share of People who do agree (Answer: 5, 6)	Share of People who do not agree (Answer: 0, 1)
Type 1 %	30,5	Type 1 % 10,2
Type 8 %	61,8	Type 8 % 0,0

Item:	Compared to others, my employer offers more money (including additional benefits).							
	do not agree at all	do not agree	do rather not agree	neutral	do rather agree	do agree	do completely agree	Total
	0	1	2	3	4	5	6	
Type 1	7	8	14	9	4	11	6	59
Type 8	6	2	2	9	9	19	8	55
Total	13	10	16	18	13	30	14	114
Type 1 %	11,9	13,6	23,7	15,3	6,8	18,6	10,2	
Type 8 %	10,9	3,6	3,6	16,4	16,4	34,5	14,5	

	Share of People who do agree (Answer: 5, 6)	Share of People who do not agree (Answer: 0, 1)
Type 1 %	28,8	Type 1 % 25,4
Type 8 %	49,1	Type 8 % 14,5

Item:	A good salary is important to me.							
	do not agree at all	do not agree	do rather not agree	neutral	do rather agree	do agree	do completely agree	Total
	0	1	2	3	4	5	6	
Type 1	1	0	1	9	14	15	19	59
Type 8	0	0	0	4	8	23	20	55
Total	1	0	1	13	22	38	39	114
Type 1 %	1,7	0,0	1,7	15,3	23,7	25,4	32,2	
Type 8 %	0,0	0,0	0,0	7,3	14,5	41,8	36,4	

	Share of People who do agree (Answer: 5, 6)	Share of People who do not agree (Answer: 0, 1)
Type 1 %	57,6	Type 1 % 1,7
Type 8 %	78,2	Type 8 % 0,0

Appendix 4.4 Detailed Analyses of Person-Job-Fit

Appendix 4.4.1 Group Statistics

	Item	Job Love Type	n	M	SD	SE
Person-Job-Fit	Scale Average	Type 1	59	3,02	1,18	0,15
		Type 8	55	5,10	0,58	0,08
Item 1	I have exactly the skills you need for the job that I do.	Type 1	59	4,15	1,45	0,19
		Type 8	55	5,40	0,71	0,10
Item 2	My job suits me.	Type 1	59	3,49	1,55	0,20
		Type 8	55	5,58	0,60	0,08
Item 3	There is no other job that would suit me better than my current job.	Type 1	59	1,42	1,39	0,18
		Type 8	55	4,33	1,29	0,17

Appendix 4.4.2 Test of Group Mean Difference

	Levene's Test for Homogeneity of Variance			t-test for Mean Difference				
	Variances are	F	Sig.	T	df	Sig. one-sided	95% Confidence Interval	
							Upper Value	Lower Value
Person-Job-Fit	equal	21,532	0,000	-11,763	112,000	0,000	-2,431	-1,730
	not equal			-12,019	85,938	0,000	-2,425	-1,736
Item 1	equal	28,490	0,000	-5,774	112,000	0,000	-1,676	-0,819
	not equal			-5,900	85,634	0,000	-1,668	-0,827
Item 2	equal	32,019	0,000	-9,386	112,000	0,000	-2,532	-1,649
	not equal			-9,635	76,057	0,000	-2,522	-1,658
Item 3	equal	1,348	0,248	-11,520	112,000	0,000	-3,403	-2,404
	not equal			-11,551	111,998	0,000	-3,402	-2,405

Appendix 4.4.3 Detailed Analyses of Scale Items (1/2)

Item:	I have exactly the skills you need for the job that I do.											
	do not agree at all	do not agree	do rather not agree	neutral	do rather agree	do agree	do completely agree	Total				
	0	1	2	3	4	5	6	Total				
Type 1	0	2	7	11	12	14	13	59	Share of People who do agree (Answer: 5, 6)		Share of People who do not agree (Answer: 0, 1)	
Type 8	0	0	0	1	4	22	28	55				
Total	0	2	7	12	16	36	41	114				
Type 1 %	0,0	3,4	11,9	18,6	20,3	23,7	22,0		Type 1 %	45,8	Type 1 %	3,4
Type 8 %	0,0	0,0	0,0	1,8	7,3	40,0	50,9		Type 8 %	90,9	Type 8 %	0,0

Appendix 4.4.3 Detailed Analyses of Scale Items (2/2)

Item:	My job suits me.											
	do not agree at all	do not agree	do rather not agree	neutral	do rather agree	do agree	do completely agree					
	0	1	2	3	4	5	6	Total				
Type 1	3	5	5	13	17	12	4	59	**Share of People who do agree** (Answer: 5, 6)		**Share of People who do not agree** (Answer: 0, 1)	
Type 8	0	0	0	0	3	17	35	55				
Total	3	5	5	13	20	29	39	114				
Type 1 %	5,1	8,5	8,5	22,0	28,8	20,3	6,8		**Type 1 %**	27,1	**Type 1 %**	13,6
Type 8 %	0,0	0,0	0,0	0,0	5,5	30,9	63,6		**Type 8 %**	94,5	**Type 8 %**	0,0

Item:	There is no other job that would suit me better than my current job.											
	do not agree at all	do not agree	do rather not agree	neutral	do rather agree	do agree	do completely agree					
	0	1	2	3	4	5	6	Total				
Type 1	21	12	12	10	2	2	0	59	**Share of People who do agree** (Answer: 5, 6)		**Share of People who do not agree** (Answer: 0, 1)	
Type 8	1	1	1	10	15	17	10	55				
Total	22	13	13	20	17	19	10	114				
Type 1 %	35,6	20,3	20,3	16,9	3,4	3,4	0,0		**Type 1 %**	3,4	**Type 1 %**	55,9
Type 8 %	1,8	1,8	1,8	18,2	27,3	30,9	18,2		**Type 8 %**	49,1	**Type 8 %**	3,6

Appendix 4.5 Detailed Analyses of Competence

Appendix 4.5.1 Group Statistics

	Item	Job Love Type	n	M	SD	SE
Competence	Scale Average	Type 1	59	4,05	1,17	0,15
		Type 8	55	5,36	0,61	0,08
Item 1	I am really good at what I do in my work.	Type 1	59	4,29	1,29	0,17
		Type 8	55	5,33	0,77	0,10
Item 2	In my work, I can show what I can do.	Type 1	59	3,59	1,40	0,18
		Type 8	55	5,36	0,70	0,10
Item 3	I feel competent in my job.	Type 1	59	4,27	1,40	0,18
		Type 8	55	5,40	0,74	0,10

Appendix 4.5.2 Test of Group Mean Difference

		Levene's Test for Homogeneity of Variance			t-test for Mean Difference				
	Variances are	F	Sig.	T	df	Sig. one-sided	95% Confidence Interval		
							Upper Value	Lower Value	
Competence	equal	13,786	0,000	-7,445	112,000	0,000	-1,662	-0,963	
	not equal			-7,596	89,072	0,000	-1,656	-0,969	
Item 1	equal	10,372	0,002	-5,182	112,000	0,000	-1,436	-0,642	
	not equal			-5,269	95,975	0,000	-1,431	-0,648	
Item 2	equal	22,757	0,000	-8,419	112,000	0,000	-2,187	-1,354	
	not equal			-8,600	86,716	0,000	-2,180	-1,361	
Item 3	equal	17,472	0,000	-5,332	112,000	0,000	-1,548	-0,709	
	not equal			-5,441	89,039	0,000	-1,541	-0,717	

Appendix 4.5.3 Detailed Analyses of Scale Items

Item:	I am really good at what I do in my work.										
	do not agree at all	do not agree	do rather not agree	neutral	do rather agree	do agree	do completely agree				
	0	1	2	3	4	5	6	Total			
Type 1	0	3	2	9	15	21	9	59	Share of People who do agree (Answer: 5, 6)		Share of People who do not agree (Answer: 0, 1)
Type 8	0	0	0	1	7	20	27	55			
Total	0	3	2	10	22	41	36	114			
Type 1 %	0,0	5,1	3,4	15,3	25,4	35,6	15,3		Type 1 %	50,8	Type 1 % 5,1
Type 8 %	0,0	0,0	0,0	1,8	12,7	36,4	49,1		Type 8 %	85,5	Type 8 % 0,0

Item:	In my work, I can show what I can do.										
	do not agree at all	do not agree	do rather not agree	neutral	do rather agree	do agree	do completely agree				
	0	1	2	3	4	5	6	Total			
Type 1	2	1	10	14	15	13	4	59	Share of People who do agree (Answer: 5, 6)		Share of People who do not agree (Answer: 0, 1)
Type 8	0	0	0	1	4	24	26	55			
Total	2	1	10	15	19	37	30	114			
Type 1 %	3,4	1,7	16,9	23,7	25,4	22,0	6,8		Type 1 %	28,8	Type 1 % 5,1
Type 8 %	0,0	0,0	0,0	1,8	7,3	43,6	47,3		Type 8 %	90,9	Type 8 % 0,0

Item:	I feel competent in my job.										
	do not agree at all	do not agree	do rather not agree	neutral	do rather agree	do agree	do completely agree				
	0	1	2	3	4	5	6	Total			
Type 1	1	2	2	11	14	17	12	59	Share of People who do agree (Answer: 5, 6)		Share of People who do not agree (Answer: 0, 1)
Type 8	0	0	0	2	2	23	28	55			
Total	1	2	2	13	16	40	40	114			
Type 1 %	1,7	3,4	3,4	18,6	23,7	28,8	20,3		Type 1 %	49,2	Type 1 % 5,1
Type 8 %	0,0	0,0	0,0	3,6	3,6	41,8	50,9		Type 8 %	92,7	Type 8 % 0,0

Appendix 4.6 Detailed Analyses of Autonomy

Appendix 4.6.1 Group Statistics

	Item	Job Love Type	n	M	SD	SE
Autonomy	Scale Average	Type 1	59	3,82	1,39	0,18
		Type 8	55	5,02	0,76	0,10
Item 1	At work, I have the freedom to choose how I do my job.	Type 1	59	4,12	1,61	0,21
		Type 8	55	5,51	0,88	0,12
Item 2	In my work, I rarely feel that others control what I do.	Type 1	59	3,59	1,96	0,26
		Type 8	55	4,87	1,11	0,15
Item 3	My employer gives me the opportunity to schedule my time freely.	Type 1	59	3,95	1,79	0,23
		Type 8	55	5,20	1,22	0,17
Item 4	My job enables me to combine work and family.	Type 1	59	3,63	1,58	0,21
		Type 8	55	4,49	1,35	0,18

Appendix 4.6.2 Test of Group Mean Difference

	Variances are	Levene's Test for Homogeneity of Variance		t-test for Mean Difference			95% Confidence Interval	
		F	Sig.	T	df	Sig. one-sided	Upper Value	Lower Value
Autonomy	equal	19,123	0,000	-5,633	112,000	0,000	-1,617	-0,775
	not equal			-5,743	90,900	0,000	-1,610	-0,782
Item 1	equal	15,595	0,000	-5,667	112,000	0,000	-1,877	-0,904
	not equal			-5,777	91,070	0,000	-1,869	-0,912
Item 2	equal	30,317	0,000	-4,255	112,000	0,000	-1,875	-0,684
	not equal			-4,333	92,856	0,000	-1,866	-0,693
Item 3	equal	9,518	0,003	-4,333	112,000	0,000	-1,823	-0,679
	not equal			-4,389	103,057	0,000	-1,816	-0,686
Item 4	equal	2,712	0,102	-3,138	112,000	0,001	-1,409	-0,318
	not equal			-3,156	111,179	0,001	-1,406	-0,321

Appendix 4.6.3 Detailed Analyses of Scale Items (1/2)

Item:	At work, I have the freedom to choose how I do my job.									
	do not agree at all	do not agree	do rather not agree	neutral	do rather agree	do agree	do completely agree			
	0	1	2	3	4	5	6	Total		
Type 1	3	1	4	11	12	15	13	59	**Share of People who do agree** (Answer: 5, 6)	**Share of People who do not agree** (Answer: 0, 1)
Type 8	0	0	0	3	5	8	39	55		
Total	3	1	4	14	17	23	52	114		
Type 1 %	5,1	1,7	6,8	18,6	20,3	25,4	22,0		**Type 1 %** 47,5	**Type 1 %** 6,8
Type 8 %	0,0	0,0	0,0	5,5	9,1	14,5	70,9		**Type 8 %** 85,5	**Type 8 %** 0,0

Appendix 4.6.3 Detailed Analyses of Scale Items (2/2)

Item:	In my work, I rarely feel that others control what I do.											
	do not agree at all	do not agree	do rather not agree	neutral	do rather agree	do agree	do complete ly agree					
	0	1	2	3	4	5	6	Total				
Type 1	4	8	6	9	8	11	13	59	Share of People who do agree (Answer: 5, 6)		Share of People who do not agree (Answer: 0, 1)	
Type 8	0	1	0	7	6	24	17	55				
Total	4	9	6	16	14	35	30	114				
Type 1 %	6,8	13,6	10,2	15,3	13,6	18,6	22,0		Type 1 %	40,7	Type 1 %	20,3
Type 8 %	0,0	1,8	0,0	12,7	10,9	43,6	30,9		Type 8 %	74,5	Type 8 %	1,8

Item:	My employer gives me the opportunity to schedule my time freely.											
	do not agree at all	do not agree	do rather not agree	neutral	do rather agree	do agree	do complete ly agree					
	0	1	2	3	4	5	6	Total				
Type 1	4	3	6	7	9	19	11	59	Share of People who do agree (Answer: 5, 6)		Share of People who do not agree (Answer: 0, 1)	
Type 8	1	0	0	5	6	11	32	55				
Total	5	3	6	12	15	30	43	114				
Type 1 %	6,8	5,1	10,2	11,9	15,3	32,2	18,6		Type 1 %	50,8	Type 1 %	11,9
Type 8 %	1,8	0,0	0,0	9,1	10,9	20,0	58,2		Type 8 %	78,2	Type 8 %	1,8

Item:	My job enables me to combine work and family.											
	do not agree at all	do not agree	do rather not agree	neutral	do rather agree	do agree	do complete ly agree					
	0	1	2	3	4	5	6	Total				
Type 1	1	4	12	10	11	14	7	59	Share of People who do agree (Answer: 5, 6)		Share of People who do not agree (Answer: 0, 1)	
Type 8	1	0	2	11	10	16	15	55				
Total	2	4	14	21	21	30	22	114				
Type 1 %	1,7	6,8	20,3	16,9	18,6	23,7	11,9		Type 1 %	35,6	Type 1 %	8,5
Type 8 %	1,8	0,0	3,6	20,0	18,2	29,1	27,3		Type 8 %	56,4	Type 8 %	1,8

Appendix 4.7 Detailed Analyses of General Appreciation

Appendix 4.7.1 Group Statistics

	Item	Job Love Type	n	M	SD	SE
Appreciation	Scale Average	Type 1	59	3,28	1,23	0,16
		Type 8	55	5,28	0,55	0,07
Item 1	In general, I feel valued as a person in my work environment.	Type 1	59	3,47	1,44	0,19
		Type 8	55	5,38	0,71	0,10
Item 2	In general, I get enough appreciation for the work I do.	Type 1	59	3,00	1,59	0,21
		Type 8	55	5,11	0,83	0,11
Item 3	I feel like I'm needed at work.	Type 1	59	3,76	1,55	0,20
		Type 8	55	5,36	1,01	0,14
Item 4	My employer gives me the feeling that I am a valuable employee.	Type 1	59	2,86	1,48	0,19
		Type 8	55	5,27	0,83	0,11

Appendix 4.7.2 Test of Group Mean Difference

	Variances are	Levene's Test for Homogeneity of Variance		t-test for Mean Difference			95% Confidence Interval	
		F	Sig.	T	df	Sig. one-sided	Upper Value	Lower Value
Appreciation	equal	29,694	0,000	-11,097	112,000	0,000	-2,365	-1,648
	not equal			-11,363	81,369	0,000	-2,358	-1,655
Item 1	equal	29,372	0,000	-8,861	112,000	0,000	-2,334	-1,481
	not equal			-9,055	85,622	0,000	-2,326	-1,489
Item 2	equal	25,355	0,000	-8,795	112,000	0,000	-2,584	-1,634
	not equal			-8,974	88,929	0,000	-2,576	-1,642
Item 3	equal	10,980	0,001	-6,500	112,000	0,000	-2,089	-1,113
	not equal			-6,594	100,433	0,000	-2,083	-1,119
Item 4	equal	18,180	0,000	-10,624	112,000	0,000	-2,857	-1,959
	not equal			-10,823	92,255	0,000	-2,850	-1,966

Appendix 4.7.3 Detailed Analyses of Scale Items (1/2)

Item:	In general, I feel valued as a person in my work environment.											
	do not agree at all	do not agree	do rather not agree	neutral	do rather agree	do agree	do completely agree					
	0	1	2	3	4	5	6	Total				
Type 1	1	7	7	10	17	16	1	59	Share of People who do agree (Answer: 5, 6)		Share of People who do not agree (Answer: 0, 1)	
Type 8	0	0	0	1	4	23	27	55				
Total	1	7	7	11	21	39	28	114				
Type 1 %	1,7	11,9	11,9	16,9	28,8	27,1	1,7		Type 1 %	28,8	Type 1 %	13,6
Type 8 %	0,0	0,0	0,0	1,8	7,3	41,8	49,1		Type 8 %	90,9	Type 8 %	0,0

Appendix 4.7.3 Detailed Analyses of Scale Items (2/2)

Item:	In general, I get enough appreciation for the work I do.											
	do not agree at all	do not agree	do rather not agree	neutral	do rather agree	do agree	do completely agree					
	0	1	2	3	4	5	6	Total				
Type 1	2	11	11	11	11	11	2	59	Share of People who do agree (Answer: 5, 6)		Share of People who do not agree (Answer: 0, 1)	
Type 8	0	0	0	2	10	23	20	55				
Total	2	11	11	13	21	34	22	114				
Type 1 %	3,4	18,6	18,6	18,6	18,6	18,6	3,4		Type 1 %	22,0	Type 1 %	22,0
Type 8 %	0,0	0,0	0,0	3,6	18,2	41,8	36,4		Type 8 %	78,2	Type 8 %	0,0

Item:	My employer gives me the feeling that I am a valuable employee.											
	do not agree at all	do not agree	do rather not agree	neutral	do rather agree	do agree	do completely agree					
	0	1	2	3	4	5	6	Total				
Type 1	2	11	11	15	10	9	1	59	Share of People who do agree (Answer: 5, 6)		Share of People who do not agree (Answer: 0, 1)	
Type 8	0	0	0	3	4	23	25	55				
Total	2	11	11	18	14	32	26	114				
Type 1 %	3,4	18,6	18,6	25,4	16,9	15,3	1,7		Type 1 %	16,9	Type 1 %	22,0
Type 8 %	0,0	0,0	0,0	5,5	7,3	41,8	45,5		Type 8 %	87,3	Type 8 %	0,0

Item:	I feel like I'm needed at work.											
	do not agree at all	do not agree	do rather not agree	neutral	do rather agree	do agree	do completely agree					
	0	1	2	3	4	5	6	Total				
Type 1	2	5	5	8	17	17	5	59	Share of People who do agree (Answer: 5, 6)		Share of People who do not agree (Answer: 0, 1)	
Type 8	0	1	1	1	2	19	31	55				
Total	2	6	6	9	19	36	36	114				
Type 1 %	3,4	8,5	8,5	13,6	28,8	28,8	8,5		Type 1 %	37,3	Type 1 %	11,9
Type 8 %	0,0	1,8	1,8	1,8	3,6	34,5	56,4		Type 8 %	90,9	Type 8 %	1,8

Appendix 4.8 Detailed Analyses of Supervisor Relationships

Appendix 4.8.1 Group Statistics

	Item	Job Love Type	n	M	SD	SE
Supervisor Relationships	Scale Average	Type 1	57	3,68	1,47	0,19
		Type 8	41	5,18	0,79	0,12
Item 1	I feel valued by my manager.	Type 1	57	3,49	1,72	0,23
		Type 8	41	5,32	0,99	0,15
Item 2	When I have a concern, my manager takes the time for me.	Type 1	57	3,95	1,48	0,20
		Type 8	41	5,27	1,03	0,16
Item 3	When I have done something well, my superior praises me.	Type 1	57	3,30	1,78	0,24
		Type 8	41	4,83	1,24	0,19
Item 4	I can count on my manager's help when I need it.	Type 1	57	3,75	1,69	0,22
		Type 8	41	5,15	1,04	0,16
Item 5	I feel that my manager trusts me.	Type 1	57	4,12	1,73	0,23
		Type 8	41	5,46	1,23	0,19
Item 6	My supervisor makes me feel thankful for my work.	Type 1	57	3,46	1,76	0,23
		Type 8	41	5,07	1,13	0,18

Appendix 4.8.2 Test of Group Mean Difference

	Levene's Test for Homogeneity of Variance			t-test for Mean Difference			95% Confidence Interval	
	Variances are	F	Sig.	T	df	Sig. one-sided	Upper Value	Lower Value
Supervisor Relationships	equal	15,169	0,000	-5,960	96,000	0,000	-2,006	-1,004
	not equal			-6,526	89,928	0,000	-1,963	-1,047
Item 1	equal	19,959	0,000	-6,100	96,000	0,000	-2,420	-1,232
	not equal			-6,632	91,920	0,000	-2,373	-1,279
Item 2	equal	2,947	0,089	-4,922	96,000	0,000	-1,854	-0,788
	not equal			-5,216	95,888	0,000	-1,824	-0,818
Item 3	equal	9,937	0,002	-4,731	96,000	0,000	-2,173	-0,889
	not equal			-5,009	95,930	0,000	-2,138	-0,924
Item 4	equal	10,927	0,001	-4,667	96,000	0,000	-1,984	-0,800
	not equal			-5,030	93,919	0,000	-1,941	-0,842
Item 5	equal	6,572	0,012	-4,245	96,000	0,000	-1,967	-0,714
	not equal			-4,484	95,986	0,000	-1,934	-0,747
Item 6	equal	13,218	0,000	-5,159	96,000	0,000	-2,239	-0,995
	not equal			-5,530	94,837	0,000	-2,198	-1,036

Appendix 4.8.3 Detailed Analyses of Scale Items (1/2)

Item:	I feel valued by my manager.											
	do not agree at all	do not agree	do rather not agree	neutral	do rather agree	do agree	do completely agree	Total				
	0	1	2	3	4	5	6	Total				
Type 1	2	8	7	10	9	15	6	57	Share of People who do agree (Answer: 5, 6)		Share of People who do not agree (Answer: 0, 1)	
Type 8	0	0	1	1	6	9	24	41				
Total	2	8	8	11	15	24	30	98				
Type 1 %	3,5	14,0	12,3	17,5	15,8	26,3	10,5		Type 1 %	36,8	Type 1 %	17,5
Type 8 %	0,0	0,0	2,4	2,4	14,6	22,0	58,5		Type 8 %	80,5	Type 8 %	0,0

Item:	When I have a concern, my manager takes the time for me.											
	do not agree at all	do not agree	do rather not agree	neutral	do rather agree	do agree	do completely agree	Total				
	0	1	2	3	4	5	6	Total				
Type 1	2	2	4	10	19	11	9	57	Share of People who do agree (Answer: 5, 6)		Share of People who do not agree (Answer: 0, 1)	
Type 8	0	1	0	0	7	11	22	41				
Total	2	3	4	10	26	22	31	98				
Type 1 %	3,5	3,5	7,0	17,5	33,3	19,3	15,8		Type 1 %	35,1	Type 1 %	7,0
Type 8 %	0,0	2,4	0,0	0,0	17,1	26,8	53,7		Type 8 %	80,5	Type 8 %	2,4

Item:	When I have done something well, my superior praises me.											
	do not agree at all	do not agree	do rather not agree	neutral	do rather agree	do agree	do completely agree	Total				
	0	1	2	3	4	5	6	Total				
Type 1	3	9	7	12	7	13	6	57	Share of People who do agree (Answer: 5, 6)		Share of People who do not agree (Answer: 0, 1)	
Type 8	0	1	1	4	7	13	15	41				
Total	3	10	8	16	14	26	21	98				
Type 1 %	5,3	15,8	12,3	21,1	12,3	22,8	10,5		Type 1 %	33,3	Type 1 %	21,1
Type 8 %	0,0	2,4	2,4	9,8	17,1	31,7	36,6		Type 8 %	68,3	Type 8 %	2,4

Item:	I can count on my manager's help when I need it.											
	do not agree at all	do not agree	do rather not agree	neutral	do rather agree	do agree	do completely agree	Total				
	0	1	2	3	4	5	6	Total				
Type 1	3	5	2	14	11	13	9	57	Share of People who do agree (Answer: 5, 6)		Share of People who do not agree (Answer: 0, 1)	
Type 8	0	0	1	3	4	14	19	41				
Total	3	5	3	17	15	27	28	98				
Type 1 %	5,3	8,8	3,5	24,6	19,3	22,8	15,8		Type 1 %	38,6	Type 1 %	14,0
Type 8 %	0,0	0,0	2,4	7,3	9,8	34,1	46,3		Type 8 %	80,5	Type 8 %	0,0

Appendix 4.8.3 Detailed Analyses of Scale Items (2/2)

Item:	I feel that my manager trusts me.										
	do not agree at all	do not agree	do rather not agree	neutral	do rather agree	do agree	do completely agree	Total			
	0	1	2	3	4	5	6	Total			
Type 1	3	3	5	5	11	17	13	57	Share of People who do agree (Answer: 5, 6)		Share of People who do not agree (Answer: 0, 1)
Type 8	0	0	0	4	3	8	25	41			
Total	3	3	5	9	14	25	38	98			
Type 1 %	5,3	5,3	8,8	8,8	19,3	29,8	22,8		Type 1 %	52,6	Type 1 % 10,5
Type 8 %	0,0	0,0	0,0	9,8	7,3	19,5	61,0		Type 8 %	80,5	Type 8 % 0,0

Item:	My supervisor makes me feel thankful for my work.										
	do not agree at all	do not agree	do rather not agree	neutral	do rather agree	do agree	do completely agree	Total			
	0	1	2	3	4	5	6	Total			
Type 1	4	6	7	8	13	13	6	57	Share of People who do agree (Answer: 5, 6)		Share of People who do not agree (Answer: 0, 1)
Type 8	0	0	2	2	6	12	19	41			
Total	4	6	9	10	19	25	25	98			
Type 1 %	7,0	10,5	12,3	14,0	22,8	22,8	10,5		Type 1 %	33,3	Type 1 % 17,5
Type 8 %	0,0	0,0	4,9	4,9	14,6	29,3	46,3		Type 8 %	75,6	Type 8 % 0,0

Appendix 4.9 Detailed Analyses of Peer Relationships

Appendix 4.9.1 Group Statistics

	Item	Job Love Type	n	M	SD	SE
Peer Relationships	Scale Average	Type 1	57	4,28	1,03	0,14
		Type 8	50	5,15	0,79	0,11
Item 1	I have a very good relationship with my colleagues.	Type 1	57	4,53	1,14	0,15
		Type 8	50	5,14	0,88	0,13
Item 2	I have the feeling that my colleagues value me as a colleague.	Type 1	57	4,61	1,10	0,15
		Type 8	50	5,20	0,90	0,13
Item 3	My colleagues support me when I need their help.	Type 1	57	4,56	1,17	0,15
		Type 8	50	5,46	0,89	0,13
Item 4	My colleagues like to spend time with me (e.g. lunch together).	Type 1	57	4,23	1,27	0,17
		Type 8	50	5,14	1,11	0,16
Item 5	I have someone at work I would call a friend.	Type 1	57	3,81	2,06	0,27
		Type 8	50	4,48	1,97	0,28
Item 6	When there is an occasion, my colleagues try to make me happy.	Type 1	57	3,70	1,73	0,23
		Type 8	50	4,78	1,28	0,18

Appendix 4.9.2 Test of Group Mean Difference

	Variances are	Levene's Test for Homogeneity of Variance			t-test for Mean Difference				
		F	Sig.	T	df	Sig. one-sided	95% Confidence Interval		
							Upper Value	Lower Value	
Peer Relationships	equal	4,670	0,033	-4,857	105,000	0,000	-1,223	-0,514	
	not equal			-4,939	103,379	0,000	-1,218	-0,520	
Item 1	equal	7,071	0,009	-3,091	105,000	0,002	-1,007	-0,220	
	not equal			-3,142	103,513	0,001	-1,001	-0,226	
Item 2	equal	2,293	0,133	-2,989	105,000	0,002	-0,975	-0,197	
	not equal			-3,027	104,596	0,002	-0,970	-0,202	
Item 3	equal	3,731	0,056	-4,442	105,000	0,000	-1,300	-0,497	
	not equal			-4,521	102,991	0,000	-1,293	-0,504	
Item 4	equal	0,992	0,321	-3,937	105,000	0,000	-1,371	-0,453	
	not equal			-3,972	104,999	0,000	-1,367	-0,457	
Item 5	equal	0,736	0,393	-1,722	105,000	0,044	-1,448	0,102	
	not equal			-1,726	104,154	0,044	-1,446	0,100	
Item 6	equal	6,864	0,010	-3,617	105,000	0,000	-1,669	-0,487	
	not equal			-3,688	102,239	0,000	-1,658	-0,498	

Appendix 4.9.3 Detailed Analyses of Scale Items (1/2)

Item:	I have a very good relationship with my colleagues.									
	do not agree at all	do not agree	do rather not agree	neutral	do rather agree	do agree	do completely agree			
	0	1	2	3	4	5	6	Total		
Type 1	0	0	1	12	14	16	14	57	Share of People who do agree (Answer: 5, 6)	Share of People who do not agree (Answer: 0, 1)
Type 8	0	0	0	2	10	17	21	50		
Total	0	0	1	14	24	33	35	107		
Type 1 %	0,0	0,0	1,8	21,1	24,6	28,1	24,6		Type 1 % 52,6	Type 1 % 0,0
Type 8 %	0,0	0,0	0,0	4,0	20,0	34,0	42,0		Type 8 % 76,0	Type 8 % 0,0

Item:	I have the feeling that my colleagues value me as a colleague.									
	do not agree at all	do not agree	do rather not agree	neutral	do rather agree	do agree	do completely agree			
	0	1	2	3	4	5	6	Total		
Type 1	0	1	1	6	15	22	12	57	Share of People who do agree (Answer: 5, 6)	Share of People who do not agree (Answer: 0, 1)
Type 8	0	0	0	4	4	20	22	50		
Total	0	1	1	10	19	42	34	107		
Type 1 %	0,0	1,8	1,8	10,5	26,3	38,6	21,1		Type 1 % 59,6	Type 1 % 1,8
Type 8 %	0,0	0,0	0,0	8,0	8,0	40,0	44,0		Type 8 % 84,0	Type 8 % 0,0

Appendix 4.9.3 Detailed Analyses of Scale Items (2/2)

Item:	My colleagues support me when I need their help.											
	do not agree at all	do not agree	do rather not agree	neutral	do rather agree	do agree	do completel y agree					
	0	1	2	3	4	5	6	Total				
Type 1	0	1	2	8	10	25	11	57	Share of People who do agree (Answer: 5, 6)		Share of People who do not agree (Answer: 0, 1)	
Type 8	0	0	0	3	4	10	33	50				
Total	0	1	2	11	14	35	44	107				
Type 1 %	0,0	1,8	3,5	14,0	17,5	43,9	19,3		Type 1 %	63,2	Type 1 %	1,8
Type 8 %	0,0	0,0	0,0	6,0	8,0	20,0	66,0		Type 8 %	86,0	Type 8 %	0,0

Item:	My colleagues like to spend time with me (e.g. lunch together).											
	do not agree at all	do not agree	do rather not agree	neutral	do rather agree	do agree	do completel y agree					
	0	1	2	3	4	5	6	Total				
Type 1	0	2	3	9	19	14	10	57	Share of People who do agree (Answer: 5, 6)		Share of People who do not agree (Answer: 0, 1)	
Type 8	0	1	0	3	8	13	25	50				
Total	0	3	3	12	27	27	35	107				
Type 1 %	0,0	3,5	5,3	15,8	33,3	24,6	17,5		Type 1 %	42,1	Type 1 %	3,5
Type 8 %	0,0	2,0	0,0	6,0	16,0	26,0	50,0		Type 8 %	76,0	Type 8 %	2,0

Item:	I have someone at work I would call a friend.											
	do not agree at all	do not agree	do rather not agree	neutral	do rather agree	do agree	do completel y agree					
	0	1	2	3	4	5	6	Total				
Type 1	5	6	6	5	7	12	16	57	Share of People who do agree (Answer: 5, 6)		Share of People who do not agree (Answer: 0, 1)	
Type 8	4	3	1	4	7	7	24	50				
Total	9	9	7	9	14	19	40	107				
Type 1 %	8,8	10,5	10,5	8,8	12,3	21,1	28,1		Type 1 %	49,1	Type 1 %	19,3
Type 8 %	8,0	6,0	2,0	8,0	14,0	14,0	48,0		Type 8 %	62,0	Type 8 %	14,0

Item:	When there is an occasion, my colleagues try to make me happy.											
	do not agree at all	do not agree	do rather not agree	neutral	do rather agree	do agree	do completel y agree					
	0	1	2	3	4	5	6	Total				
Type 1	3	5	6	9	11	15	8	57	Share of People who do agree (Answer: 5, 6)		Share of People who do not agree (Answer: 0, 1)	
Type 8	1	0	1	5	11	14	18	50				
Total	4	5	7	14	22	29	26	107				
Type 1 %	5,3	8,8	10,5	15,8	19,3	26,3	14,0		Type 1 %	40,4	Type 1 %	14,0
Type 8 %	2,0	0,0	2,0	10,0	22,0	28,0	36,0		Type 8 %	64,0	Type 8 %	2,0

Appendix 4.10 Detailed Analyses of Client Relationships

Appendix 4.10.1 Group Statistics

	Item	Job Love Type	n	M	SD	SE
Client Relationships	Scale Average	Type 1	38	4,16	1,02	0,17
		Type 8	41	4,99	0,82	0,13
Item 1	I think most of the people I work for appreciate my work.	Type 1	38	4,39	1,24	0,20
		Type 8	41	5,12	0,81	0,13
Item 2	It's rare that I get criticism for my work from my customers.	Type 1	38	4,37	1,32	0,22
		Type 8	41	5,12	0,95	0,15
Item 3	I often get a "thank you" from my customers for my work.	Type 1	38	3,71	1,69	0,27
		Type 8	41	4,73	1,23	0,19

Appendix 4.10.2 Test of Group Mean Difference

		Levene's Test for Homogeneity of Variance		t-test for Mean Difference					
	Variances are	F	Sig.	T	df	Sig. one-sided	95% Confidence Interval	
							Upper Value	Lower Value
Client Relationships	equal	1,021	0,315	-4,006	77,000	0,000	-1,249	-0,419
	not equal			-3,972	70,940	0,000	-1,253	-0,415
Item 1	equal	3,800	0,055	-3,102	77,000	0,002	-1,194	-0,260
	not equal			-3,054	62,991	0,002	-1,203	-0,251
Item 2	equal	4,792	0,032	-2,918	77,000	0,003	-1,268	-0,239
	not equal			-2,883	66,854	0,003	-1,275	-0,232
Item 3	equal	4,060	0,047	-3,090	77,000	0,002	-1,679	-0,363
	not equal			-3,053	67,074	0,002	-1,689	-0,354

Appendix 4.10.3 Detailed Analyses of Scale Items (1/2)

Item:	I think most of the people I work for appreciate my work.											
	do not agree at all	do not agree	do rather not agree	neutral	do rather agree	do agree	do completely agree					
	0	1	2	3	4	5	6	Total				
Type 1	1		2	3	11	16	5	38	Share of People who do agree (Answer: 5, 6)		Share of People who do not agree (Answer: 0, 1)	
Type 8	0		0	1	8	17	15	41				
Total	1		2	4	19	33	20	79				
Type 1 %	2,6	0,0	5,3	7,9	28,9	42,1	13,2		Type 1 %	55,3	Type 1 %	2,6
Type 8 %	0,0	0,0	0,0	2,4	19,5	41,5	36,6		Type 8 %	78,0	Type 8 %	0,0

Appendix 4.10.3 Detailed Analyses of Scale Items (2/2)

Item:	It's rare that I get criticism for my work from my customers.											
	do not agree at all	do not agree	do rather not agree	neutral	do rather agree	do agree	do complete ly agree					
	0	1	2	3	4	5	6	Total				
Type 1	1		1	8	7	14	7	38	**Share of People who do agree** (Answer: 5, 6)		**Share of People who do not agree** (Answer: 0, 1)	
Type 8	0		0	4	4	16	17	41				
Total	1		1	12	11	30	24	79				
Type 1 %	2,6	0,0	2,6	21,1	18,4	36,8	18,4		**Type 1 %**	55,3	**Type 1 %**	2,6
Type 8 %	0,0	0,0	0,0	9,8	9,8	39,0	41,5		**Type 8 %**	80,5	**Type 8 %**	0,0

Item:	I often get a "thank you" from my customers for my work.											
	do not agree at all	do not agree	do rather not agree	neutral	do rather agree	do agree	do complete ly agree					
	0	1	2	3	4	5	6	Total				
Type 1	3	2	2	8	8	11	4	38	**Share of People who do agree** (Answer: 5, 6)		**Share of People who do not agree** (Answer: 0, 1)	
Type 8	0	1	1	5	6	16	12	41				
Total	3	3	3	13	14	27	16	79				
Type 1 %	7,9	5,3	5,3	21,1	21,1	28,9	10,5		**Type 1 %**	39,5	**Type 1 %**	13,2
Type 8 %	0,0	2,4	2,4	12,2	14,6	39,0	29,3		**Type 8 %**	68,3	**Type 8 %**	2,4